Snow Goer's Vintage Snowmobiles

Memorable Machines and Highlights from Snowmobiling's Golden Age

Volume One

DAVID WELLS
and *Snow Goer* magazine

Enthusiast Books

Introduction

From the Vietnam War in Southeast Asia to the civil rights movement across the United States, plus rallies and protests of those affairs and more, the 1960s were a tumultuous era. However, deep in the Snowbelt there was another uprising – one centered around fun and enjoyment, and around winter.

Utilitarian over-snow machines had been around for a few decades, but the recreational side of the sport was in its infancy. In that background, *Snow Goer* magazine was launched in the Northwoods of Wisconsin. And, on the inside cover of the very first issue – labeled as December 1966 – were these words.

"The publishers of *Snow Goer* are proud to announce the newest, most complete, comprehensive, informative publication in its field – devoted to the users, the industry and the unlimited future of the snowmobile.

Our primary interest is to promote and increase the development of the snowmobile for family and sporting enjoyment. *Snow Goer* is dedicated to the World of Snowmobiling!"

Through more than 50 years of publishing and the various ups and downs of the sledding market, that dedication to promoting snowmobiling and the joys it brings to winter has never waned. *Snow Goer* was the first nationwide snowmobiling publication, and today it is still the largest paid-circulation magazine in the industry.

Aside from celebrating the current and future aspects of the sport, however, *Snow Goer* also celebrates snowmobiling's captivating past. The interesting machines and the benchmark technologies, and the colorful personalities and intriguing folklore behind them are captured in each issue in the Flashback or Timeline section, plus occasional feature articles that cover broader aspects of the sport's history.

The vast majority of those articles in the past three decades have been penned by veteran snowmobile journalist and historian David Wells. In fact, Wells' dedication to preserving an accurate and authentic history of the sport and sharing its stories on the pages of *Snow Goer* and some of its sister publications over the years led to his induction into the International Snowmobile Hall of Fame in 2015.

Many of those great *Snow Goer* articles have been collated here – in the first edition of *Snow Goer*'s *Vintage Snowmobiles* – for your reading enjoyment. As you'll see, the sport's history is marked by ideas good and bad, triumphs and failures, inspiring conquests and hard-to-believe blunders – and that's what makes it so interesting.

Special thanks to the unnamed hundreds, if not thousands, who shared their stories, clarified details, provided photos and relived many of their great memories with us in the writing of all of these articles.

John Prusak
VP, Group Publisher, Editor
EPG Media & Specialty Information

About the Author

David Wells is a long-time snowmobiler who has chronicled the sport on the race track, on the trail, and in the show room since the early 1970s for *Snow Goer* magazine, *Snow Week* newspaper, *Snowmobile Business* magazine, and numerous other publications as well as on radio and television.

Over the years he has made tracks in the snow from the edge of the Atlantic Ocean to the heights of the Continental Divide and north into the Arctic Ocean watershed. He rode many vintage snowmobiles when they were new, used them to participate in many snowmobile club activities, skinned a few knuckles working on them, and generally had a great time along the way.

Drawing on a background in the snowmobile business with multiple brands and in user organizations at all levels in his native New York State, Wells brings a well-rounded perspective to vintage snowmobiling. And he is a frequent visitor to vintage snowmobile events and institutions across the eastern part of the continent.

Wells was inducted into the International Snowmobile Hall of Fame in Eagle River, Wisconsin, in September, 2015.

Enthusiast Books
Copyright 2019 David Wells
All rights reserved. No part of this work may be reproduced or used in any form by any means. . . graphic, electronic, or mechanical, including photocopying, recording, taping, or any other information storage and retrieval system. . . without written permission of the publisher.

The information in this book is true and complete to the best of our knowledge. All recommendations are made without any guarantee on the part of the author or Publisher, who also disclaim any liability incurred in connection with the use of this data or specific details.

We acknowledge that certain words, such as model names and designations, mentioned herein are the property of the trademark holder. We use them for purposes of identification only. This is not an official publication.

ISBN-13: 978-1-58388-351-8

For more books of interest or to contact the publisher, visit us at www.enthusiastbooks.com

Printed in USA

Contents

1967 Ski-Doo Super Olympique	4
1969 Yukon King Grizzly	6
1969 Ski-Doo T'NT 669	8
1970-72 AMF Ski-Daddler	10
1970 Wheel Horse Safari	12
1971 Boatel Grand Prix	14
1971 Dauphin	16
1971 Moto-Ski Capri 292	18
1971 Suzuki Nomad	20
The Swinger	22
1972 Alouette Eliminator	24
1972 Arctic Cat Kitty Cat	26
1972 Bolens Super Sprint 440	28
1972 Poloron Tornado	30
1972 Skiroule RTX 447	32
Ski-Lark & Wee-Lark	34
Sears Sportsters	36
1972 Sno Jet SST	38
1973 Ariens 450SX	40
The Chaparral SS/III	42
1973 Evinrude Trailblazer	44
1973 John Deere JDX	46
1973 Massey Ferguson Ski Whiz	48
1973 Moto-Ski 'F' Series	50
1973 Raider TT	52
Last Stand of the Axial Fan Stocker	54
1973 Rupp American	56
1973 Scorpion Super Stinger TK	58
1973 Ski-Zoom Comet	60
The Alouette Super Brute	62
1974 Arctic Cat Panther VIP	64
The 1974 Boa-Ski SS	66
1974 Chaparral Thunderbird	68
1974 Johnson JX	70
1974 Northway Interceptor 15 440D	72
1974 Roll-O-Flex Wild One	74
1974 Sno Jet Sabre Jet	76
1974 Yamaha GPX	78
The MTD Columbia	80
1975 John Deere 340/S	82
The Rupp Nitro F/A	84
Scorpion Whip	86
1976 Arctic Cat Pantera	88
1976 Polaris Colt S/S	90
1976 Ski-Doo T'NT RV	92
The First Yamaha Exciter	94
Arctic Cat Jag	96
1977 Kawasaki Sno Jet SST	98
1977 Polaris TX-L	100
The Sno-Runner Saga	102
1980 Kawasaki Invader LTD 4/6	104
The Vintage SRX	106
1981 Arctic Cat El Tigré 6000	108
1981 Yamaha SRX	110
1983 John Deere Sprintfire	112
Moto-Ski Mirage III	114
1986 Ski-Doo Formula SP	116
Snow Bikes	118
Rebadged & Rejected	120
The Great Stock Racing War	124

1967 Ski-Doo Super Olympique
The Sled That Started It All

If you don't believe in love in first sight, here's proof that it actually can happen. In 1967, Bombardier produced 44,421 Ski-Doo snowmobiles, including many called the Super Olympique, a model that had been introduced for the prior year as the line's performance leader.

One of these 1967 Super Olympiques was the first snowmobile I ever rode. It happened during the winter of '67 in a field near Potsdam in northern New York. I had always known that winter was good for something, and that ride showed me what it was. I was hooked.

That particular Super Oly belonged to my buddy Ted Perkins, and we have enjoyed many snowmobile adventures together in the many years since then.

Primitive Plaything
The '67 Super Olympique carried a new 299cc two-stroke Rotax engine situated right in the operator's lap. Equipped with a cast iron cylinder containing a three-ring piston, it also had a new intake silencer to reduce induction noise and warm the air as it entered the engine, plus a new choke for easier cold starting. But operators still had to be careful that the intake body didn't suck in their clothing to plug the carb. And the engine could backfire right into the operator's crotch, too.

Nevertheless, buyers were willing to put up with these perils to get the Super Oly's big 14.5 hp engine that was claimed to drive the machine to the unheard of snowmobile speed of 48 mph. Of course, the cab, or hood, was still permanently secured to the chassis with a series of screws, so opening it to change the spark plug, adjust the carb or otherwise work on the engine or clutching was nearly impossible in the field.

Other notable improvements on the '67 Super Oly included nylon-covered throttle and brake cables for freeze

4

resistance, new polyurethane drive sprockets to improve drive efficiency and a new track with nylon fibers instead of cotton to reduce stretching and increase track life. The new and improved seat had a second layer of foam and new vinyl for increased comfort during those rare times when you might actually be sitting on it. And the rear bumper/grab handle swung down to become a warm-up stand or to keep the track from freezing to the ground overnight.

The Super Oly really was a hot sled for the day, as shown by Duluth, Minnesota, resident Alan Bartlet winning the 300 class at the first Duluth Indoor, a major race at that time, with a '67 model as Ski-Doo took 13 of the 15 classes contested.

Snow Goer editors at the time tested the 1967 Super Olympique and had some interesting things to say.

"An added improvement could be a hood that would tip up for easy access to the engine compartment. Of course, this feature could be put on ALL snowmobiles as far as we are concerned. …We do believe, however, that eventually all machines will have some sort of flip-up or 'take off' affair." They also loved the pop-up headlight, and went on to a very complimentary conclusion. "It met all our standards and even went above some, so it rates high on stars. We would recommend it for an individual as well as a family."

So what was using this machine like? It liked to go straight, so the only way to get it to turn was to stand up, lock your feet into the stirrups, lean forward and out over the inside ski as far as possible, and use body English to force turning. Riding standing up made more sense than sitting down because you could use your legs as suspension. Kneeling on one knee was a good compromise that offered more comfort than sitting without sacrificing too much maneuverability and still allowing you to proceed at something faster than walking speed.

In 1967 New York State permitted snowmobiles to be licensed for on-road operation with a small metal license plate attached to the seat back. So Ted licensed his and legally operated it on roads including a run into downtown Syracuse. He also rode it in New York City's Central Park, becoming undoubtedly the first and very likely only snowmobiler ever ticketed for riding there.

"Trouble found us shortly in the form of a NYPD patrol car with a flashing red light," Ted recollects. He and his female companion were told to leave immediately. "So we started back in the general direction of the restaurant [and his car and trailer], but via a scenic route. The episode ended when we were stopped for a second time because we 'didn't follow orders to leave right away,'" Ted recalls. The historic citation was for "vehicle on foot path."

Post-Olympique Perspective

Model year 1968 was the last hurrah for the Super Olympique, but the Olympique line was built by the thousands all the way through 1979. And along the way it introduced many thousands of people to snow riding, so the venerable Oly is one of the most important models in the long history of our sport.

1967 Ski-Doo Super Olympique

MANUFACTURER
Bombardier Ltd., Valcourt, Quebec

POWERTRAIN
Engine: 299cc Rotax Type 300 air-cooled piston-port single with one Tillotson HR diaphragm pumper carb, breaker point ignition and single pipe into muffler
Lubrication: Pre-mix at 20:1
Power Output: 14.5 hp @ 5,200 rpm
Clutches: Bombardier

CHASSIS
Type: Welded and painted one-piece steel with stirrups, chrome steel tube front & rear bumpers, and fixed fiberglass hood
Claimed Dry Weight: 265 pounds
Front Suspension: Triple-leaf springs
Ski Stance: 24 inches
Rear Suspension: 14 bogie wheels with torsion springs
Track: Bombardier 15-inch, 3-ply, nylon-reinforced molded rubber with dual sprocket drive and 50-inch footprint.
Brake: Drum
Fuel capacity: 3.6 gallons
Standard Equipment: Ignition and lighting switch, decompression switch, choke, retractable head light, chrome handlebars, anti-slip running board mats, dashboard glove box
MSRP: $875

1969 Yukon King Grizzly
The Biggest Fall Ever

Photo by collector Kevin Hancock

Yukon King suffered perhaps the farthest fall from glory of any snowmobile ever manufactured. In less than four years, it went from a totally undefeated racing season to serving as a bad example in another brand's ads.

Here's the whole story.

In the early 1960s, veteran marketer Don Thompson at Mercury Marine recognized that the snowmobile could be a counter-seasonal product for the company's dealers. After failing to persuade Mercury patriarch Carl Kiekhaefer to enter the snowmobile business, Thompson left and established his own marketing company to sell a wooden tow-behind sleigh called a Yukon King, apparently named for movie Mountie Sgt. Preston's faithful police dog.

Thompson then merged his business with boat builder Moorhead Plastics of Moorhead, Minnesota, and was named manager of its snowmobile division to produce a Yukon King snowmobile for the 1967 season. Soon after, Moorhead Plastics changed its name to Silverline, Inc., after the company's increasingly popular boat line.

The Undefeated Season

Thompson knew that the fledgling Yukon King brand required something dramatic to set it apart from the other 100-plus snowmobile makes on the market. Boat racing experience at Mercury gave him some important insight. He decided to concentrate Yukon King's scant resources where the big competitors were not involved, so he chose USSA's new 295cc Stock class.

After considerable effort, Thompson obtained exclusive snowmobile use of the German Lloyd alternate-firing, 20 hp twin as a stock factory engine option for Yukon King's mid-line Grizzly model. Fitted with a Tillotson HD-13A carb, the industry's first silenced tuned exhaust from the Donaldson Muffler Company, the first drive clutch with engagement speed tuned to the engine torque curve, and the first torque-sensing driven clutch, the Grizzly went racing. The team had a $5,000 budget for the 1968 season, five drivers, five of the orange sleds and four helmets, plus one personally loaned to the team by Thompson.

When it was all over, the Yukon King factory team and its Grizzly sleds had won its class at every sanctioned race it entered during the 1967-68 season: the racers dominated their class at Eagle River, won at several other Midwestern events, and notched a first-through-fifth-place class sweep to close the season. The team was slightly over budget, but that seemingly didn't matter.

And thanks to Thompson's industry connections, Yukon King joined four of the industry's biggest manufacturers for a late-season *Playboy* magazine snowmobile photo shoot. Things seemed to be going great for the upstart brand.

The King Is Dead
But Yukon King snowmobiles, like the Grizzly 15 that was virtually identical to the race winners other than its 15 hp JLO engine, just weren't selling very well. Returns for manufacturing defects were one of multiple issues that dogged sales efforts. The company touted its amazing 1968 race results in its 1969 ads and brochures, stressing that the race team did it with stock-class sleds, but that just wasn't enough.

Yukon King was financially forced to stop racing and 1969 models were closed out for as little as $450. In February 1969, Gilson Brothers announced acquisition of the Silverline snowmobile business, but the deal fell through. Further negotiations to sell it to Chrysler Corporation were unsuccessful, and Yukon King was dead.

Parent company Silverline, Inc. was sold to Arctic Enterprises in fall 1969. Arctic wanted the very viable Silverline boat business, with its considerable fiberglass operations to augment its growing Arctic Cat snowmobile business. Arctic Cat also inherited about 150 brand new, crated Yukon Kings as part of the deal.

In 1971, Arctic's advertising agency Carmichael-Lynch came up with some attention-grabbing ads for the 1972 Cats. One consumer ad was headlined "What are you doing this weekend?" and showed a snowmobiler puzzling over a torn apart orange sled. The ad talked about doing a lot less tinkering and a lot more riding if you owned a Cat. The orange sled in the picture was a Yukon King, one of the batch that Cat inherited in the Silverline acquisition. You could even read the Yukon King hood decal in the background.

A similar dealer recruitment ad for snowmobile trade publications used a pile of crated orange sleds, also Yukon Kings, as background to help drive home the point that Cat dealers had essentially sold out of sleds in 1971 while dealers handling most other brands had way too much carryover inventory.

These Arctic Cat ads marked the final appearance of Yukon King in any kind of promotional activity, a truly ignominious end for the sled that earned a racing record that will never be beaten.

1969 Yukon King Grizzly 15

MANUFACTURER
Silverline Inc., Moorhead, Minnesota

POWERTRAIN
Engine: 292cc, JLO, rotary fan-cooled, piston-port single with one Tillotson HD diaphragm pumper carb, breaker point ignition and single pipe into "Sof-Tone" muffler
Lubrication: Pre-mix at 20:1
Power Output: 15 hp
Clutches: Yukon King / Atlas Sense-O-Matic transmission

CHASSIS
Type: Welded and painted steel with stirrups, chromed tube steel bumpers and fiberglass hood
Estimated Dry Weight: 330 pounds
Front suspension: Triple leaf springs
Ski Stance: 23.5 inches
Rear Suspension: 12 bogie wheels
Track: Scorpion 15-by-122-inch Frigid Flex steel-reinforced molded rubber with dual drive
Brake: Drum
Fuel Capacity: 5 gallons
Standard Equipment: Primer, fold-down warm-up stand, dual headlights, bustle-type rear storage compartment, passenger grab handles, "Snow Guard" snow flap

MSRP: $799

1969 Ski-Doo T'NT 669
The One That Changed Everything

Through the 1960s, most snowmobiles were modestly powered two-seaters that placed utility above performance. They emphasized qualities like carrying and towing ability and good flotation to break trail where none existed instead of flat-out speed and handling.

One of the milestones in the development of the modern snowmobile occurred in December 1967 when Bombardier turned loose a race model called the Super 370 in the Olympique chassis. A modified, beefed-up version of that model was fitted with Rotax's brand new 599cc axial fan-cooled vertical twin — the first Rotax engine built exclusively for snowmobiles — in a new model called the T'NT. The initials were short for Track and Trail, reflecting the intended dual use for this model that was engineered as a trail sled that could win in both the Stock and Modified racing categories. Only 117 were built that first year, and you had to be a recognized racer with good connections to get one. Halvorson Ski-Doo racer Steve Ave rode the 1968 T'NT to his second Eagle River World Championship in three years, and many other Ski-Doo racers recorded wins with the new machine that winter.

But the real significance of the T'NT was that it began the long march for the snowmobile from a two-seat utility machine that you could have a little fun with to a single-seat pure recreation machine that placed performance far above any utility consideration.

The next step in this process was the new 1969 T'NT 669, the first T'NT to be built on something other than a modified Olympique platform. And unlike the very exclusive '68 T'NTs, plenty of the '69s were available for sale to anyone who had the money.

The Big Bomber Takes Flight
Although Bombardier continued to build lower-powered T'NT models on the Olympique platform, the top of the line T'NT 669 was built on the new Nordic family luxury machine chassis. The 18-inch tracks on these sleds were the widest yet fitted to any Ski-Doo, and Bornbardier's dual sprocket drive put the power to the track. Sporting a new Rotax 669 axial fan-cooled twin with a single carb, the engine could also be equipped with an optional manifold that unconventionally mounted twin carbs in a unique vertical V configuration.

This largest T'NT variant also featured unique styling to set it apart from other Ski-Doo models. The new forward-tilting hood was an improvement because it allowed much easier access for engine and clutch work than the prior fixed hoods. Side scoops and internal shrouds moved cooling air to the engine and clutches, and a shorter windshield gave the machine a racier look. The two-piece chromed front bumper visually separated the hood from the belly pan inline with the seat instead of curving down to running boards as on older models. And although the seat was long enough to accommodate a passenger, it lacked the traditional passenger backrest. Elimination of the rear bumper saved a few more pounds and made the big T'NT four inches shorter than its chassis-mate Nordic.

On The Track
The 669 T'NT began its competitive life with high hopes at the Duluth, Minnesota, Indoor on the

first weekend of December, 1968. But with Stock classes limited to 400cc the big bomber had to run in the 800 Modified class where it was simply outgunned by other brands with larger, more powerful engines.

Still, the 669s enjoyed some competitive successes. Willie Rousin and Maurice Mongeau shattered the existing snowmobile distance jumping records at Eagle River with them. But both riders also shattered bones while landing, and the United States Snowmobile Association immediately stopped competitive jumping on the spot.

Four 669s, including one ridden by defending champion Steve Ave, made the Eagle River World Championship final, but Arctic Cat swept the top three finishing spots. However, Dan Planck, of LaPeer, Michigan, and a relief driver won the inaugural Soo I-500 endurance race in Sault Ste. Marie, Michigan, on a T'NT 669 at an average speed of 36 mph over the grueling 14-hour race.

The following year, Bombardier expanded the T'NT series with 292, 340, 399, 640 and 775 engines to cover most of the racing classes, also adding smoother riding slide rail suspensions.

On The Trail

As a trail sled, the T'NT 669 was a real handful. "Starting the sled was an adventure" says vintage snowmobile collector Mark Elwell of Arkport, New York. "It takes a strong man to pull this thing over." The combination of high compression and a small recoil handle had a tendency to rip the handle right out of the operator's hand, and recoil failure was an ongoing issue. Owners learned to carry a pocket full of spark plugs when riding, and the gas mileage was poor. Handling was good for the day, with the wide track keeping the sled flat, but the sled was heavy and "headstrong" in deep snow. Ride quality was poor as with all bogie wheel sleds, and the sled was not comfortable to ride sitting down due to the low seat.

But the T'NT 669 definitely appealed to the macho guys who wanted the biggest and baddest sled. To say that the performance image sold well is an understatement.

Other companies quickly took notice of what Ski-Doo was doing with the T'NT. They began creating their own performance models, like the Arctic Cat Puma, Polaris TX, Moto-Ski Grand Prix and Rupp Nitro, to compete with the T'NT. Aided greatly by the Stock racing war that erupted in 1972, these new performance models evolved into single-seat thoroughbreds with more horsepower, wider ski stances, better suspensions and narrower tracks that generally limited them to racetracks and established trails.

The 1969 Ski-doo T'NT 669 was the sled that had triggered this landmark change. It's the great-great-granddaddy of the sled that you're probably riding this season, and that makes it one of the most influential designs of all time.

1969 Ski-Doo T'NT 669

MANUFACTURER
Bombardier Inc., Valcourt, Quebec, Canada
Model number: 942

POWERTRAIN
Engine: Rotax axial-fan-cooled piston-port twin
Displacement: 668.6 cc
Carburetion: Tillotson HD21A diaphragm pumper
Compression Ratio: 10:1
Ignition: Magneto & breaker points
Lubrication: Pre-mix at 20:1
Exhaust: Single pipe with can muffler
Power Output: 45 hp
Electrical Output: 75 watts
Drive and Driven Clutch: Bombardier

CHASSIS
Type: Welded and painted steel with stirrups, steel belly pan, chromed steel front bumper, and fiberglass hood
Weight (dry, claimed): 385 pounds
Front Suspension: Five leaf springs
Ski Stance: 27 inches
Rear Suspension: 12 rubber bogie wheels with springs on three trucks
Track: 18-by-114-inch molded rubber with steel reinforcing rods and double sprocket drive
Brake: Single shoe mechanical drum
Fuel Capacity: 6.25-gallons (US)
Standard Equipment: pop-up headlamp, Kelch fuel gauge
Options: Dual carb kit, speedometer, tachometer

Price: $1,395

1970-72 AMF Ski-Daddler

The sports car approach to snowmobiling didn't work

In 1965, American Machine and Foundry Co. (AMF) became the second large corporation (after Outboard Marine Corp.) to enter the snowmobile business by introducing its 10 hp Ski-Daddler for the 1966 snowmobile season.

The company was assembling a broad portfolio of leisure products that would include AMF bowling equipment, Ben Hogan golf clubs, Head skis, Voit athletic equipment, Slickcraft boats, Alcort Sunfish sailboards, Roadmaster bicycles, Whitley exercise machines, AMF lawn and garden equipment and Harley-Davidson motorcycles. With all the "fun" in its lineup, snowmobiles were a natural addition.

But the boxy Ski-Daddlers of the late '60s earned a poor reputation for quality and reliability, and the company realized that it would have to overhaul its product and promotion to survive in the skyrocketing snowmobile business.

So for 1970, AMF transferred snow sled production from Des Moines, Iowa, to York, Pennsylvania, and rolled out a collection of sleek new orange sleds. Failing to comprehend that snowmobilers were more interested in hot rods, pick-up trucks and tractor pulling than sporty imported automobiles, the company began to promote the new sleds as "the sports car approach to snowmobiling." This was explained as engineering a Ski-Daddler to look and feel like a sports car.

Orange Roll Out

The new orange Ski-Daddlers looked great. A retractable headlight and a chrome wrap-around front bumper aided an unusually sleek and clean execution of contemporary snowmobile styling. They also had a console to separate the engine from the driver, a relatively novel feature in 1970.

But the sleds were cast in the traditional mold. A Hirth engine, or a JLO for the low-end model, was mounted atop a welded steel chassis. With Salisbury clutching, bogie wheels and minimal or no instrumentation, these new sleds failed to advance snowmobile engineering.

Although all the models looked very much alike, there were actually four series of orange Ski-Daddlers. The sporty Mark IV series had 15-inch tracks, while the upscale Mark V series had 18-inch tracks, electric start, a bigger (6-gallon) fuel tank and rear turn signals. The short-lived Mark VI was essentially a Mark IV with a 634 Hirth engine, a cut down seat and the bigger gas tank. The Mark XX series were limited-edition race sleds. One interesting feature was a rear lift handle that folded down to become a track stand. It was fitted to most of the Mark IV and Mark V models.

Sports Car For The Snow?

The 1970 Ski-Daddler brochure described the Mark V as the "nearest thing to a Porsche you can ride on the snow." Then it claimed that, "the Mark VI takes off like a Ferrari, handles like a Maserati, maneuvers like an Alfa-Romeo." These comparisons were absolutely laughable to anyone who knew anything about these vehicles, and meaningless to those who didn't.

Oblivious to the fact that real sports cars almost always had manual transmissions, AMF tried to pass off its snowmobile automatic "variable speed torque sensitive drive" as "sports car-type engineering." The company also claimed "a rubber track designed for traction under all conditions" was a further example of this "sports car-type engineering."

Maybe the biggest disconnect was suspension technology. Sports cars are known for their superior underpinnings, but AMF tried to pass off its dirt-common and already outdated undercarriage as something special. Despite the accelerating move to the better riding slide rails by competitors, all non-competition SkiDaddlers were stuck with bogies until 1972 when sliders appeared on just one trail model – the Mark IV 400D. And ski shocks were never even an option, let alone standard. So the sports car analogy made no sense here either.

Yet AMF completely missed one sports car claim that would have made great sense: a disc brake. Popularized by Jaguar's historic racing victories at Le Mans, fade-resisting disc brakes were not yet an automotive or snowmobile standard. But a disc brake was the lone advanced engineering feature on the orange Ski-Daddler.

Sports car racing was popular, and so was snowmobile racing, so AMF went racing with its new sleds. It did not go well. Aside from one USSA World Series Stock class victory before anyone cared about Stock racing, AMF sleds were also-rans on the track as well as in the showroom.

Another Rebuild

AMF's promotional theme lacked any relevance to the snowmobile market and was largely unsupported by its engineering. Sleek and modern appearing as they were, orange Ski-Daddlers were still a "me too" product. It had questionable reliability that saw little development over its brief life in an industry that was rendering last year's sleds obsolete.

Despite building about 14,000 sleds for the 1970 and '71 model years, the Ski-Daddler was phased out in favor of the company's forthcoming Harley-Davidson snowmobile. Only about 1,000 Ski-Daddlers were built for 1972, and all remaining inventory of AMF brand sleds were sold to a liquidator who retailed them direct to consumers at heavily discounted prices.

Even as the orange Ski-Daddlers were being introduced, the basic design was being thoroughly re-worked and re-powered with exclusive Aermacchi engines. Eighty of these improved units were built as prototype 1971 Harley-Davidson snowmobiles. The Harley sleds went to market in 1972, the last year of the Ski-Daddler, and AMF tried to use the Harley mystique to market them. But that didn't work, either. The snow hogs remained on the market essentially unchanged through the 1975 model year when AMF finally gave up on the snowmobile business for good.

1972 AMF Ski-Daddler Mark IV 400D

MANUFACTURER
Western Tool Division of AMF Inc., Des Moines, Iowa, and York, Pennsylvania

POWERTRAIN
Engine: Hirth 210R axial-fan-cooled twin
Displacement: 399cc
Carburetion: One Tillotson HD diaphragm pumper
Ignition: Magneto and breaker points
Lubrication: Pre-mix at 25:1
Exhaust: Single pipe into muffler
Power Output: 28 hp
Drive Clutch: Salsbury
Driven Clutch: Salsbury

CHASSIS
Type: Welded steel with a fully removable fiberglass hood
Weight: Claimed 355 pounds dry
Front Suspension: Triple-leaf springs
Ski Stance: 25.5 inches
Rear Suspension: Slide rails with torsion springs
Track: 15-inch molded rubber with riveted-on steel cleats
Brake: Mechanical disc
Fuel Capacity: 5 gallons in a removable tank
Standard Equipment: Retractable headlight, low profile seat, under-seat storage compartment, zippered in-seat storage pouch, passenger grab strap, tinted windshield, gas gauge
Key Options: Electric start, cigarette lighter (ES required), tachometer

Price: $1,080

1970 Wheel Horse Safari

The No Horse Sense Sled

Wheel Horse Products Inc. was formed in 1946 to produce lawn and garden tractors and related outdoor power equipment. By the late 1960s, it was yet another hard goods manufacturer attracted to the overheated snowmobile market.

With a home base in the Snowbelt, a reputation for quality products and 3,000 American dealers selling similarly sized and priced wheeled goods using similar technology, Wheel Horse appeared to be a great candidate for snowmobile success. And it wasn't lost on management that several of the company's direct competitors, including AMF, Bolens, Poloron and Sears, were offering snow sleds.

But Wheel Horse officials didn't display any horse sense, which the dictionary defines as common sense, when they entered the snowmobile business.

Inexplicably, Wheel Horse decided not to engineer its own machine. In April, 1969, the company made an expedient entry into the sled business by purchasing the Sno-Flite brand that had been built for the 1968 and '69 seasons by the C.E. Erickson Company Inc. (Cee-Co) of Des Moines, Iowa. Cee-Co was a manufacturer of cabinetry, display fixtures and advertising novelties that had also built go-karts, apparently unsuccessfully, and this probably should have raised a red flag for Wheel Horse. But apparently it didn't.

Sno-Flite To Safari

Sno-Flite was another of the dozens of "me, too" snowmobile brands flooding the market in those days. With nothing to differentiate it from dozens of competitive sleds, and hampered by unattractive styling that made them look clumsy and appear heavier than they really were, the Sno-Flite sleds sold very poorly in the intensely competitive snowmobile market.

Wheel Horse moved sled production to its tractor plant in South Bend, Indiana, where the workers reportedly experienced considerable difficulties building snowmobiles. Sno-Flite became Safari, with a red color scheme to differentiate the new machines from the yellow Sno-Flites. An air scoop was added to the top of the hood, the front bumper was switched from flat to tube stock and most models got a new rear storage compartment, but the uninspired design was otherwise left pretty much as it was.

About 2,000 left over Sno-Flites were re-manufactured as Safaris, a common industry practice of the time, and another 4,000 new Safaris were built for 1970. All six models had Kohler power, ranging from an 18 hp 295 to a 30 hp 440, with five on 15-inch tracks and one with a 22-inch wide track. Positioned as "rugged as any Wheel Horse tractor" and promoted by a National

Football League (NFL) endorsement as the "pick of the pros" with an NFL logo on ads and literature, Safari models were priced from $845 to $1,195.

The company signed up many dealers with inducements of free freight and free dealer floor plan financing until February 1, 1970. Attractive sales literature, color TV commercials and a big schedule of national magazine ads supported the effort. Dealers were also encouraged to demonstrate the machines and many did. SnowCo trailers, a leading brand of the day, were also offered as Wheel Horse branded accessories. Retail sled sales were slow but not totally dead.

"We had a single-cylinder, low-horsepower Wheel Horse snowmobile," recalls my long-time riding buddy Wayne Farley. "It was my dad's. He bought it brand new from our Wheel Horse dealer in town [Avon, New York]. It was the biggest piece of crap you ever did see. Ride it 15 minutes to an hour and it would break something in the suspension – shaft, bearing, this, that and the other thing. The hood was the most incredible thing on it, though. It was some sort of plastic. It got rolled down hills and never got a crack in it. We used to ride with this whole crew in the neighborhood. And we were young bucks, ex-military and all that. We'd go across a field, 25 or 35 miles an hour, next thing you know I'm rolling over. Sled couldn't go 35 without rolling. It was horrible."

Failure Came Fast
With about 2,500 of the 1970 Wheel Horse sleds unsold at the end of the season, no new Safaris were built for 1971. Reinhard Brothers, the company's Midwest distributor, bought 2,000 of the left-overs and blew them out in the '71 season at about half off the suggested retail price with a full one-year warranty, a rarity back then.

The limited production 1972 Safari line was just three models with new decals and a few minor improvements including more power for the wide track, but not even a parts book, just a four-page list of supplemental parts. Sales remained slow, so the company dropped snowmobiles and sold the remaining Safari assets to Parts Unlimited, which supported the brand until the parts ran out.

Wheel Horse showed no horse sense in acquiring the failing Sno-Flite, or frankly for entering an already over-saturated market. With barely two years of actual production over a three year period, the Safari was one of the fastest flops on record for a nationally distributed name-brand snow machine. The Wheel Horse name departed the lawn and garden industry in 2007, sparking renewed interest in everything with the company's logo, but decent examples of the failed Safari snowmobile are rare these days because most of them were deservedly junked long ago.

1970 Wheel Horse Safari 309

MANUFACTURER
Wheel Horse Inc., South Bend, Indiana

POWERTRAIN
Engine: 309cc Kohler radial-fan-cooled piston-port single with one Tillotson diaphragm pumper carb, magneto and breaker point ignition, and single exhaust into tuned muffler
Lubrication: Pre-mix at 20:1
Power Output: 20 hp
Drive Clutch: Salsbury

CHASSIS
Type: Welded and painted steel with stirrups, chrome steel bumpers and acrylonitrile-butadiene-styrene (ABS) hood
Claimed Dry Weight: 315 pounds
Front Suspension: Triple leaf springs
Ski Stance: 26.5 inches
Rear Suspension: Bogie wheels with torsion springs
Track: Goodyear 15-inch wide molded rubber
Brake: Mechanical disc
Fuel Capacity: 3 gallons
Standard Equipment: Dual 35-watt headlights, removable gas tank with Kelch cap, non-slip foot rests, dash glove box, rear seat storage compartment, passenger grab handles, snow flap

MSRP: $995

1971 Boatel Grand Prix
The Snow Yacht Slowly Sinks

The Boatel Company was a houseboat and pontoon manufacturer that entered the booming snowmobile business in 1964 by purchasing the Trailmaker iron dog from The Mathews Company. Boatel's first conventional sled was the 1966 Ski-Bird. Its major claim to fame was being the first celebrity-endorsed snowmobile, by Minnesota Vikings coach and ex-Philadelphia Eagles QB Norm Van Brocklin.

But it was the failure of the Snow-Bird that led to a notable next step for the Boatel line, according to veteran snowmobile ad man Phil Little, who worked with the brand.

"The Ski-Bird had a giant plus. It was so ugly and slow selling that Boatel company President Jim E. Klapmeier and former Polaris employee Roy Baumgartner decided to dump it for a more progressive model," Little said.

The result was a model with many forward thinking features, and more than a few rough edges.

New Ideas & Old Shortcomings
That model was the Boatel Grand Prix, a visually-appealing and somewhat high-tech snow yacht presented with a marketing strategy of exclusivity and high per-unit profit for dealers when it made its debut in 1970.

"I was working for the Erle Savage advertising agency," Little said, pointing out that the agency had earlier worked for Polaris. "Happily [Klapmeier and Baumgartner] involved me in the process largely on cosmetic and graphics issues." But his influence extended a bit farther.

"One feature I was responsible for was the butterfly steering. During my Polaris days I received a 1968 Colt. On one of my many rides before I went sled racing, there was a mishap that made an impression on me. The handlebar grip popped off in a turn and I made a hole in the snow. That got my ergonomics brain thinking about another design where the grip would not free itself. My thought was a handlebar with a vertical grip. It was a cast and plastic-coated part that I'm sure added unnecessary cost to the machine. It did, however, have 'talk' value."

The Grand Prix was different in other ways, too. An early adopter of aluminum for the chassis and skis, and of plastic for the belly pan, other progressive Grand Prix features included a fully-enclosed engine compartment, a lightweight 20-inch polyurethane track, a wide 33-inch ski stance, a governor on the carb to restrict speed for young operators, and a Donaldson muffler with an enclosed megaphone that was said to produce more speed with less sound.

The unitized power package containing the engine, clutches, jack shaft and steering gear insured drive system alignment and was attached to the chassis with four bolts.

Another good idea saw the brake mounted on the drive axle so that a chaincase failure would not render it useless. The big machine also included a boatload of items usually found as accessories on other brands like electric start, ski shocks, full instrumentation and under-seat storage with a flashlight, an adult beverage flask, a spare quart of oil and a fitted cover.

Initially advertised with a choice of a 440 (a 28 hp, 434cc JLO twin) at $1,695 or a limited availability 760 (a 45 hp, 744cc JLO twin) at $1,850, the stylish 1970 Grand Prix was claimed to be "60-pounds lighter than the most common wide-track snowmobile" in Boatel promotions and was backed with a very strong warranty. But the 760 was never produced. And despite the company's often-repeated performance claims, the remaining 440 was still a big, heavy and very expensive snowmobile with leg-breaker stirrups, an obsolete bogie wheel suspension and an outdated band brake.

Marketed as a machine for the select few with the theme line "It's not for everyone," the Grand Prix had a position of exclusivity. Boatel approached successful major brand snowmobile dealers with the proposition that the Grand Prix would provide high profit margins from sales to riders who only wanted the best that money could buy. But not enough dealers signed up.

Rude Welcome To The Real World
Sometimes big promises don't result in big results. *Invitation To Snowmobiling* magazine tested a new 399 model and found the Grand Prix to be well-built, well-equipped and unusually quiet, but also slow, ponderous and very pricey. The magazine's final remarks suggested the Grand Prix was for people who wanted a sled but didn't really like to go snowmobiling. Others agreed. One user said that the big luxury sled was "not real good in deep snow, even with the 20-inch track." Reviewers were split on the butterfly handlebars, some liking them, others maintaining that they hurt maneuverability.

Little's personal experience on the race track wasn't much different.

"I was so pumped about the Grand Prix as a racer that I spent huge money to build a fuel-injected 440cc CCW engine with everything including stuffed [crank] cases," Little said. "I did a nifty paint job and took it to its first race. The course was a rough swamp bottom. The Grand Prix started bucking so much that it threw the hood off. That race and the machine were so disgusting to me that I parted it out and never rode it again.

"A lot of snowmobilers looked at the Grand Prix, but few bought," Little said. "Boatel threw in the towel in 1972 and went back to building boats." The Grand Prix was sold to Glarco Inc. of Aitkin, Minnesota, which continued to manufacture essentially the same sled for the 1973 season with the name altered to GP Mark II. A few more were assembled from left-over parts for 1974 and '75.

The Grand Prix did innovate in engineering and marketing, but the size and weight, obsolete suspension and other features, and especially the huge price, were all negative factors that could not be overcome. It's really a wonder that this large barge was afloat as long as it was.

1971 Boatel Grand Prix 399

MANUFACTURER
The Boatel Company, a subsidiary of Telecheck International, Mora, Minnesota

POWERTRAIN
Engine: 398cc Canadian Curtis-Wright (CCW) axial-fan-cooled piston-port twin with one Tillotson HR diaphragm pumper, Kokusan magneto and breaker point ignition, and single pipe into "power tuned" Donaldson muffler
Compression Ratio: 8.5:1
Power Output: 30 hp @ 5,800 RPM with 27.3 pound-feet torque @ 5,500 RPM
Electrical Output: 75 watts
Clutches: Salsbury drive and torque-sensing driven

CHASSIS
Type: One-piece anodized aluminum with chromed tube steel stirrups and bumpers, Cycolac acrylonitrile-butadiene-styrene (ABS) belly pan and fiberglass hood
Claimed Dry Weight: 420 pounds
Front suspension: Triple leaf springs with hydraulic shock absorbers
Ski Stance: 33 inches
Rear Suspension: Bogie wheels (19) with torsion bars
Track: Gates 20-inch wide, 5-ply molded polyurethane with internal drive
Brake: Band type on drive shaft
Fuel Capacity: 5 gallons
Standard Equipment: Electric start, choke, butterfly steering wheel, speedometer/odometer, tachometer, gas gauge, padded dash with emergency shut-off switch, side marker lights, passenger grab handles, under seat storage compartment with flashlight and refreshment flask, spare quart of oil, tow hitch, fitted cover

MSRP: $1,795

1971 Dauphin
A Big Splash Quickly Disappears

Photo by Mark Elwell

At the height of the vintage snowmobile era in the late 1960s and early '70s, builders and brands were coming and going, some buying and building other brands while trying to stay afloat in an insanely competitive environment.

And no company made a bigger splash or packed more activity into fewer years than Dauphin Industries of Grand-Mere, Quebec.

The Splash
Organized in 1969 by Ovide Desaulnier, the fledgling manufacturer was one of literally dozens to produce a copy of the classic Ski-Doo.

With a Hirth industrial engine perched atop a steel tunnel over bogie wheels and a molded rubber track, there really wasn't much to differentiate the 1969 Dauphin from most of its competition except for its sleek styling with a distinctive royal purple and white color scheme, and a disc brake as its one advanced feature.

Dauphin is French for dolphin, and the company adopted the aquatic mammal that had been popularized by the "Flipper" television show as its identity, using a dolphin logo liberally on its sleds. But unlike most other fledgling sled manufacturers, the company quickly built a respectable distribution network across the North American snowbelt on both sides of the border. It was one of the first brands that I became aware of when I got into the business in 1970.

The 1970 Dauphins were available in two series. Standard models had manual start single-cylinder engines and single headlights. DeLuxe models had either twin-cylinder engines or electric start if not both, with dual

16

headlights and a white belly pan. The company was one of the first to adopt the new Eastern drive clutch, replacing the Power Bloc found in the earliest Dauphins, and dependability and ease of operation were stressed as key selling points.

In addition to dealerships handling the Dauphin brand, the company also became a private brand supplier to J.C. Penney, one of the leading chain stores of the day. Known as the Penney's Manhandler, only decals differentiated the machines from Dauphins.

The rapidly growing company completed calendar year 1970 by introducing the Dauphin Flipper, the company's version of the short-lived Chimo mini-sled built by Somovex of L'Isletville, Quebec. That sled was also being sold by Penney's as the Mini-Manhandler. Somovex was a parts supplier to Dauphin, and Dauphin apparently acquired assets of Somovex following that company's bankruptcy in December 1970. But the Flipper never entered full production.

The 1971 Dauphins got a mild restyling but no significant changes. A few Grant's stores, another big dry goods retail chain, also became Dauphin dealers. The mini-sled was continued for Penney's, but with the name changed to Snow Tamer. The company also built a series of Sno-Chief models for Dufrane Motor Distributors of Malone, New York. The 1971 and '72 Sno-Chiefs were rebadged Dauphins built in Grand-Mere, with the '71s differing little from the Dauphins except in color. But the 1972 Sno-Chiefs had JLO power and a different track.

B.C.R. Auto-Neige of St. Henedine de Beauce, Quebec, was also a customer. Its 1972 Super Star sleds were bright blue Dauphins with Kohler or CCW power and a few other minor changes.

According to reports from the day, Dauphins were not particularly fast or smooth riding, but they were tough, relatively dependable and handled pretty well for what they were. Janice Brewer, a western New York teenager when her father brought home a new Dauphin 240E, remembers that she and her sister rode it for several seasons.

"We had a lot of fun on it," she said. "We had no problems making it operate. [We] didn't have any problems steering it." That particular machine was fully restored a few years ago by versatile vintage authority Mark Elwell of Arkport, New York, and is now owned and exhibited by Cindy Mayka of Syracuse, New York.

The Ripples Fade
Like most small snowmobile manufacturers, Dauphin Industries was undercapitalized for the difficult and cash intensive sled business. The company was badly hurt by slow payment for the Penney's sleds, delivery of which fell behind schedule due to slow parts deliveries to Dauphin, and then by cancellation of Penney's orders for thousands more snowmobiles.

Dauphin went bankrupt in 1972 and the dolphin sled died. Penney's cleared its inventory in the '73 season, with Manhandler 240E prices slashed from the original $1,160 to $799. Pull start 292 single cylinder models were cut to $560, and Snow Tamers dropped to only $388.

Dufrane Motors purchased the Dauphin tooling, fixtures and parts at the bankruptcy auction and moved them down to Malone. The sled re-emerged as an improved Sno-Chief and lasted through a final 1977 prototype, but that's a tale for another time.

Ultimately the Dauphin was just one more flop in the long line of Ski-Doo clones that didn't make it. But in its four-year existence, Dauphin Industries and its dolphin sled made more waves than many brands that lasted longer than they did, and that makes the nearly forgotten Dauphin one of the more interesting and important brands of the fabulous vintage era.

1971 Dauphin 240E

MANUFACTURER
Dauphin Industries Ltd., Grand-Mere, Quebec

POWERTRAIN
Engine: 438cc Hirth 211R piston-port axial-fan-cooled twin with one Keihin 407 diaphragm pumper carb, breaker point ignition and single pipe into muffler
Power Output: 24 hp @ 5,500 rpm
Electrical Output: 75 watts
Drive Clutch: Eastern

CHASSIS
Type: Welded and painted steel with stirrups, chrome steel bumpers and fiberglass hood
Claimed Dry Weight: 365 Pounds
Front Suspension: Triple-leaf springs
Ski Stance: 24.5 inches
Rear Suspension: Bogie wheels (12 on 3 trucks) with torsion springs
Track: 15.5-inch, three-ply molded rubber with nylon and steel reinforcement
Brake: Mechanical disc
Fuel Capacity: 5.4 gallons
Standard Equipment: Electric start, dual headlights, seat back storage compartment

MSRP: $1,099

1971 Moto-Ski Capri 292

Affordable Family Fun

Photo courtesy of Jayson Bryant

When Bombardier acquired Moto-Ski from bankrupt Giffen Recreation in January 1971, the orange sled builder had 840 employees, mostly at its newly expanded production facility on the south shore of the St. Lawrence River. It also had a big following. The company was using much of its 50,000 sleds per year capacity, and annual production gave it something approaching 10 percent of the market against roughly 25 major competitors and dozens of lesser ones.

By the time the 1971 model year was over, Moto-Ski had moved well over 37,000 units through their 1,200 dealers, with almost 21,000 in the United States and the balance in Canada. It was enough to put the company in second place in Canada, and third overall trailing only Ski-Doo and Arctic Cat in total unit sales.

Nobody knew it at the time, but this was the high water mark for Moto-Ski, an honest machine built with above average product integrity when many brands were mechanical and electrical atrocities.

The Capri 292, a no-frills single-cylinder family sled, was one of the brand's best sellers in that peak season, and it provides good perspective on why Moto-Ski had become such a success.

Our Economical One

Moto-Ski described the 1971 Capri 292 as "our economical one" since it was the price leader of the company's full-sized sleds. The entire line had been restyled with a sleek, angular cowl replacing the outdated round hood used in the 1960s. The new cowls were initially made from fiberglass but molded plastic was introduced late in the production year as a rolling change.

Safety improvements included Mota-Ski's first handlebar-mounted kill switch and a passenger grab strap. In the rush to get completed units out the door, equipment like carburetors, bumpers, hinges and seat covers tended to vary somewhat, depending on what was on hand when the sled was assembled.

The '71 Capri was offered in five models with four engine choices. Two different 292 singles were offered, along with a 338 Hirth single with or without factory-installed electric start, and a 399 JLO twin. This use of multiple European engine brands was typical of many sled manufacturers of the day, as companies used whatever they could get from the industry's major suppliers to power their products.

To keep costs down, all Capri models were pretty Spartan, lacking gauges and the engine cover that equipped more expensive Moto-Skis.

The 292s didn't even have the two-color seat or the snow flap that were found on more expensive Capri models. One big selling point was a two-year track guarantee on Moto-Ski single- cylinder models and one year on twins. This was part of the company's famous "Tougher Seven Ways" marketing communications platform. Developed by the giant New York City advertising agency Young & Rubicam, this theme was used to describe specific engineering features like the hand-welded steel chassis, "airplane-type control cables that won't freeze up;" ball and socket steering and twin headlights "that won't leave you in the dark."

A Value Story

When it was all said and done, the Capri 292 was a lot of snowmobile for the money. Big enough to handle two adults, and tough enough to endure the rough treatment that was handed out to snow machines back before organized trails were commonplace, the Capri 292 was one of the least expensive genuine two-seaters available. And it was also more reliable than many competitive sleds, too.

The nice price combined with Mota-Ski's well-earned reputation for durability to make the Capri a family favorite across the snowbelt. Many Moto-Ski owners were passionate about their rides. They were proud of their orange machines and didn't want anything else. Consequently many of them became very unhappy when Bombardier later acquired the brand.

Moto-Skis in general and the Capri variants in particular did tend to last pretty well. There were still a couple of them in my snowmobile club when I joined a decade later. Their ride and handling were totally obsolete by then, but they were still running strong. And some of them still are today, too.

End Of An Era

By 1971, the bogie wheel Capri with its engine in the rider's lap was becoming pretty dated, and its replacement was on the drawing board, to be carried forward under Bombardier ownership. But the Capri did stay in the line for a couple more years until it was superceded by the much more sophisticated F series that made its debut in 1973.

But the Capri 292 and its running mates established a reputation for quality and value that made Moto-Ski a leading name in the industry for many years. The brand from the south shore of the St. Lawrence River lasted longer and sold more snow machines than any of the non-survivors. And there are still lots of Moto-Ski partisans around to this day.

1971 Moto-Ski Capri 292

MANUFACTURER
Les Industries Bouchard, Lte., Sainte-Anne-de-la-Pocatiere, Quebec, Canada, a subsidiary of Giffen Industries, Inc., Miami, Florida

POWERTRAIN
Engine: 292cc Hirth 193R or JLO L295 radial-fan-cooled piston-port single (both were used)
Carburetion: One Tillotson HR44A or Keihin 406 (JLO only) diaphragm pumper
Compression Ratio: 12:1
Ignition: Magneto and breaker points
Lubrication: Pre-mix at 20:1
Exhaust: Single pipe into muffler
Power Output: 19 hp (Hirth)/ 21.5 hp (JLO)
Drive Clutch: Moto-Ski "camdrive glide"

CHASSIS
Type: Hand-welded and painted steel belly pan and tunnel assembly with stirrups and rear lift handle, chromed steel front and rear bumpers, fiberglass or molded plastic hood
Dry Weight (claimed): 325 pounds
Front Suspension: Four leaf springs
Ski Stance: 24 inches
Rear Suspension: Rubber bogie wheels on ball bearings with torsion springs
Track: 15-3/16-by-117-inch Moto-Ski utilizing two Uniroyal 3-ply rubber belts with full-width rubberized cleats and single (center) sprocket drive
Brake: Mechanical shoe on driven pulley
Fuel Capacity: 6.15 gallons

STANDARD EQUIPMENT
Dual headlights with protective cover, simulated walnut dash panel, primer, decompression switch (Hirth only), kill switch, side reflectors, non-slip footrests, passenger grab strap, seat back tool box, tow hitch

MSRP: $745

1971 Suzuki Nomad

Durability Didn't Do It

While engineering their first-ever snowmobile, Suzuki engineers correctly concluded that most snow machines of the day were essentially disposable devices.

So the new 1971 Suzuki SM10 snowmobile, marketed as the Nomad 360, was constructed to last and introduced with the theme "Built stronger than it has to be."

Attention-grabbing ads carried headlines like "Suzuki thinks a snowmobile should last longer than three years." The company then backed it up with a longer-than-standard warranty and attention to detail in many key areas. But would it be enough to grab attention in a crowded market?

Some New, Some Not

A new purpose-built snowmobile powerplant was specifically engineered to combat vapor lock, a major reliability issue of the day. The Nomad was one of the first sleds in the industry to use the Mikuni VM-series float bowl carburetor with an external fuel pump. Other anti-vapor lock measures included a large radial cooling fan and a carefully-engineered exhaust system to fight under-hood heat that caused this sled-immobilizing problem.

The Nomad's engine also utilized reed valve induction for better low-end grunt. Outboard Marine Corp. (maker of Evinrude and Johnson) brought this concept to the sport but never promoted it, allowing Suzuki to appear to be the first to use it. A dual-coil ignition also improved reliability, and the electrical output of 180-watts more than doubled that of typical sled engines of the day.

At 360cc, the Nomad's engine didn't fit the industry's established size hierarchy. But the modest power output was in line with the typical 340 fan of the day and provided a quick glimpse of the future. Later Arctic Cat Spirit engines from Suzuki also used larger-than-normal displacements to generate additional torque and last longer due to de-stressed components.

The Suzuki chassis was decidedly old school, and despite promotion of its "aircraft-type ball joints" in the steering, the Nomad's handling, side-to-side stability and ride quality were sub-standard. However, an engine shroud, kill switch, adjustable handlebars and disc brake were all advanced features. Suzuki also emphasized its "double-strength aluminum drive wheel," which was how it confusingly described the plastic-covered drive sprocket.

Warranty of six months or 1,500 miles, whichever came first, was better than most.

The Market Yawns
Despite instant credibility from the Suzuki name backed up with extensive attention-grabbing advertising, the market greeted the Nomad with a big collective yawn as the "Suzuki lives longer" message simply failed to resonate with buyers.

Suzuki handicapped its sled sales by limiting them to full-line dealers only. No snowmobile-only franchises were allowed, significantly limiting the number of outlets because the financial and floor-space requirements for major-brand motorcycle dealerships were much higher than for a sled dealership. And many Suzuki motorcycle dealers simply had little interest and even less experience in the snowmobile market so they were not effective representatives for the sled line.

Popular Snowmobiling magazine did run a feature on the new Suzuki sleds, commenting that "the Nomad … is no slouch on performance." The publication also noted that the Nomad "is well-equipped electrically for night driving" and went on to comment that "we see a lot of hardware that can come loose after a few hours riding, but in general the machines look well made." The magazine concluded that "Instead of trying to capture the market with tricky little mini-snowmobiles or appearing years behind in development, Suzuki has introduced a well-developed machine worthy of the buyer's consideration."

Nevertheless, sales of the 1971 Nomads just sputtered along as riders generally ignored the maybe 5,000 Suzuki sleds of all three models (two Nomads and the very similar original XR-400) that were built that year.

Moving On
The Nomad anchored the Suzuki snowmobile line throughout the brand's five-year run, with engine options tweaked and expanded along the way. But by 1975 Suzuki had a big pile of unsold snowmobile inventory, and it was clear that its product engineering and marketing strategy built on durability had failed. The company exited the business as a vehicle marketer after the '75 season to become Arctic Cat's primary engine supplier.

Nomad restoration parts are hard to find now, but reproductions of some items are available, and many Yamaha parts will reportedly fit the chassis and suspension. It is likely that the Hamamatsu, Japan-based factories of the two companies used many of the same component suppliers.

Durability didn't make the Suzuki snowmobile successful, but quality original Nomads still exist today because they were built to last.

1971 Suzuki Nomad

MANUFACTURER
U.S. Suzuki Motor Corp., Santa Fe Springs, California, by Suzuki Motors Co., Ltd, Hamamatsu, Japan

POWERTRAIN
Engine: 359.3cc Suzuki radial-fan-cooled reed-valve twin
Carburetion: One Mikuni VM float type
Ignition: Magneto and breaker points with dual coils
Lubrication: Pre-mix at 20:1
Exhaust: Single pipe into muffler
Power Output: 28 hp @ 6,500 RPM with 23 pound-feet of torque @ 5,500 RPM
Clutches: Salsbury 910 drive and Suzuki driven

CHASSIS
Type: Welded and painted steel belly pan and tunnel with stirrups, chrome bumpers and lift handle, and fiberglass hood and engine shroud
Claimed Dry Weight: 358 pounds
Front Suspension: Triple-leaf springs
Ski Stance: 23.9 inches
Rear Suspension: Bogie wheels with torsion coil springs
Track: 15.5-inch center-drive steel-reinforced molded rubber with 50.5 inch footprint
Brake: Mechanical disc
Fuel Capacity: 4.2 gallons
Standard Equipment: Engine shroud, adjustable handlebars, kill switch, speedometer/odometer, dipstick gas gauge, storage compartment in seat, non-slip footrests, passenger hand grips, towing hitch, snow flap, electric start on otherwise identical model SM10D

MSRP: $895 ($995 with electric start)

The Swinger

Pick a pair

In the heady days of the 1960s sexual revolution, "swinging" was a code word for wife-swapping. So Swinger made an attention-grabbing name for the all-new mini-sled introduced by Sportscraft Industries for the 1971 model year.

The Swinger wasn't the first mini-sled on the market, but it had a more fully developed marketing platform than most sleds of any size at the time. "Pick a pair and have twice the fun" was the basic pitch, emphasizing that two Swingers could be purchased for essentially the same price as one standard sized sled – and at a price of $575 per Swinger, that was basically true. Most of the initial advertising and sales literature showed a man and an attractive woman with two Swinger snowmobiles. Although the literature talked about the kids, they were rarely seen.

A tiny Chrysler two-stroke engine with no electrical charging circuit powered the first Swinger. It was said to be capable of propelling the sled at speeds up to 35 mph. But it also tended to over-heat, causing under-hood components to warp and fail. A 12-volt battery with an on-off switch powered the lights.

Like many sleds from the 1960s, the Swinger's hood was permanently attached to the frame instead of being hinged or at least easily removable. But unlike the majority of its contemporaries, the Swinger had a console that covered the moving parts, and this was promoted as the excellent safety feature that it was. However, these design decisions made under-the-hood service like charging the battery or tuning the carburetor very difficult in the garage and impossible in the field.

Up front, a transverse leaf spring provided the ski suspension. This inexpensive front-end arrangement was tried and quickly discarded by several of the mini-sled manufacturers because it resulted in sub-standard ski tracking and poor side-to-side stability, making the small sleds difficult to ride in anything other than ideal conditions. In back, the Swinger had a simple rack suspension with torsion springs that was somewhat similar to the later Scorpion Para-Rail. Six bogie wheels were mounted solidly to the rack, and there were two sprockets on the axle at each end of the track, but only the front ones were powered.

However, the Swinger did have some important positive attributes. It was very small at just 72 inches long including the skis, 26 inches tall excluding the windshield and 28 inches wide. And at only 175 pounds, it was a featherweight even for the time. This was actually small and light enough to allow loading two of the tiny machines side-by-side into the back end of a full-sized station wagon (remember them?) for transport to the trailhead. No truck or trailer was needed. And the machines could be stored in the garage by standing them on their rear bumpers like a rear-engine riding lawnmower, greatly reducing the space they occupied.

Before WKRP, actress Loni Anderson modeled with the 1973 Swinger snowmobile.

At a time when most brands had a single signature color, Swinger offered a choice of two bright "with it" colors, lime green and plum purple, along with a choice of snow white or much more practical black upholstery. The color selections were supposed to appeal to the wife who might be apprehensive about having a snow machine, making Swinger one of the very first brands to use color choice as an element of its marketing plan.

A serious effort to recruit dealers was conducted, but pitching the Swinger as a great second line for dealers already handling other brands was not very successful. And the Swingers that did reach the trail proved to be less than satisfactory.

In March of 1971 Griswold Industries acquired Sportscraft Industries. No 1972 Swingers were produced, but Griswold continued to sell off left-over 71s on a discounted customer-direct basis for $489.95 each.

Swingin' Some More
Griswold heavily re-engineered the Swinger for the 1972-73 model year. A conventional ski suspension with multi-leaf springs solved the handling and stability issues. Upgraded power came from a 15.5-horsepower JLO 230cc one lunger with a Tillotson HD carb, Donaldson muffler, a charging circuit and a Salsbury 500 drive clutch. The hood was hinged for under hood access. Vents on the front and both sides of the hood helped cool the engine better, and a chrome headlight bezel improved the looks.

Claimed speed capability rose to over 40 mph, and a kill switch was added for safety. Dry weight rose to 255-pounds. Company owner F.W. Griswold claimed that every machine was tested on a chassis dynomometer prior to shipment, a practice that would become commonplace in the snowmobile industry.

But the 1973 Swinger had limited distribution and no serious marketing or advertising campaign behind it. The considerably improved little machine was generally overlooked by the snowmobile press who were infatuated with sexy Skiroules, smoking hot El Tigrés, revolutionary liquid-cooled Bruts, big new rotary-engined Evinrudes and Johnsons, rear-engine Raiders and dozens of other brands with new "look at me" features. Few dealers carried mini-sleds and few buyers chose to "pick a pair" so the Swinger snowmobile was clearly going nowhere.

Swingin' Comes To A Hault
Griswold Industries apparently had big plans for the Swinger, including an all-new full-sized model. According to a midwestern Vintage sled enthusiast, at least one prototype of the full sized Swinger was actually constructed. But that was as far as Swinger or Griswold ever got in the snowmobile industry.

In truth, none of the mini-sled brands ever found much of a market or lasted more than a few seasons. Furthermore, 1973 proved to be a pivotal year in snowmobiling. Gross overproduction had finally caught up with the industry, and demand for snow machines crashed following a relatively light winter and the economic shock of the first Arab oil embargo.

So despite Swinger's color option innovation and solid initial marketing programs, the little sled joined the quickly lengthening list of the industry's failed brands.

Today Swinger is an object of affection for a handful of collectors, particularly women, who have fallen under the seductive spell of this petite and interesting snowmobile pioneer.

1971 Swinger

MANUFACTURER
Sportscraft Industries Inc., St. Paul, Minnesota

POWERTRAIN
Engine: 134cc Chrysler radial-fan-cooled reed-valve single
Carburetion: One Tillotson HL diaphragm pumper
Ignition: Magneto and breaker points
Lubrication: Pre-mix 16:1
Exhaust: Single pipe with tube muffler
Power Output: 10 hp
Electrical Output: None
Drive Clutch: Salsbury 330

CHASSIS
Chassis: Welded 16-gauge steel with electrostatic coating, chromed steel front bumper, plastic tunnel close-off panel and fixed fiberglass hood
Claimed Dry Weight: 175 pounds
Front Suspension: One transverse mono-leaf spring with helper leaf
Ski Stance: 22.5 inches
Rear Suspension: Rigid rack with two torsion springs and six bogie wheels
Track: 12- by 90-inch steel-reinforced molded rubber with 34-inch footprint
Fuel Capacity: 3.6 gallons
Standard Equipment: Choke, wood-grained dash panel, non-slip running boards, zippered storage compartment in front of seat, "flat back" rear end for vertical storage
Options: Machine color, seat color

MSRP: $575

1972 Alouette Eliminator

Bangor Punta Punts The Snowmobile Business

Featherweight Aluminum Corporation started building Alouette snowmobiles in 1966 for the 1967 season by following the successful Ski-Doo template. In 1968 the company began producing re-bodied Alouettes as Arlberg snowmobiles for Alcock, Laight and Westwood of Bramlea, Ontario. But Arlberg only lasted two seasons (model years 1969 and '70) before failing financially.

In the meantime, Greenwich, Connecticut-based industrial conglomerate Bangor Punta Ltd. purchased Featherweight and provided fresh capital to expand the operation. One of America's 200 largest companies at the time, Bangor Punta already owned Piper Aircraft, Smith & Wesson firearms, Starcraft Campers, four boat companies building everything from day sailers to ocean racers, and a number of other successful businesses. Observing that almost every hard goods company seemed to be selling sleds, and that many manufacturers were building multiple brands, Bangor Punta had Alouette build more thinly disguised clones as Starcraft snowmobiles. Brought to market for the 1970 season, they sold very poorly.

In spring 1971, Bangor Punta announced that Starcraft sleds would be discontinued after just two seasons because they were diluting Featherweight's snowmobile effort, and that the best of both lines would be combined under the Alouette name.

The Beautiful Brutes

One of the few assets that Alouette inherited from the defunct Starcraft snowmobile brand was the Eliminator model name. Offered with 295, 340 and 440 twin-cylinder Sachs engines, the 1972 Eliminators replaced the previous GT series as Alouette's trail performance offerings in a lineup that was pared down from eight to just five models.

Improvements to the GT series to create the new Eliminators included evolutionary restyling and a switch to Sachs power for the 440, new handlebars and grips for better comfort, a kill switch, a seat strap for a passenger, wider skis and improved steering stops that prevented damage to the ball joints in the steering gear. Still light-

24

weight machines with an outstanding power-to-weight ratio, *Invitation To Snowmobiling* magazine found the Eliminator to be the lightest 440 tested that year.

But the machines were still small and narrow with a high center of gravity, so they weren't particularly stable.

"The first option you sold a guy was ski spreaders," recalls Alouette enthusiast Brian Berger, whose father-in-law, Ray Moyer, was an Alouette dealer in Bangor, Pennsylvania. "They widened it 4 inches."

"And they came in two styles," said Ray's son Brian Moyer, "straight and stepped." This illustrates one of Alouette's strong points: more options than most other brands. Some, like a speedometer/odometer and a tach, were factory installed. Others, like slide rail suspension and electric start, were dealer installed. Sleds were all pre-wired to make the key start installation easier for the dealers. Performance parts like free-air cylinders and pistons, tuned pipes and gears were also available. Other options included a snow flap, chrome skis and a cargo sleigh.

Billed as the Beautiful Brutes, the 1972 Alouettes got solid marketing support including good sales literature, a serious advertising and product publicity campaign in snowmobile magazines and a massive, well promoted sweepstakes. Top prize was a red Piper Cherokee four-place aircraft, with a couple of boats and 24 Alouette snowmobile suits as consolation prizes.

Snow Goer tested the '72 Eliminator 440 near Park City, Utah. The editors praised the excellent under-seat storage compartment, multi-density foam seat, convenient rubber hood latches and overall dependability. "The Alouettes have plenty of leg room," commented the reviewers, who concluded that Alouette sleds were "classy and sassy."

Punted

Despite lots of publicity and some positive reviews for the new Eliminators and other Alouette models, there was just one thing wrong: Alouette snowmobile sales were declining in the face of overall industry sales increases. Melting down from 18,000 in 1970 when Bangor Punta bought Featherlite, to 15,000 in 1971 when it became obvious that Starcraft sleds were failing, to only 12,000 in 1972 when Alouette was Bangor Punta's only snowmobile brand, the trend was clearly in the wrong direction and Alouette had fallen out of the top 10 brands in sales.

So Bangor Punta became one of the first of several major conglomerates to leave the snowmobile business. They sold Featherweight to Coleco, another conglomerate, and Alouette passed into the hands of the third owner in its short history.

The Coleco years would bring Alouette some of the most fearless engineering that the snowmobile world has ever seen, including the unique Ski Sorber front suspension on the 1973 models, a highly influential, handlebar-mounted headlight pod that became a major success story years later for another brand, and a World's Championship in oval sprint racing. But that's a story for another time.

1972 Alouette Eliminator 440

MANUFACTURER
Featherweight Corporation, a subsidiary of Bangor Punta Ltd, at Montreal, Quebec

POWERTRAIN
Engine: 437cc Sachs SA2-440 axial-fan-cooled piston-port twin with one Tillotson HD-88A diaphragm pumper carb, breaker point ignition and a single pipe
Compression Ratio: 10.3:1
Power Output: 35 hp @ 6,500 RPM
Drive & Driven Clutches: Salsbury

CHASSIS
Type: Welded and painted steel with stirrups and chromed tubular steel bumpers, fiberglass hood
Claimed Dry Weight: 345 pounds
Front Suspension: Triple-leaf springs
Ski Stance: 22 inches
Rear Suspension: Rubber bogie wheels with torsion springs
Track: 15-inch polyester-reinforced rubber with single sprocket drive
Brake: Mechanical disc
Fuel Capacity: 5 gallons
Standard Equipment: Engine console, primer, kill switch, reflective side stripes, non-slip foot rests, passenger grips and grab strap, under-seat storage area, tow hitch, dual tail lights

MSRP: $1,195

1972 Arctic Cat Kitty Cat

All-Time Champion Kids Sled

The second annual USSA World Series of Snowmobiling was held in March, 1971, in Boonville, New York. But race sleds weren't the only snow machines in the public eye that weekend, as the pint-sized Arctic Cat Kitty Cat was unveiled to the public for the first time.

Although youth-sized snowmobiles had been around for several years, the new Cat for kids was aimed at an even younger crowd, the 5- to 10-year olds. Crammed full of safety features and restricted to a top speed between 8 and 12 mph, depending on where the engine governor was set, the Kitty Cat clearly wasn't a real trail sled but more of a motorized toy for the back yard.

Arctic officials emphasized that the Kitty Cat was small enough to go in the trunk of a car, yet it was styled to look just like a big Cat, right down to its molded plastic hand controls, black hood and Arctic trademark spotted vinyl seat cover over the high-density foam seat. Price was initially announced as "about $250."

Little did anyone know at the time that this unique machine would become a snowmobile icon for decades to come, and the most successful kid sled ever built. It would also be the machine that introduced many sledheads to the sport – from average Joe trail rider to mountain riders to world championship-winning snowmobile racers.

Into Production

The pilot-build of approximately 50 Kitty Cats, including the one shown at Boonville, used a Clinton two-cycle engine under a chrome hood grille from the Kohler/Wankel big Cat hood, with trim decals that were patterned after the 1971 EXT race sleds.

The production models released for the 1972 season had many changes. Most obvious was a Kawasaki engine, just like big brothers Cat sleds, with the choke relocated from the now smaller dash panel to under the hood where little hands wouldn't find it easily. The hood lost the chrome grille in favor of a molded-in black one, but gained side louvers. The belly pan switched from metalflake silver to plain gray.

The chassis was heavily reworked with a different bulkhead, improved hood hinge, redesigned steering and skis, and deletion of the tubular rear bumper in favor of an integrated plastic lift handle and reflector unit. An engine kill switch was added, just like on the big sleds, and new triangular hood decals were used. And in addition to Arctic Cat black, they were also produced with hoods in a choice of red or yellow (50 of each) to sell to families who owned other brands of sleds.

Initial production was at Arctic's recently acquired General Leisure lawnmower plant in Omaha, Nebraska, with the actual retail price set at $269.95 plus freight. Promotion included a ton of product publicity in snowmobile magazines and demos at many snowmobile events.

Small as it was, the Kitty Cat wasn't the bottom end of the Arctic Cat line up. That distinction went to the House Cat; a plastic inflatable "snowmobile" introduced a short time after the Kitty Cat. Propulsion was by the leg muscles of the toddlers that it was

26

designed to indoctrinate and prepare for the big move up to the gasoline-powered Kitty Cat.

On The Snow
The tiny machine was an instant hit. Even though the Kitty Cat was an expensive toy that was helpless in any kind of serious snow, families eagerly snapped them up for their youngsters. Their low speed and solid construction kept them running for years. It was incredible how much abuse they could absorb. My touring buddy Ted has a funny video of his seven-year-old son driving his Kitty Cat flat out into a square hit on a cinderblock house foundation. Sled and helmeted rider simply shrugged off the impact without damage to either one. Another of my buddies bought one for his five-year-old son, but his two year old kept jumping on it and riding it away any time his older brother abandoned it even momentarily.

Many Kitty Cats were passed down from one sibling to another, and then eventually sold for use by other families. Once the initial depreciation hit had been absorbed, the little sleds maintained their value amazingly well. The only serious maintenance issue was the inevitable track deterioration from age and use.

Kitty Cat racing was added to all kinds of snowmobile events, and it was amazing how almost everyone would stop whatever they were doing to watch the rug rats run their Kitty Cats. More than a few winning racers got their start in competition this way.

Time And Changes
The Cat for kids evolved quite a bit over the years. The alternate hood colors were dropped after the first year and the fuel tank went from metal to plastic in 1973. Graphics and trim began evolving in 1976 and changed considerably over time, getting extensive and very colorful in later years. One of the biggest changes occurred in 1977 when the Suzuki AA06A1 60cc engine replaced Kawasaki power, one year after the same engine supplier change in the big Cats. The carb was eventually changed to a Mikuni butterfly type. A handlebar pad became standard equipment in 1979. Unfortunately Arctic Enterprises went out of business in 1981, so no Kitty Cats were built for the 1982, '83 or '84 model years.

Arctco, Inc., the successor to Arctic Enterprises, began building Kitty Cats in 1985. This later series included an always-on headlight and a windshield as standard equipment. Both were previously available as options. Other materials changes later in life included switching to a steel chassis with an ABS hood. A real rear bumper was added in 1995.

Production ran through the 2000 model year when the new, larger, and more capable four-stroke Z 120 pushed the then $1,349 Kitty Cat aside.

Little Legacy
The Kitty Cat introduced thousands of youngsters to the joys of snow riding, with many of those kids eventually graduating to their own full sized snow sleds. It proved to be the most popular and longest lasting of the more than half-dozen snowmobiles built specifically for kids over the years, it and paved the way for the later 120-class sleds from Arctic and others.

Many Kitty Cats are still out there entertaining tiny tykes across the snowbelt and preparing them to participate in our favorite outdoor past time. Some of them actually resell repeatedly for more than their original list price, so many of them are likely to be around as long as there are tracks available to keep them moving. And that makes the Kitty Cat one of the great classic sleds of all time.

1972 Arctic Cat Kitty Cat

MANUFACTURER
Arctic Enterprises, Inc., Thief River Falls, Minnesota, at Omaha, Nebraska

POWERTRAIN
Engine: 60cc Kawasaki T5A060S1A piston-port radial-fan-cooled single
Carburetion: One diaphragm pumper
Ignition: Magneto and breaker points
Lubrication: Pre-mix at 25:1
Exhaust: Single pipe into muffler
Power Output: 2.85 hp @ 7,000 RPM
Drive Clutch: Arctic Cat centrifugal

CHASSIS
Type: Riveted aluminum with extruded aluminum front bumper, and fiberglass hood & belly pan
Claimed Dry Weight: 95 pounds
Front Suspension: Mono-leaf springs
Ski Stance: 17.5 inches
Rear Suspension: None, rigid wheel frame with zero travel
Track: 10-by-54.3-inch molded rubber with dual sprocket drive and a 14-inch footprint
Brake: Mechanical band type
Fuel Capacity: 0.5 gallon
Standard Equipment: Key lock ignition, choke, imitation walnut dash panel, engine governor, kill switch, padded ski tips, side and rear reflectors, snow flap

Price: $ 269.95 MSRP excluding freight

1972 Bolens Super Sprint 440
The real deal arrives too late

In the 1960s, the Bolens Division of Food Machinery Corporation (FMC) was a very old, very well known and unusually innovative manufacturer of quality lawn and garden equipment. Wanting to provide a counter-seasonal product for its northern dealers, the company jumped into the snowmobile business in 1965 by purchasing the Canadian-built Hus-Ski.

An articulated two-piece machine, the Hus-Ski was a twin-tracked power unit that pulled the riders on a ski-mounted sulky. Under Bolens ownership, this odd and occasionally hazardous design was renamed the Diablo Rouge (red devil) and got an appropriate color change. Pushed onto sometimes-reluctant dealers and heavily promoted by the company, it did sell in some numbers. "They wanted every one of the tractor and power equipment dealers to take some sleds," recalls former Bolens dealer George Burdick of Salisbury, New Hampshire.

But FMC soon realized that it needed a more mainstream product. For the 1969 season, the company created a conventional sled and christened it the Bolens Sprint. The company sold the two types side-by-side for one winter, then dropped the Diablo Rouge and forged ahead with the Sprint. A nicely styled but otherwise pretty unremarkable machine, it did have a few plusses, like superior gas capacity and optional turn signals. But despite above average promotional support, it just didn't sell well.

After using several of the common engine brands of the day, including JLO, Hirth and Kohler, the company tried differentiating the Sprint by creating its own captive powerplants. Engineered by Bolens but manufactured in West Germany, these new twins and unique three-cylinder air-cooled engines carried the Gutbrod name. But they were unreliable, with the triples notoriously bad, and they killed what equity had been built for the Bolens Sprint brand name.

Back To The Drawing Board
The snowmobile market was still booming, so Bolens returned to the drawing board to try to re-engineer their Sprint into a winner. One obvious need was a new engine.

Carl Kiekhaefer had been the driving force behind Mercury outboards and snowmobiles, but had left the company after Brunswick Corporation gained control of the business. His performance boat start-up venture, Kiekhaefer Aeromarine, began building snowmobile engines as a sideline.

Bolens jumped at the opportunity to ally with Kiekhaefer's performance image and became one of two brands (along with Northway) to use a version of his sled engine. Interesting fuel mixture flow control with ports in the pistons and "power pockets" in the cylinder walls, plus early use of CD ignition with surface gap spark plugs, made these some of the most technically advanced and powerful snowmobile engines of their time. A beefed-up Salsbury drive clutch was also provided for these engines.

The 1972 Bolens Sprint line was reduced from nine to six models, and all but the low-end 293 got an engine kill switch as part of the industry's response to safety criticism. The three Kiekhaefer-powered models, all 440s, were among the very few truly all American-made snowmobiles available. Gutbrod twins were retained in the low-powered models but relabeled as Bolens engines.

One of the six '72 Sprints was a new performance model, the Super Sprint 440. The first Bolens with a slide rail suspension, this Kiekhaefer-powered line leader also used a polyurethane track instead of the rubber one on other Sprints. New, reflective, multi-color striping set off the chassis and nicely restyled hood, but a smaller gas tank was fitted.

"I sold just one of that particular model" Burdick recollects. "This sucker, as I remember it, would just about fly. One of the guys around here had a T'NT 669, and it would eat that T'NT right up."

Snow Goer testers were enthusiastic, too, saying that the Super Sprint 440 performed admirably under what were described as difficult test conditions, noting that it did not tend to vapor lock at high altitudes, and concluding that "these machines deserve a hard look for '72."

But even this hot new model had issues. "They had a lot of track problems," Burdick says. *Snow Goer* also noted that a larger windshield would provide better rider protection, more storage space would have been welcome and a larger taillight would be more visible.

The Finish Line
Despite the hot new Kiekhaefer 440 engine, slide rail suspension and sleek styling that was definitely above average for the day, the Bolens Sprint brand had simply suffered too much damage. The company pulled the plug on the snowmobile business during the winter of 1972, leaving distributors and dealers to liquidate remaining inventory. Key service parts soon became difficult to obtain, and running Bolens Sprints are relatively rare today.

The Super Sprint 440 was the real deal, a genuine hot sled, but it quickly faded into snowmobile history as just one more really good machine that was just too little, too late to save a company's winter recreation business.

1972 Bolens Super Sprint 440

MANUFACTURER
Bolens Division of FMC Corporation,
Port Washington, Wisconsin

POWERTRAIN SPECS
Engine: Kiekhaefer Aeromarine 440S axial fan cooled piston-port twin
Displacement: 433cc
Carburetion: One Tillotson HD94A diaphragm pumper
Compression Ratio: 10.5:1
Ignition: K-tron capacitor discharge (CD) with surface-gap spark plugs
Lubrication: Pre-mix at 20:1
Exhaust: Single pipe into muffler
Power Output: 40 hp @ 6,800 rpm
Electrical Output: 75 watts
Drive Clutch: Salsbury heavy duty

CHASSIS SPECS
Type: Welded and painted steel with stirrups, painted tube steel rear bumper, chromed steel front bumper and fiberglass hood
Claimed Dry Weight: 335 pounds
Front Suspension: Triple-leaf springs
Ski Stance: 26 inches
Rear Suspension: Slide rails
Track: 15.5-inch-wide one-piece molded polyurethane with dual drive sprockets
Brake: Mechanical disc
Fuel Capacity: 5 gallons
Standard Equipment: Speedometer/odometer, tachometer, kill switch, storage compartment in seat, passenger grab strap, tow hitch, snow flap, reflective side stripes
Options: Dual carb kit, expansion chamber kit, racing sprockets, skidframe wheel kit

MSRP: $1,245

1972 Poloron Tornado
Nice Try, But No Cigar

Color photo courtesy of www.vintagesnowmobiles.50megs.com

Founded in 1937, Poloron Products evolved into a mini-conglomerate. Headquartered in the New York City suburb of New Rochelle, New York, the company built such diverse products as charcoal braziers, picnic coolers, lighted Christmas decorations, institutional furniture, modular homes, riding lawn tractors and travel trailers in a dozen factories scattered across the eastern United States.

And like many hard goods manufacturers of the 1960s, it answered the siren song of the booming snowmobile business.

The rare Poloron Stallion is virtually forgotten, but the very different 1970 Poloron established the company in the snowmobile business. Sleds were assembled at the company's Michigan City, Indiana, lawn tractor plant with components sourced from typical industry suppliers including Polaris. Engines were up front. Appearance, features and pricing were definitely competitive, and sleds were backed by a full one-year warranty that exceeded most contemporaries.

The 1970 Poloron single-cylinder Cyclone and twin-cylinder Tornado models also introduced an emergency shut-off switch mounted on the fake wood dash above the handlebars. In a couple more years, virtually every new sled would include a "kill" switch as an industry-wide safety upgrade to stave off threatened legislation.

Building A Brand

Although the Poloron name wasn't as familiar as Mercury or Suzuki, it wasn't totally unknown to the American public, and that gave the company's machine some credibility against the dozens of Ski-Things and Sno-Turkeys from two-car-garage companies that nobody had ever heard of. Vintage Snowmobile Club of America (VSCA) National Champion Tom Todd's father was a multi-line dealer in the Cooperstown, New York, area who took on the Poloron sled.

"My dad sold as many of them as AMF and Bolens (sleds)," Todd says.

Poloron sleds got extensive newspaper coverage for delivering food, medicine, and fuel during a big January 1970 snow emergency in Pennsylvania's Pocono Mountains east of Scranton, where the company had another manufacturing plant.

The company also filed their sleds with the United States Snowmobile Association (USSA) for Stock class racing. But they had to settle for crumbs like Clyde Dickens of WADR radio in Remsen, New York, taking second in a media event on a Poloron Cyclone at Boonville's huge New York State Championships in February, 1970.

For 1971, Poloron sleds were upgraded with new styling, dual headlights, an improved dash, metalflake green hoods, disc brakes and more engine options. The 1972 models were essentially re-badged 1971s.

"They ran good, and handled good for their day," Todd recalls. "The chassis was well designed. The only real difference between them and Arctic Cat was that Cat had slide rails. And I thought that metalflake green was the neatest color."

Actually a better product than most of us gave them credit for back in the day, and one of the first with what is now a standard safety feature, Poloron sleds were killed by intense competition and subpar marketing. Today they are a seldom-seen rarity.

1972 Poloron Tornado 804

MANUFACTURER
Poloron Products, Inc., New Rochelle, New York, at Michigan City, Indiana

POWERTRAIN
Engine: 398cc Kohler K399-2 axial-fan, air-cooled, piston-port twin.
Carburetion: One Tillotson HR43A diaphragm pumper
Ignition: Magneto & breaker points
Lubrication: Pre-mix at 20:1
Exhaust: Single pipe into a Donaldson "power-tuned" muffler
Power Output: 28 hp
Drive Clutch: Salsbury

CHASSIS
Type: Welded phosphate-dipped and painted 18-gauge steel belly pan and tunnel with stirrups, Apex chain case, chromed steel bumpers and fiberglass hood
Claimed Dry Weight: 320 pounds
Front Suspension: Triple leaf springs
Ski Stance: 28 inches
Rear Suspension: Bogie wheels (12) with torsion springs
Track: 15.5-inch wide Goodyear steel & polyester reinforced 3-ply rubber with center drive
Brake: Mechanical disc
Fuel Capacity: 4.5 gallons
Standard Equipment: Stewart-Warner speedometer/odometer, choke, kill switch, gas gauge, dual headlights and tail lights with on-off switch, non-slip running boards, console storage compartment, snow flap, ring gear for electric start

MSRP: $1,095

Bumps In The Trail

Overwhelmed by more established manufacturers, Poloron found it hard to compete. The free air "hot stocker" ended the company's hopes in racing. And its other businesses were selling on price to discount stores and the military, so they did not know how to market effectively to consumers.

The company's sales literature was amateurish. Initially it used illustrations of the sleds, leaving the impression that the machines weren't quite real. A switch to photography for 1971 was disastrous. Unlike most sled manufacturers that did outdoor photography in the winter or settled for studio product shots, Poloron tried to do studio shots that looked like the outdoors in winter. But bareheaded people with no headgear or eye protection pretending to ride sleds while surrounded by Styrofoam snow and fake trees just didn't work. It was hard to take Poloron snowmobiles seriously when shown in these obviously staged settings, especially when the company's slogan was "Capture the real excitement of winter," but sales inquiries were directed to Louisiana where there's never any snow.

Not surprisingly, sales never met anticipated levels.

Pulling The Plug

Poloron blew its sled inventory out cheap ($799 for a top-of-the-line Tornado 399) and quit the business. Holding company Poloron Products completely ceased operations in 1981.

1972 Skiroule RTX 447

Sexy On The Snow

Photo courtesy of www.vintagesnowmobiles.50megs.com

"Snowmobiles used to be pretty much the same . . . then came Skiroule"

That line from the 1972 Skiroule sales brochure was no product puffery dreamed up by some advertising agency. The jaw-dropping new RTX absolutely revolutionized the way people thought about snow machines. It was the first snowmobile to emphasize appearance, liberally augmented by the use of beautiful women, as a primary feature to attract attention and win customers. Furthermore, these sleek new sleds also introduced engineering ideas that were subsequently adopted by other brands.

The Beautiful Difference
"Performance doesn't have to look like a box… just look at Skiroule."

Born in 1966 in Rejean Houle's Quebec garage, Skiroule had resembled a green Ski-Doo because that's pretty much what it was.

But in 1972, that all changed. Now owned by the Coleman Company of Wichita, Kansas, "Skiroule shook the industry with the sharpest styling ever" according to our *Snow Goer* predecessors.

The super-sleek new design was based on its successful 1971 factory racers who had taken the Mod 340 class at the Eagle River, Wisconsin, Snowmobile Derby and Mod 440 at the second annual United States Snowmobile Association World Series in Boonville, New York. The later was the first major victory for an unknown named Gilles Villeneuve.

Long and low, the sleek new Skiroule was highly aerodynamic while all the others were still ugly crates or tadpole shapes. Even the Skiroule headlight was covered with a streamlined, clear lens.

With the engine moved to a forward position, a much lower center of gravity took the acrobatics out of maneuvering even though Skiroule retained the leg-breaker stirrups from the old engine-in-your-lap layout. Comparative tip-over testing by *Snow Goer* verified that these low-slung beauties had some of the best side-to-side stability in the industry.

More new ideas included instruments mounted on the handlebars, externally mounted rear suspension for more travel and improved ride quality, and a completely enclosed engine console that, according to the brochure, "not only looks great but also reduces the sound of the engine."

The premium RTX series featured slide rail suspension and full instrumentation, while the lower-powered RT series had bogie wheels. Most models had 15-inch wide tracks, but the top models in each series had higher-flotation 17-inch tracks, a common practice of the day for top-of-the-line offerings.

It certainly didn't hurt that Skiroule often showed its rakish new design with attractive young ladies. Whether clad in one of Skiroule's elegant snowmobile suits, their stunning White Lightning casual jump suit, or a floral print bikini, tastefully posed mademoiselles were definitely a big part of the marketing effort.

Consumer acceptance was quick, and the "green bullet" was voted Best in Styling in a poll conducted by *Invitation To Snowmobiling* magazine.

But The Beauty's Only Skin Deep
My touring buddy, Ted Perkins, purchased an RTX 447 after satisfactory ownership of an earlier Skiroule. Problems began immediately.

Unlike its race sled predecessors with free air engines sticking out in the breeze, the RTX was subject to classic vapor lock with its fully enclosed, fan-cooled engine. "Out of the box, the new 447 always took many pulls and much playing with the choke to start, even when cold," Perkins recalled. And restarting when warm was even worse, as I can attest from watching him on numerous occasions. "I just could not understand how the factory could have knowingly allowed the product to ship with these starting problems," he said.

Fixes began with removal of the wire mesh screens over the hood vents, and quickly proceeded to installation of a Grosse Jet in the carb. Clutching changes were also made. "The changes made a noticeable improvement," Perkins said, "but the 447 was always somewhat temperamental starting or restarting. You had to know it."

Another design defect showed up later. Moisture would collect in the throttle cable and freeze, making the cable sticky and sometimes inoperative. "I would have to put my hands around any exposed part of the cable to loosen it up," Perkins explained, going on to relate how this resulted ultimately in a stuck-throttle tree smash. "A test program should have found this design problem," he said.

Still, he really liked his 447, calling it "an otherwise nice running sled,' and rode it as his primary machine until 1980. "I do not recall any design problems with the chassis, suspension or front end," Perkins said.

Down The Trail
Skiroule became a first-tier brand with its breakthrough design, but never really challenged the market leaders for dominance. However, the new Skiroule led to much more emphasis on styling throughout the industry, and enclosed engine compartments were soon standard practice to meet new sound emission restrictions. Handlebar mounted instruments and outboard rear suspension also showed up on other brands.

Coleman soon tired of the snowmobile business and sold Skiroule to a private owner who kept the basic RTX/RT platform in production relatively unchanged until the brand expired in 1977. By then its age was definitely showing, but its styling was still turning heads across the snowbelt.

1972 Skiroule RTX 447

MANUFACTURER
Skiroule Ltd., a subsidiary of the Coleman Co., Wickham, Quebec, Canada

POWERTRAIN
Engine: Sachs axial fan twin
Displacement: 436cc
Carburetion: One Tillotson HDR diaphragm
Compression Ratio: 10.3:1
Ignition: 75W magneto and breaker points
Lubrication: Pre-mix 25:1
Exhaust: Single pipe with muffler
Power Output: 40 hp @ 6,500 rpm
Drive Clutch: Skiroule aluminum, balanced
Driven Clutch: Skiroule steel

CHASSIS
Type: Formed and welded 18-guage steel with stirrups and aluminum chaincase
Claimed Dry Weight: 386 pounds
Front Suspension: Double-leaf springs with hydraulic shocks
Ski Stance: 26 inches
Rear Suspension: Skiroule Super-Slide Bar with twin rear external coil-over-shock assemblies and front shock
Track: 17.125-inch-wide 4-ply molded rubber reinforced with nylon and fiberglass rods; 5/8-inch lug height
Brake: Mechanical disc, self-adjusting
Fuel Capacity: 5.4 U.S. gallons (4.5 Imperial gallons)
Standard Equipment: Speedometer, tachometer, console storage compartment, double row heavy-duty chain with automatic tensioner, trailer hitch
Key Options: Electric start, chrome front grab handle, clip-on back rest, matching tow-behind

Price: $1,299 U.S. MSRP

Ski-Lark & Wee-Lark
The Simple Snowmobiles

Could a California-based company that specialized in vintage airplane restoration make a legitimate mark in the snowmobile market? There was only one way to find out. The Larkin Aircraft Company was incorporated in December, 1968, by World War II Army Air Corps pilot and flight instructor Keith Larkin in Watsonville, California, south of San Francisco on the Monterey Bay coast.

The company's foundation was renovating and restoring WWII airplanes, but it also began manufacturing mini-bikes and tiny utility vehicles based on the mini-bikes. When it moved to snowmobiles, it created two low-tech but interesting and memorable machines most notable for their diminutive size and affordable price.

On A Lark
Conceived at least in part by Walter Zurowski, the Larkin Ski-Lark made its debut for model year 1971. Since California snowmobiles were going to be transported across the state to the Sierra Nevada Mountains to be ridden, the Ski-Lark was engineered to be as compact, simple, light and inexpensive as possible. The manufacturer stressed that it was built with aircraft quality from standard snowmobile industry parts, but there really wasn't much to the claim.

The tiny sled had a 10-inch wide rubber track and bogie wheels in the back, and a single transverse leaf spring shared by the skis. It was attached to a vertical steering post extending up through the hood, where it connected to the handlebars with a tiller bar. A Tecumseh four-stroke lawnmower engine delivered its 4 hp through a Salsbury clutch and a small jackshaft across the tunnel to a motorcycle sprocket and chain drive in a thin fiberglass housing. A motorcycle-type twist throttle was used, and there were some reports of it freezing up in cold weather.

It was so underpowered and minimalistic that the prototype Ski Lark didn't even have a brake. It did have a simple windshield but that was quickly discontinued. The machine weighed just 106 pounds and was small enough to fit in the trunk of a Cadillac or the back end of a station wagon.

Advertised as being one-third of the size, and one-third of the price, of a conventional snowmobile, the Ski-Lark was claimed to have the same power-to-weight ratio and performance of full-sized sleds. But the claimed top speed of 20 to 25 mph was certainly not in the big sled class. Neither was the ride quality or the handling with the transverse ski spring, an idea that had been tried and rejected by numerous mini-sled manufacturers. And since there were no lights or alternator to run them it was a daytime-only machine, although a lighting kit was supposedly available.

By the following fall, an even smaller sibling appeared that was based on the original Ski-Lark prototype that had been upgraded before going into production. The Wee-Lark was positioned strictly as a kid's sled. It was pretty much the same machine as the Ski-Lark but its tunnel was 8 inches shorter and it also had a shorter track, plus it was powered by a smaller engine – a 3 hp two-stroke.

Testing The Tiny Twins
Los Angeles-based *Popular Snowmobiling* magazine was produced by exactly the kind of people that these machines were intended to serve, so a couple of the magazine's writers took their wives and kids to test a group of 1972 Ski-Larks and Wee-Larks in spring snow of the High Sierras. They said the sleds ran all week from early morning until after dark and "gave no trouble at all – probably because they're made by a builder of airplanes."

The testers advised keeping the Ski-Lark out of deep powder if the rider weighed more than 125 pounds because the larger rider would cause the sled to sink. But they did say that it would go most places a big sled would go, and noted that it handled a 180-pound rider while pulling three kids and two dogs on a toboggan.

"The engine is fairly quiet," the magazine reported. Testers emphasized that "It's certainly not a toy," concluding that "all of us agreed that this sled is FUN!" emphasizing the word in capital letters.

The magazine testers also found that the sub-mini Wee-Lark was "very quiet with a tuned muffler, and that's something the neighbors will appreciate as the little kids churn up the snow by the hour in the backyard." They concluded that "the little chugger does about 12 miles an hour and will keep the little guys happy all day long."

Evolution
Larkin Aircraft relocated from Watsonville to nearby Freedom, California, and continued to develop the Ski-Lark. Production rights for the tiny twins were later sold to Watsonville-based Zurowski Enterprises. Newer Ski-Larks were a couple of inches longer, had a cleated track and a grab bar on the back end, but otherwise stayed pretty much the same through the mid-1970s, although some had a slightly larger 5 hp, 133cc Teke engine.

The most simple and basic snowmobile ever seriously marketed, the Ski-Lark and Wee-Lark actually sold in decent numbers, probably due to their incredibly low prices. They still show up at today's vintage shows, where they usually draw a crowd of curious onlookers.

1972 Ski-Lark and Wee-Lark

MANUFACTURER
Larkin Aircraft Company, Watsonville, California

POWERTRAIN
Engine: Tecumseh HS-40 four-stroke (Ski-Lark); Clinton 92cc two-stroke with tuned muffler (Wee-Lark)
Power Output: 4 hp (Ski-Lark); 3 hp (Wee-Lark)
Drive Clutch: Salsbury

CHASSIS
Type: Unitized welded steel with fiberglass hood
Claimed Dry Weight: 106 pounds (Ski-Lark); 82 pounds (Wee-Lark)
Front Suspension: One transverse mono-leaf spring
Ski Stance: 20 inches
Rear Suspension: 4 bogie wheels on one truck (Ski-Lark); none on Wee-Lark
Track: 10-inch wide nylon-reinforced molded rubber
Brake: Mechanical drum

MSRP: $349 (Ski-Lark); $248 (Wee-Lark)

Sears Sportsters
Large Retailer's Last Shot At Selling Sleds

At the beginning of the 1960s, Chicago-based Sears, Roebuck and Company billed itself as the "World's Largest Store" – which, by the way, is how the giant Chicago radio station WLS, founded by Sears, got its call letters. As such, Sears tried to carry almost anything that anyone would ever want to buy, and was the first of the big chain stores and catalog marketers to add snowmobiles to its product selection when it offered an ice scooter under its David Bradley brand early in the decade.

By the mid-60s, sales of conventional snowmobiles were starting to boom and Sears began selling private-brand sleds from suppliers that eventually included Fox Trac, Robin Nodwell, Trail-A-Sled (Scorpion), AMF and the Trade Winds division of Outboard Marine Corporation.

And by the beginning of the 1970s, snowmobiles were definitely changing again. The handwriting was on the wall for traditional Ski-Doo clones with bogie wheels and engines on top of the tunnel. Sears knew it needed something more competitive than the old-style 309 and Hillary models from Trade Winds, so it turned to the most prolific private brand manufacturer in the snowmobile business, Polaris Industries. A Sears product announcement said that its new snow machines from Polaris would have "performance and designed features most desired, as determined by Sears consumer research."

Realization

In spring 1971, a letter from Polaris President Herbert Graves announced to its distributors and dealers that it would be manufacturing sleds for Sears, and that these machines would be built to Sears specs to be sold and serviced primarily through Sears retail stores in metropolitan areas of the snowbelt. It stated that these sleds would provide Polaris dealers with additional opportunities for parts sales and service work, including warranty repairs, with Sears parts available to Polaris dealers for this purpose. The manufacturer encouraged its distribution to look at the new Sears relationship as a marketing asset, not a competitor, though the dealers and distributors at the time took varying views of the situation.

The new machines turned out to be slightly de-contented variants of the Polaris Charger and Mustang with a new name, Sears Sportsters. Done in an attractive deep blue color scheme with black trim, they carried engines not available in directly equivalent Polaris models – a 244 single, a 335 fan twin, a 432 free air twin and a 432 fan twin with a 20-inch track. Far more advanced than any previous Sears sleds, they featured front-mounted Polaris Star engines with Mikuni slide valve carbs – but not the CD ignitions on the Polaris brand sleds. They also had Polaris clutching that was widely regarded as the best in the industry, powerful hydraulic disc brakes that were unavailable on other machines of the day and cleated tracks with smooth-riding slide rail suspensions on all but the bogie-suspended wide track. Chrome ski shocks were originally an option, but apparently became standard equipment at some point in the fall of 1971. Electric start for the twins, covers, tachometers and survival kits were some of the other Polaris-sourced options and accessories

36

available, but Sears snowmobile apparel was purchased from other vendors.

Sportster prices were competitive, starting at just $649 for the 244 single. The sleds were also available on installment credit just like any other major purchase from Sears. These new Sears snowmobiles were supported with full-color brochures, timely and informative big newspaper ads in markets where Sears retail stores carried the sleds and product publicity in many leading snowmobile magazines of the day.

Judging by how many have survived, the Sportster 335 seems to have been the best-selling model by far, with the 432 free air probably the next most popular. But the Sportsters were only around for one season, and were closed out at heavily discounted prices later in the winter. In March of 1972, Sears announced that it would leave the snowmobile business.

So What Happened?

Why didn't the Sears Sportsters make it? They were clearly more advanced than most popular competitive models. And unlike many failing snowmobile brands, Sears advertised and otherwise promoted its sleds, although the company completely avoided racing which was an important but very costly promotional activity back then.

Considering that the similar Polaris models sold acceptably, that Sears' research on desired performance and features was apparently right on target, and the similar lack of success of other chain stores and catalog merchandisers – J.C. Penney, Montgomery Ward, Herter's, Eaton's in Canada and several others – with snowmobiles, the conclusion has to be that snowmobilers rejected the mass merchant distribution channel in favor of the franchised dealer channel, not the Sportster sleds themselves.

1972 Sears Sportster 335

MANUFACTURER
Polaris Industries, a Textron company, at Roseau, Minnesota, for Sears, Roebuck and Company, Chicago, Illinois

POWERTRAIN
Engine: 335cc Fuji Heavy Industries EC34P piston-port fan-cooled twin with dual Mikuni VM30 slide valve carbs, magneto and breaker point ignition, and single tuned pipe into muffler
Lubrication: Pre-mix at 20:1
Power output: 24 hp @ 6,000 RPM
Clutches: Polaris Torque-O-Matic with flyweight drive and torque sensing driven

CHASSIS
Type: Welded and painted steel with chrome steel bumpers and fiberglass hood
Claimed Dry Weight: 400 pounds
Front Suspension: Triple leaf springs with hydraulic shock absorbers
Ski Stance: 25.5 inches
Rear Suspension: Polaris fiberglass slide rails with torsion springs and two hydraulic shocks on the rear arm
Track: 15.5-inch polyester-reinforced rubber with steel cleats and dual-sprocket drive
Brake: Hydraulic disc
Fuel Capacity: 4.5 gallons
Standard Equipment: Kill switch, passenger grab strap, rear seat storage compartment, snow flap
Options: Electric start

MSRP: $999

1972 Sno Jet SST
Sporty, Seductive Trendsetter

One of the more successful brands of the vintage era, Sno Jet was definitely in snowmobiling's big league by the beginning of the 1970s. The bright blue sleds from Quebec had better distribution than most brands, and were gaining notoriety as attractively priced snow machines with good performance.

For 1972, the sporty new SS'T was introduced. The apostrophe in the name departed quickly but the SST became the most successful model in the Sno Jet trail sled lineup.

Better By Design
Sno Jet's theme in the early 1970s was "Better By Design," but the exterior appearance of the sleds really had not been anything unique. So to launch the new SST, Sno Jet stylist Charles Beaudet created a revised hood design that moved the headlight from the typical raised notch atop the hood's centerline to a recessed position offset to the (rider's) right side of the hood. The sleek, attractive, asymmetrical styling continued behind the windshield with the gauges recessed into the top of the hood to the right of the handlebars. This unusual appearance definitely set the SST apart from the literally hundreds of other sleds on the market. The company claimed that the offset headlamp revealed objects more clearly when cruising at night.

Meanwhile, Sno Jet was moving from Hirth to Yamaha for power. With the SST positioned as Sno Jet's trail

38

flagship, it was given a series of Yamaha engines that included the higher output Sport (S) series 292 single, 340 twin and 440 twin, plus another 440 twin with power that was more like a 400. Bogie wheels were standard, but all models were also available with the optional new Multiflex slide rail suspension, and it appears that few of the machines with hotter S series engines were actually sold with bogies. Other improvements over older Sno Jets included upgraded muffler, cooling system, track and seat.

Snow Goer testers lauded the new machine, saying, "The Sno Jet SST for '72 turns out to be as good as it looks. And with the brightest new styling of the year, the whole sled has been updated and looks like tomorrow." Many reviewers applauded the SST's handling, and it was also a quiet sled for the day.

By the following year, the SST had become Sno Jet's most successful model, selling well and also doing well in Stock-class racing when "stock" still meant family trail sleds, not sizzling hot stock racers.

Improvement & Influence

If 1972 was the year of the facelift, 1973 was the year that the engineering caught up. The SST looked pretty much the same, but it was quite different in detail. *Snow Goer* reviewers were impressed with the changes. "With the Sno Jet engineers determined to build a sled of a quality to match the forward-looking design of the '72 machines, the 1973 SST offers a number of minor refinements that add up to a major package."

The 4-gallon steel gas tank on the 1972 that was integrated into the front of the chassis was subject to rusting, so it was replaced with a 5.7-gallon plastic tank with improved filler. A new ACS muffler was added. The now-standard equipment Multiflex slide suspension was improved, and ski shocks were standard. A new headlamp put out 25 percent more light, and a brake light, kill switch and padded engine cover were safety upgrades. The rear seat storage area was removed to provide more passenger room, so a front mounted tool box was added.

Invitation To Snowmobiling magazine also liked the changes, especially the extra seat room and overall performance. "Want a mover, an action machine? Quickness is yours with the sporty SST," the publication advised its readers.

Sno Jet extended the SST's unique and attractive asymmetrical styling into the lower priced Star Jet series and created a completely different version of it for the new Whisper Jet family sled. The off-center headlight became a Sno Jet styling standard and was used on still more models including the Astra Jet, Strata Jet and Thunder Jet F/A racer. Several other companies began to pick up on the offset headlight look, too, often but not always for free air models where it was more than just a styling exercise because it allowed maximum air to be rammed in directly over the cooling fins of engines that were offset to the left for better race track cornering.

The SST got a complete make-over for 1974 that retained the offset headlamp. But for 1975, the asymmetrical styling was dropped. The SST line was split into fan and free air versions but continued as Sno Jet's most popular trail sled right on through the end of the brand as the Kawasaki Sno Jet in 1977.

But many think the 1972-73 SST that started the whole asymmetrical headlight look was easily the best looking of them all. Charles Beaudet got it right the first time.

1972 Sno Jet SST-S 440

MANUFACTURER
Sno Jet division of Glastron Boat Company, a subsidiary of The Conroy Company, Inc. of Quebec, at Thetford Mines, QC

POWERTRAIN SPECS
Engine: 433cc Yamaha Sport (S) series axial-fan-cooled reed-valve twin with Tillotson HD diaphragm carb and single ACS exhaust
Ignition: Magneto and breaker points
Power Output: 37 hp
Clutches: Yamaha drive and Sno Jet driven

CHASSIS SPECS
Type: Welded, painted steel with stirrups, chromed steel bumpers and fiberglass hood
Dry Weight (claimed): 355 pounds
Front Suspension: Triple-leaf springs with hydraulic ski shocks
Ski Stance: 23.5 inches
Rear Suspension: Bogie wheels or Multiflex flexible steel slide suspension
Track: Positrak 15.5-by-115-inch nylon reinforced rubber with molded-in cleats
Brake: Mechanical disc

MSRP: $1,250

1973 Ariens 450SX

"Super Sleds" Just Weren't Super Enough

If there was any outdoor power product manufacturer that really knew snow, it had to be Ariens. After all, the company had already invented the modern snow thrower that everyone else had copied to get into that market. Its oft-repeated tag line was "Come snow, go Ariens'. The company also had a great reputation for high-quality lawn mowers including a very popular line of rear-engine riders. Those products gave the company a solid network of distributors and servicing dealers who could sell other powered goods.

So in 1968, Ariens jumped into the burgeoning snowmobile market. Its new 1969 Arrow 300/III snowmobile was patterned after the classic Ski-Doo, including an old-fashioned hood that extended all the way down to the running boards. The Sachs-powered "me too" machine was solidly built and carried a recognizable brand name, so it was well accepted by Ariens distributors and got good reviews from the media. Unfortunately acceptance by the buying public was less enthusiastic and first-year production had to be cut back.

But Ariens persevered and gained a measure of consumer acceptance for its snow sled. The company gradually expanded its model line up using both Sachs and Kohler engines, and even established its own "Track 'em Down" snowmobile club for Ariens Arrow owners. But sales still weren't meeting company expectations.

The "Super Sleds" Appear
Observing that racing and high performance was becoming the name of the game, Ariens introduced its first high

40

performance models, the SX series "super sleds" for the 1972 season. Marketed as racing machines, the SX series got the requisite kill switch, tachometer, wedge seat and a mostly black paint job to make it look mean and fast.

Actually the new SX machines were very similar to existing Ariens Arrow models in most respects. Like all Ariens snowmobiles, the chassis was actually produced by Skiroule, a company in which Ariens had invested to ensure supply of this basic building block. Besides this same old chassis, the S-models also used many of the same components including hood, steering, "arctic-dynamic" skis and ski suspension with shocks added.

However, the SX twins were the first Ariens sleds fitted with slide rail suspensions. The top-of-the-line 450SX had a 35 HP 437cc Sachs engine, while the 350SX used a 28 HP 338cc Sachs instead of the Kohlers and smaller displacement Sachs engines used in other Ariens models.

But the "super sleds" were still old style machines with the engine in the rider's lap, leg-breaker stirrups on the steel tunnel and styling that was hopelessly stuck in the 1960s.

Ariens filed its sleds for Stock class competition with the United States Snowmobile Association (USSA), but with the coming of the free-air-powered "hot stockers" in the early 1970s, the throwback Ariens SX just wasn't anywhere near competitive on the race track.

Taking It To The Trails

It was pretty clear that the SX series would have to make it as trail sleds. But none of the Ariens models were selling very well. And almost unbelievably in this time of great annual improvements in snow sleds, the 1973 SX models were virtually identical to the 1972 versions except for some noise reduction upgrades.

When *Snow Goer* tested the 1973 450SX, editors found that it turned out an above average power curve on the chassis dynamometer, and that combined with relatively light weight to give it a very attractive power-to-weight ratio. It was also one of the most stable sleds tested with a tip-over angle of 40 degrees. However, they found comfort, handling and suspension performance definitely lacking, commenting that "the muscle required to keep the 450SX in rein also came under a heavy barrage of negatives by the test crew."

The editors final summary put the sled in market perspective. "While the *Snow Goer* crew found the 450SX hard put to compete with the outstanding styling and performance of '73s from a number of other companies with machines in Wyoming (the test site), it still gets a lot of gold stars for its basic good qualities."

Time To Go

What wasn't reported, or even known at the time, was that Ariens had already decided to exit the snowmobile business before the *Snow Goer* spring testing was done.

"We could see the handwriting on the wall," said Michael Ariens, company President and later Chairman of the Board. "We weren't making our annual (sales) increases that we thought we needed to make to be viable in the business."

Realistically, the snowmobile product diverted company resources from their core lawn, garden, and snow thrower business. Also, the Ariens snowmobile dealer organization wasn't big enough and wasn't expanding fast enough. And the first signs of an industry-wide inventory problem were already appearing. It was time for Ariens snowmobiles to go away as one of the first recognizable names to drop out of the industry.

1973 Ariens 450SX

MANUFACTURER
The Ariens Company, Brillion, Wisconsin

POWERTRAIN
Engine: 437cc Sachs SA-2 440 axial-fan-cooled piston-port twin
Carburetion: One Tillotson HD diaphragm pumper with ram tube
Ignition: Magneto & breaker points
Lubrication: Pre-mix at 24:1
Exhaust: Single pipe into a Donaldson muffler
Power Output: 35 hp @ 6,500 RPM
Drive Clutch: Salsbury

CHASSIS
Type: Welded and painted steel with stirrups, chromed tube steel bumpers and acrylonitrile-butadiene-styrene (ABS) hood
Dry Weight (claimed): 355 pounds
Front Suspension: Triple-leaf springs with inboard-mounted hydraulic shock absorbers
Ski Stance: 26 inches
Rear Suspension: Slide rails with torsion springs
Track: 15-inch nylon-reinforced molded rubber with double sprocket drive
Brake: Mechanical disc on driven pulley
Fuel Capacity: 5 gallons
Standard Equipment: Speedometer/odometer, tachometer, kill switch, twin sealed-beam headlights, non-slip foot rests, storage compartment, snow flap

MSRP: $1,350

The Chaparral SS/III
Fast Fan From The West

By 1972, Chaparral was on a roll. Armco Steel had acquired Powered Products Corp. and its Snow Birdie snowmobile in 1969. The new owners changed the brand name to Chaparral, which was previously the low-end model in the Snow Birdie line, and poured on the product development dollars.

Deemed 'America's fastest growing major snowmobile' Chaparral was well on its way to becoming an industry leader when it introduced its 1973 models. At the top was a new series of trail performance sleds that evolved from the earlier Firebird SS. Although saddled with one of the least memorable model names ever – SS/III – its eye-opening performance more than offset its uninspiring nomenclature. Packed with advanced engineering, save the engine inexplicably mounted atop the tunnel, the new candy-apple red sled from Colorado made a big splash.

Editors Are Impressed
"*Snow Goer* riders agreed that this machine is one of the best," summarized our review in a 1973 issue.

"This could be the best of all the '73s," declared *Invitation To Snowmobiling* magazine.

What allowed the SS/III to win this high praise? It started with its lightweight construction, using a riveted aircraft aluminum tunnel with no stirrups, extruded aluminum bumpers and a die-cast aluminum chaincase at a time when most contemporaries were still using formed and welded steel for these parts. The SS/III's hood and belly pan were formed from sheet molding compound (SMC), the dash panel was high-impact ABS plastic, and the molded polyurethane track was unencumbered by heavy steel cleats. This kept the overall dry weight in the range of a claimed 320 to 345 pounds, depending on equipment.

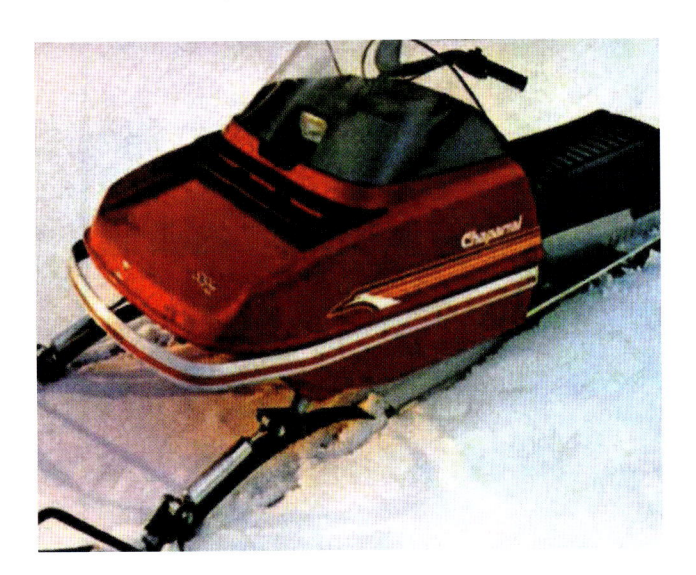

The other side of the performance equation was power. All 1973 Chaparral trail sleds had purpose built axial fan-cooled engines from Fuji Light Industries.

The five-port Fuji Lights with capacitor discharge ignition (CDI) and Teflon-coated piston rings were unusually powerful across the board, including the 45 hp 440 that was the hottest choice for any Chaparral trail sled in 1973.

By contrast, Arctic Cat's Kawasaki 440 axial fan was only good for about 35 hp, and very few other 440 fans could honestly top 40 hp. One secret to the Fuji's awesome power was higher compression than other similar engines. At 12:1, it was nearly double some of the competition including the Kawasaki's 6.5:1 compression ratio.

My friend Gil purchased an SS/III with the 42 hp 400 engine so he could grass race the sled in the top USSA Stock class of the day. He already owned a 440 Hirth-powered 1971 Chaparral Executive wide track that he liked a lot, but there was no 440 Stock racing class at the time.

A 34 hp 340 was also available in the SS/III. A planned 30 hp 295 model was listed in the first printing of the 1973 Chaparral full-line brochure, but the small-bore model was dropped prior to release. Subsequent brochures and publicity made no mention of it.

The E-Z Rider progressive-rate track suspension was Chaparral's unique design. Engineered to transfer weight under acceleration and then level off, it featured fully enclosed but adjustable coil-over shock damping units mounted parallel to the ground on each side of the slide rail skid. Pre-drilled holes allowed for the easy addition of up to four sets of wheels for grass drags or marginal snow conditions.

A Kelsey-Hayes mechanical disc brake provided the stopping power, with a hydraulic disc upgrade available. Speedometer, tachometer, handlebar pad, emergency engine kill switch, wrap-around taillight, and passenger handgrips were standard, with heat gauge, cigarette lighter, electric start, stirrup kit, chrome skis and 2.25-gallon auxiliary gas tank available as dealer-installed options.

Real World Tests
The SS/III would definitely run with the best of its contemporaries, if not flat outrun them. *Invitation To Snowmobiling* reported that it was the fastest sled it tested

that year, beating 13 other machines including a Rupp Nitro 440, a Scorpion Super Stinger 440 and the lighter Alouette 440. However, they didn't test any of the new free-air stock racers like the Arctic Cat El Tigré or Ski-Doo TN'T F/A.

Gil was never really serious about drag racing his 400. He prepped it himself with assistance from several others, including some minimal help from me, and sporadically entered events with an assortment of riders ranging from Chaparral factory-branch mod racers to his teenage son, John. But the sled was mostly a trail rider that I got a chance to enjoy every once in a while.

Maybe the most startling trait of the SS/III was its handling. *Snow Goer* testers uniformly praised its steering. I can say from personal experience that the sled was phenomenal on twisty trails considering that it retained the old-fashioned engine-on-the-tunnel configuration. The high center of gravity gave it only average roll-over resistance despite a relatively wide 28-inch ski stance, but the tight-turning skis and good tracking in just about any snow conditions allowed a smaller turning circle than most contemporaries.

If the SS/III had a shortcoming, it was rider ergonomics. It was a little noisier than the average sled and some riders complained of being bent-over too far while operating it. Personally I never had a problem with either, but I never rode it all day.

Still, the days of an axial fan machine as a top performance model were numbered. The new free-air stock racers were taking over the track and the trail, and liquid cooling was starting to creep in slowly. Chaparral skipped right over the free air stage, and discontinued the SS/III after just one season in favor of the liquid-cooled SSX that offered a little more power and refinement, but not quite as good of power-to-weight ratio. This made the 1973 SS/III 440 arguably the hottest Chaparral trail sled ever built.

Epilogue

On February 11, 1974, Armco Steel Corporation announced it would immediately liquidate the entire Chaparral line, even though the 1975 line was ready to go. The decision was based on "general conditions," but everyone knew the 1973 Arab oil embargo played a major role.

More than 40,000 registered Chaparral snowmobile owners were left with orphan machines.

This proud brand, which had pioneered or been an early adopter of many advanced engineering ideas, now pioneered the mass exodus of major manufacturers from the suddenly stone cold snowmobile business.

1973 Chaparral SS/III 440

MANUFACTURER
Chaparral Industries Inc. (Subsidiary of Armco Steel Corp.), Denver, Colorado

POWERTRAIN
Type: Fuji Light Industries axial fan-cooled twin-cylinder
Displacement: 432cc
Carburetion: Single Keihin
Ignition: Capacitor Discharge
Lubrication: Pre-mix at 20:1
Exhaust: Single pipe with Torque-Tuned muffler
Power Output: 45 hp @ 6800 rpm
Clutch: Chaparral asymmetric variable speed

CHASSIS
Type: Riveted aircraft aluminum
Claimed Weight: 345 pounds dry
Front Suspension: Multi leaf springs with chrome-plated hydraulic shocks
Ski Stance: 28 inches
Rear Suspension: Chaparral E-Z Rider progressive-rate slide rail with dual enclosed coil springs over hydraulic shocks
Track: 15.5-inch fiberglass reinforced polyurethane directional pattern with internal drive
Brake: Kelsey-Hayes dual pad mechanical disc
Fuel Capacity: 5 gallons

Price: $1,375

1973 Evinrude Trailblazer

The American Rotary Engine

In June 1964, Outboard Marine Corporation (OMC) became the first big name manufacturer to enter the rapidly expanding snowmobile market. But soon more performance-oriented companies were leaving OMC in the snow dust. Something was needed to refocus consumer attention on this industry pioneer.

For the 1973 model year, that something became the industry's first domestically produced Wankel rotary engine.

The Rotary Revolution

Perfected in the late 1950s by Dr. Felix Wankel of West Germany's NSU Motorenwerke, the rotary engine design was licensed to other companies for commercial development. A three-sided rotor spins inside a trochoid (two slightly overlapping circles like the Master Card logo) combustion chamber to open the intake port, compress the air-fuel mixture and expel the burned charge. Light and compact with few moving parts, non-critical of fuel, virtually vibration free and quiet for the day, rotaries produced more horsepower and much greater low-end torque than heavier two-strokes of like displacement.

By 1971, several companies including Skiroule and Polaris had built sleds powered by Fichtel & Sachs Wankels. Arctic Cat was selling all the Sachs 303cc rotary-powered sleds that it could produce, with the Wankel Lynx frequently retailing at or above list price. Other manufacturers were clamoring for more rotary engines, and Sachs could not begin to meet the demand.

OMC had acquired a Wankel development license in 1963 for use in outboards, but never followed through. During the winter of 1970-71, the company decided to try the Wankel in sleds and began work on the project D471 rotary. At 528cc, the 35 hp OMC Wankel was the first rotary engine developed specifically for snowmobiling, the most powerful rotary to go into a snow sled at the time and the first production rotary to be built in North America. Yet it was essentially the same size and weight as the very popular but considerably less powerful Sachs 303 Wankel.

The D471's novel compound porting produced very smooth idling while allowing better high-speed breathing for improved top-end performance. Capacitor Discharge ignition (CDI) with unique 12mm surface gap spark plugs fired the fuel charge. A centrifugal cooling system made of lightweight magnesium was used instead of the conventional fan on the Sachs Wankel.

In February 1972, 150 pilot-build rotary-powered sleds were shipped to OMC dealerships across the continent for extensive field-testing by dealers and lucky customers. Some of these test sleds logged as many as 1,600 miles during the balance of that unusually lengthy winter.

Deemed ready for production, the OMC Wankel was initially offered for sale in the 1973 Evinrude RC-35-Q Trailblazer and its identical twin in alternative trim, the Johnson Phantom.

Big Sled, Big Features, Big Bucks

OMC believed that customers would pay a premium for the advantages of this new engine, so it was placed in its top-of-the-line models. Loaded with safety and convenience features, the Trailblazer was just about the heaviest single-track machine on the market, and at $1,850, it was one of the most expensive. An Arctic Cat Panther with the improved Sachs 295 Wankel

44

weighed 100 pounds less and cost only $1,325, albeit without many amenities of the RC-35.

Sled magazines praised the D471 rotary engine, but were less enthusiastic about other aspects of the OMC rotary twins. "The engine has tremendous potential, but it deserves to be fitted to a lighter chassis," said *Invitation To Snowmobiling*. "Turning the Phantom involves a lot of body English to overcome the considerable understeer that dominates this new family sled," reported the *Popular Science Snowmobile Handbook*.

Both publications commented that the big OMC would be really tough to get unstuck if you did get it bogged down to the point that you couldn't back it out with its reverse gear.

But performance sleds were taking over and 2-ups were entering a decline, so there simply wasn't much of a market for a big, heavy and expensive family machine with sub-standard handling and obsolete bogie suspension, especially when sold by dealers who generally looked at snowmobiles as something to do only when boats were in hibernation.

Moreover, the rotary engine craze had peaked and gone sour. Problems with side seals were beginning to discredit the Wankel and consign many rotary sleds to the junkyard. And unlike a couple of years earlier when Wankels could command a premium price, very few snowmobilers were now willing to pay more to get one, if they were willing to accept the engine at all. Add the 1973 energy crisis and chronic industry overproduction, and the big OMC rotary just never had a real chance to make it.

The D471 was reworked to produce 45 HP without an increase in displacement for 1974, and the sled was improved cosmetically, but it made no difference. All Evinrude and Johnson snow machines were selling poorly, and 1976 was OMC's last year in the snowmobile business.

The innovative and powerful OMC D471 Wankel engine just couldn't overcome everything stacked against it. Terrible timing, an overweight and outdated chassis, sub-standard marketing, high price and an organization not dedicated to snowmobiling doomed the first and only snowmobile with an American-made Wankel engine.

1973 Evinrude Trailblazer RC-35-Q

MANUFACTURER
Outboard Marine Corp., Milwaukee, Wisconsin, and Peterborough, Ontario

POWERTRAIN
Engine: 528cc OMC D471 air-cooled single chamber rotary
Carburetion: One Bendix float-type with labyrinth air box and remote fuel pump
Compression Ratio: 8.5:1
Ignition: OMC Firepower Capacitor Discharge (CD)
Lubrication: Pre-mix at 50:1
Exhaust: Single pipe into OMC muffler
Power Output: 35 hp and 33.5 lb-ft of torque @ 5,500 rpm
Drive System: OMC 507 with neutral and reverse gear

CHASSIS SPECS
Type: Welded and painted steel with chromed tube steel bumpers and fiberglass hood
Wet Weight: 555 pounds (as tested by *Invitation To Snowmobiling* magazine)
Front Suspension: Triple-leaf springs
Ski Stance: 28 inches
Rear Suspension: Bogie wheels (15 wheels on 3 trucks) with torsion springs
Track: 20.5-inch polyurethane with 41-inch footprint
Brake: Mechanical disc
Fuel Capacity: 5.5 gallons (high-octane required)
Standard Equipment: Electric start, primer, choke, kill switch, handlebar pad, speedometer/odometer, tachometer, fuel gauge, cigarette lighter, full-length under-seat storage compartment, passenger grab handles, snow flap

MSRP: $1,850

1973 John Deere JDX

Muscle sled Masquerader

When Deere and Company began developing a snow machine in 1969 it joined many others by copying market-leader Bombardier's successful layout with the engine atop a welded steel tunnel and bogie wheels underneath. Introduced for the 1972 model year, the initial John Deere snowmobiles were well built and reliable, but hamstrung by the inherent ride and handling limitations of Bombardier's concept that had now become outdated.

The market was moving toward better performance, so Deere again followed many other brands by adapting the outmoded template for its new JDX series. Two versions were available for 1973: the top-of-the-line JDX 8 with a CCW 440 engine and a Salsbury 850 drive clutch; and the JDX 4 with a Kohler 292, a Salsbury 780 drive clutch and less standard equipment.

Performer Or Pretender?
As the new flagship of the line, the JDX series was promoted in John Deere sales literature as having "superior performance and distinctive styling." Superlatives were flung around like macaroni salad in a food fight, always a good indication of a bunch of baloney. "From ski tip to snow flap, the JDX 8 is a totally new sled," said the brochure. "The ultra-low silhouette, bold 'blitz-black' color, and unique trim treatment suggest eager speed and agile handling."

But observation of the '73 Deere spec sheets and new model photos would lead you to believe that there was no difference between the carryover Model 500 green machine and the JDX models except for color, a lower windshield and ski shocks on the new additions to the line.

Actually that wasn't quite correct because the JDX 8 did get a similar but completely different engine. A 438cc CCW KEC 440/21 motor replaced the 436cc CCW KEC 440/4 powerplant of Model 500. Bore and stroke were slightly different, the 438 got a slightly bigger carb, and the final gearing was changed. Rated at 38 to 40 hp (depending on SAE test method) instead of the 36 hp engine in Model 500, the slightly hotter engine helped justify a $100 price premium for the JDX 8 over the green machine.

But with the old style chassis and bogie wheels, this was a very tame ride compared to the new 55 hp Arctic Cat El Tigré 400 and 440, or any other of the emerging free air Stock racers. Even worse, many directly competitive fan-cooled machines – like the lighter 46 hp Chaparral SS/III 440, the 44 hp Northway Interceptor 440 and the racy red Rupp Nitro 440 - had the power and handling to blow the JDX into the weeds. Plus, all these competitive machines had slide rail suspensions and disc brakes, and most had capacitor discharge ignitions, too.

Performance-oriented sled magazines largely ignored the new JDX series. But *Invitation To Snowmobiling* tested the JDX 8 and had some unusually candid observations. Editors called it "sporty but not overly quick," noting that it finished next to last among seven machines in their time trials. And although ride quality was rated slightly above average, the review noted that one editor was thrown off the sled by an unexpected bump while side-hilling. Worse, with the second highest center-of-gravity of all 21 machines tested, the JDX 8 was anything but stable. Testers said it was agile, but also called it "touchy" and "demanding" in the turns despite the standard carbide runners. The archaic 4.25-inch external band brake with the drum on the secondary shaft wasn't impressive, either. "The JDX was next to last in stopping distance of the eight machines tested," the publication reported.

On the plus side, the magazine found the JDX 8 to be the second quietest sled among the 21 tested that spring. They lauded the flip-up hood panel for easy refueling and the safety spill tray atop the steel gas tank. Other positive comments covered numerous additional safety features and service provisions including an under-hood troubleshooting decal and Deere's excellent dealer service.

But in the end, *Invitation To Snowmobiling* went on the record with a negative summation. "The machine offers distinctive styling and, in some areas, superior performance. However, we can't give it a top-grade rating because balancing the JDX on uneven terrain or whirling through tight turns with it demands inordinate skill."

Lesson Learned

The maladroit JDX series hung around for a couple more years with some upgrades to areas like clutching, and with yet another model, the seldom seen 399cc JDX 6. But even financing with deferred payments and deferred interest plus a free snowmobile suit with the sled couldn't make the JDX series a winner on the sales floor. The lesson was obvious. A black paint job, a short windshield and a couple extra horsepower just did not make a performance sled. The JDX was obsolete at introduction and doomed to failure no matter how well Deere promoted the outdated design.

But unlike several of its snowmobile competitors, Deere and Company would not repeat this mistake with its next consumer performance sled. The 1976 Liquifire was a thoroughly modern machine that could hold its own against the best from the rest of the industry.

1973 John Deere JDX

MANUFACTURER
Deere & Company - Horicon, Wisconsin

POWERTRAIN
Engine: 438cc Kioritz/ Canadian Curtis Wright KEC 440/ 21 fan-cooled, case-reed twin with one Walbro WDA-34 diaphragm pumper carb and single exhaust
Ignition: Magneto and breaker points
Power Output: 40 hp @ 6, 750 rpm
Clutches: Salsbury 850 drive and John Deere driven

CHASSIS SPECS
Type: Painted aluminum tunnel and belly pan with chromed steel bumpers and fiberglass hood
Dry Weight (claimed): 386 pounds
Front Suspension: Triple-leaf springs with hydraulic shock absorbers
Rear Suspension: Trailing arm bogie type, with 15 polyurethane wheels on six trucks
Ski Stance: 28 inches
Track: 15.5-by-118-inch steel-reinforced molded polyurethane
Brake: External band drum type

MSRP: $1,435

1973 Massey Ferguson Ski Whiz

Success Was Fleeting

The ads for the 1973 Massey Ferguson Ski Whiz announced, "This one's the most improved sled on the trail." And strictly speaking, that was true.

The Canadian agricultural giant had entered the snowmobile business for the 1969 season with a big, well-built machine from the company's Des Moines, Iowa, plant. Styled and hued after the company's very successful line of farm tractors, and propelled by an industry-first internal drive track, Ski Whiz sleds were sold predominantly through a well-developed network of rural dealers and backed by Massey's established parts and service operations. The company thought its snow machine would be a solid hit.

But by the time Massey had a couple of seasons under its belt, the company understood that it had to add some style and sizzle to its heavy, homely, underperforming snow tractor or it was not going to succeed. So for the 1973 season the Ski Whiz was redesigned.

Twenty-Eight Improvements

"Dramatically new from the handlebars right down to the snow," the brochure read. And they weren't kidding. Advertising and sales literature pointed out 28 areas of improvement that took 50 pounds off the new 1973 Ski Whiz snowmobiles compared to the older models.

It started with a decidedly better overall appearance. Clean, new styling rounded off the corners and sharp edges while maintaining the basic Ski Whiz shape. The trademark red hood remained, but the chassis changed color from silver to black. Many details were upgraded including the windshield, seat, front bumper, ski spindles, storage compartment, gas tank, drive belt, passenger hand holds and snow flap. Safety improvements included an engine kill switch, side reflectors, larger taillights and a bigger handlebar pad. Germany's JLO continued as the only Ski Whiz engine supplier, but the new models had more horsepower across the board and better mufflers made them quieter, too.

The company also made a serious effort to improve the ride and handling of the big sleds. The skis were shortened to reduce steering effort and brackets for optional ski shocks were added to most models. The three-position front spring mount for ski pressure adjustment was retained from earlier models.

Engines were moved lower and further forward for improved stability and the bogie wheels were repositioned further forward to improve deep snow performance and hill climbing ability. A new polyurethane track featured a deeper, more aggressive profile and had easier tension adjustment, too. Finally, two new well-equipped wide track (WT) models with 18-inch tracks were added to the lineup, the balance of which continued with 15.5-inch tracks. Unfortunately, all these changes did not dramatically improve the ride and handling, and side-to-side stability remained unimpressive.

Drive clutches also continued to be a problem. Unhappy with the off-the-shelf Salsbury, St. Lawrence and Drummond pulleys used on early Ski Whiz snowmobiles, Massey Ferguson had engineered its own drive clutch and began using it on 1972 models. The 1973 Ski Whiz sleds had a major drive clutch recall, and updated machines received a Series II decal, but placement of these decals on the machines was not uniform by any means.

Success Doesn't Last

Sales jumped about 60 percent for the redesigned Ski Whiz, but success was fleeting. The expanded 1974 Massey lineup was essentially some warmed over 1973 models with a red-trim-on black color scheme and some additional equipment choices. The energy crisis from the 1973 Arab oil embargo and the growing industry-wide glut of unsold inventory hurt sales of all brands, and Massey was certainly no exception.

But the heart of the problem was that the redesigned Ski Whiz retained too much obsolete technology- particularly the heavy, steel chassis and bogie wheel suspension. It's sub-standard ride and handling received tepid magazine reviews when it got press at all. And lacking any kind of a performance image - because the company was one of the few recognizable names that wasn't into racing- Massey could not compete for the trail racer buyers who were becoming a key segment of the fast evolving snowmobile market.

Massey discontinued production of the Ski Whiz in 1974. It turned to competitor Scorpion to supply its snowmobile needs starting with the 1975 model year before exiting the market for good following the 1977 snowmobile season.

The redesign of the original Ski Whiz had definitely improved the company's snowmobile, but just didn't go far enough to drive Massey Ferguson to lasting sales success in the highly competitive snowmobile industry.

1973 Massey Ferguson Ski Whiz 440WT

MANUFACTURER
Massey-Ferguson, Inc., Des Moines, Iowa [Subsidiary of Massey-Ferguson Industries Limited, Toronto, Ontario, Canada)

POWERTRAIN
Engine: Rockwell JLO L-440/2 axial fan-cooled twin
Displacement: 428cc
Carburetion: One Tillotson HD diaphragm pumper with M-F air-intake silencer
Compression Ratio: 7.5:1
Ignition: Magneto and breaker points
Lubrication: Pre-mix at 20:1
Power Output: 40 hp @ 6,500 rpm
Exhaust: Single pipe with a Donaldson muffler
Drive Clutch: Massey Ferguson
Driven Clutch: Massey Ferguson

CHASSIS
Type: Welded and painted steel tunnel and belly pan with molded fiberglass hood
Weight: 390 pounds
Front Suspension: Triple-leaf springs with 3-position front end adjustment
Ski Stance: 26 inches
Rear Suspension: Bogie wheels with torsion springs
Track: 18-inch wide internal drive, molded polyurethane with ice cleats
Brake: Mechanical disc
Fuel Capacity: 5.5 U.S. gallons
Standard Equipment: Speedometer/odometer, fuel primer, engine kill switch.
Options: Electric start, tachometer, hour meter, ski shocks, rear view mirror, tow-behind sleighs

Price: $1,275 MSRP

1973 Moto-Ski 'F' Series
More Than Just Tough

They grew up tough. Les Industries Bouchard began manufacturing Moto-Ski snowmobiles in 1962, and the orange machines from the south bank of the St. Lawrence River earned a reputation for durability.

The famous "Tougher Seven Ways" ad campaign enhanced that reputation with commercials that featured a Moto-Ski on a roller coaster and another one bouncing along a bone-dry rocky creek bed. By the time the 1971 sales season was over, Moto-Ski was the second best-selling brand in Canada and third best in the world. But financial complications led to its acquisition by Bombardier early in calendar year 1971. However, big yellow decided to operate Moto-Ski as a separate division that would stand on its own in the increasingly turbulent snowmobile industry.

Enter the 'F'

Snowmobilers were demanding machines that were not just faster and more reliable, but also ones that rode and handled better and went farther on a tank of gas. Plus, new industry-mandated noise and safety requirements meant that snowmobiles were changing in ways beyond performance parameters.

For 1973, Moto-Ski introduced its first models developed under Bombardier ownership. The all-new 'F' series was engineered for family snowmobiling with style and verve – sort of a "sport sedan" for the snow. The sales literature explained, "Just because you've got your girl along, you don't have to ride an old ladies' machine at an old ladies' pace."

Marketed alongside Moto-Ski's traditional engine-on-top-of-a-steel tunnel Zephyr, Capri and Cadet lines, the 'F' was a significant departure in almost every way. Prior to its release to the public, the 'F' series Moto-Ski was tested by more than a thousand consumers. Along with its sibling, the "S" series sled, Moto-Ski figured the two snowmobiles would account for one-third to one-half of the production for the 1973 model year, according to a report in the October 1972 issue of *Snow Goer*. The 'F' series showed up on the last day (due to a memo mix up) of *Snow Goer* magazine's annual test ride in Wyoming. In all, editors tested 26 different snowmobiles in the spring of 1972.

Borrowing styling and engineering concepts from Moto-Ski's pre-Bombardier Bullett oval racers, the F series was noticeably sleeker and wider, and had a lower center of gravity than the other Moto-Ski family sleds. Compared to the 1972 Zephyr 340 or 440 and the MS-18, the 'F' series was 7 inches shorter and the ski stance was 3 inches wider.

"The machine's overall stability matched other sleds well respected for good handling, something Moto-Ski's consumer test program confirmed last spring," *Snow Goer* editors wrote.

The low forward-mounted engine, aluminum tunnel, slide rail suspension and ski shocks were just some of the features adapted from the oval tracker for this new trail model. Editors and consumer test riders liked the slide rail rear suspension.

"The dual slides cut through tough ruts in our test area like a German torpedo, without excessive bounce or fish tailing," editors noted.

The Japanese-built "Bouchard Special Engine" was available in three sizes (295 F, 340 F and 440 F), and even the 295 was a twin, not a one-lunger like most of the sub-300cc engines of the day.

The engine was fully enclosed to reduce noise and the backside of the engine compartment was padded for operator protection. A larger gas tank increased range, a multi-foam racing-style seat improved comfort and a wider track provided better flotation in deep snow. The 'F' also one-upped other family sleds by providing a tachometer along with a speedometer.

Other standard equipment included chrome steel bumpers at both ends, nonskid footrests, passenger handles, a tool box and a cutter hitch. Side reflectors and an engine kill switch on the handlebars were standard on all 1973 Moto-Skis for improved safety.

Test editors noted that the thick, padded seat was top notch and added, "[The] 6.5-gallon gas tank is ingeniously molded into the console making it the most unique concealment of a gasoline tank we've seen on a sled."

A backrest was optional on all three F models, and the 340 and 440 could also be fitted with electric start, although my friend Dave's 340 'F' that I enjoyed occasionally until it wore out many years later, had neither.

The competition-derived features of this family snowmobile made it fun and easy to ride, and it would out perform most of its contemporaries of similar displacement.

"The 'F' was quite a sled," said Bill Monette, a vintage collector and son of a former New York state Moto-Ski dealer. "They were really nice handling machines."

Overall *Snow Goer* editors gushed over the Moto-Ski 'F' series snowmobile.

"Last year we said Moto-Ski lacked pizazz, like the difference between kissing your sister and your sweetheart, but that's all changed now," editors wrote. "It rides well and has all the qualities necessary to keep snowmobiling the sport it should be."

Evolution And Dissolution

For 1974, the 'F' was given a graphic facelift and a price increase to become the first Futura, a designation that would grace top-of-the-line Moto-Skis for nearly another decade. At the same time, the 'F' was also stretched 5.5 inches to become the Chima, replacing the Zephyr as the limousine of the line. Both lasted for one more year while Ski-Doo-based Moto-Skis made their initial appearance. By 1976, Moto-Ski had become a series of orange Ski-Doos with some minor differences from their yellow brothers. These orange Bombardiers embodied the modern features that the 'F' had introduced to the historic brand, and the transitory 'F' series quietly slipped into snowmobile history.

1973 Moto-Ski 'F' Series

MANUFACTURER
Moto-Ski Limited, a subsidiary of Bombardier Limited, at Sainte-Anne-de-la-Pocatiere, Quebec

POWERTRAIN
Type: Bouchard Special Engine axial fan cooled two-cycle twin
Displacement: 293.5cc (295 F), 336cc (340 F) or 435cc (440 F)
Carburetion: Mikuni
Ignition: Magneto
Lubrication: Pre-mix at 20:1
Exhaust: Single pipe with muffler
Power Output: 24 hp (295 F), 32 hp (340 F) or 40 hp (440 F)
Drive Clutch: RPM-Sensing centrifugal type
Driven Clutch: Torque-sensing

CHASSIS
Type: Riveted aluminum with steel sub-frame
Listed Dry Weight: 380 pounds (295 F); 395 pounds (340 F and 440 F)
Rear Suspension: Slide rail with one shock absorber on rear arm
Front Suspension: Multi-leaf springs with shock absorbers
Ski Stance: 28.5 inches
Fuel Capacity: 6.5 gallons
Track: 17-inch wide three-ply molded rubber with sprocket-drive on steel cleats
Brake: Mechanical disc

MSRP: $1,095 (295 F); $1,145 (340 F); $1,245 (440 F)

1973 Raider TT

Twin Tracks For Snow Trails

Detroit native Bob Bracey was an automotive engineer who had worked for each of the American-Big Three automakers and for the company that built Ford's successful GT-40 race car. Bracey also loved snowmobiles and was intent on producing a revolutionary sled that would outperform conventional snow machines.

After two years of development, his original Raider twin track appeared in 1971, with about 500 built by Michigan manufacturer Leisure Vehicles Inc. The radical Raider wasn't the first twin-track snowmobile by any means because big, double-track utility sleds like the Ski-Doo Alpine and Valmont had been around for years. But this was really different.

The Raider was more like a race car because the operator sat in it instead of on it, and relied on its low center-of-gravity with four points of ground contact for excellent stability and superior handling. It also provided excellent protection for the rider, so it was promoted as offering safety with sports car maneuverability.

Enlarged and heavily re-engineered for 1972, Raider moved into the mainstream by adding distribution across the snowbelt, and the sled started to sell in significant numbers. But the design still had a lot of issues, so the basic machine was heavily re-worked again for 1973.

While this work proceeded, Honda attempted to buy Raider, or to partner with the company, and a number of Honda-powered prototypes were built and tested by Honda dealers. But Honda was not impressed with Raider management and business practices, and terminated the partnership.

Refined & Rewarded

The model year 1973 refinements included smoothing the body contours and windshield, and adding new reflective graphics. The chassis got shocks mounted forward of the coil spring ski struts and revised springs on the rear suspensions to improve ride quality. Urethane foam on the inside of the engine cover helped meet new industry noise emission standards.

The engine was tilted to make room for a larger carb, and this further lowered the center of gravity and also reduced vibration. Power choices were reduced to a 400 (in the 34TT) or a 440; a kill switch was added and a Salsbury 850 drive clutch replaced two other Salsbury

52

models previously used. But weight increased to 100 pounds more than the original 1971 units.

The resulting machines were rewarded with generally favorable magazine reviews.

"Its ride is much improved over last year," *Snow Goer* editors commented. And they loved the new front bumper. "Smash it, and all you have to do is remove the screws and it pops back to original shape since it's the same miracle 'memory' plastic used in Pontiac LeMans front bumpers." They were also very impressed with the Raider's incredible stability and overall ease of operation, but not with the thin seat cushion or the acceleration of the 34TT that they tested. And they were disappointed that the machine was too wide to fit on their chassis dynamometer.

Invitation To Snowmobiling magazine editors were also generally impressed with the machine except for comfort issues, starting with the thin seat cushion. They noted that with the weight of the engine in the rear, the skis tended to skitter and bounce more than on a conventional sled, affecting comfort but not steering. Reviewers commented that the ski shocks helped, but were "not a final solution." And one female editor said she never realized until late in the test that the foot bar inside the cowling was adjustable for operator leg length. However, the magazine noted that the 1973 44TT went even farther on its tip-over test than the '72 model, offering a good 12-degree stability advantage over the best conventional sleds. Plus, it was even quieter than the already quiet '72 Raider models. "Performance is not the Raider's long suit," the editors reported, but they did love its climbing ability and novelty value.

The Tracks Get Faint
Model year 1973 turned out to be the high water mark for Raider snowmobiles, with more machines built and sold than any other model year. But despite generally good media reviews and increasing acceptance of the radical concept, the '73 Raiders failed to sell out as industry overproduction, declining snowfall and the 1973 Arab oil embargo shook the entire powersports world to its core.

Left-over '73 TTs were converted to the new 1974 Eagle model. Dealers were provided with an update kit consisting of new decals and a 1974 owner's manual. And 1975 was Raider's last year. Leisure Vehicles succumbed to trends affecting the whole industry as well as to the loss of visionary President and Chief Engineer Bob Bracey who had resigned, partly due to the Honda situation, to pursue a new project - the ARBE Manta twin track racer. In fact, Bracey's pursuit of the twin-tracked, cockpit style snowmobile continued all the way to 2001 with his Trail Roamers. But that's another story.

Still, Raider had reportedly sold something approaching 20,000 sleds in five years, substantially more than many well-known snowmobile manufacturers of the vintage era, and proving that the radical twin track trail sled that resembled a race car actually had something going for it.

1973 Raider 44TT

MANUFACTURER
Leisure Vehicles Inc., Troy, Michigan

POWERTRAIN
Engine: 438cc Canadian Curtiss Wright (CCW) KEC-440/21 axial-fan-cooled, piston port twin with one Walbro WDA-38 diaphragm pumper carb, Kokusan magneto and breaker point ignition, and single pipe into a Donaldson muffler
Lubrication: Pre-mix at 20:1
Power Output (claimed): 40 hp @ 6,500 rpm
Electrical Power: 120 watts
Clutches: Salsbury 850 drive and torque-sensing driven

CHASSIS
Type: Painted tubular steel with painted tube steel rear bumper, urethane front bumper and fiberglass body shell
Claimed Dry Weight: 420 pounds
Front Suspension: Coil spring struts with external hydraulic shock absorbers
Ski Stance: 25.5 inches
Rear Suspension: Single slide rails with leaf springs and one hydraulic shock per side
Tracks: Two, 8-inch wide, double belted arid fiber reinforced, with full-width steel cleats and single sprocket drive
Brake: Kelsey-Hayes mechanical caliper on the driven pulley
Fuel Capacity: 5.6 gallons
Standard Equipment: Electric start, speedometer/odometer, tachometer, fuel gauge, adjustable foot rest, twin snow flaps, passenger seat and grab strap

MSRP: $1,399

Last Stand of the Axial Fan Stocker
1973 Rupp Nitro

Rupp Industries had always been a performance-oriented company, starting right from the day that Mickey Rupp opened the doors as a kart builder in 1959. The company successfully moved into snowmobiles in 1965, and for 1972 it introduced its new Nitro stock racer, a machine that was engineered to leverage racetrack success into showroom sales.

The company wanted to take full advantage of a new United States Snowmobile Association (USSA) rule that required offering the full slate of Stock, Women's and Junior Stock classes at all sanctioned races. Most major snowmobile racing events had offered only the loud, fast and expensive Modified classes, so Stock classes had only run at the local races and the season-ending USSA World Series of Snowmobiling.

The Nitro series was similar to existing competitive machines like the Ski-Doo Tn'T and the Arctic Cat Puma. Single-seaters built on a shorter chassis than the more common 2-Ups of the day, they featured sporty styling and axial fan-cooled engines. This cooling system uses an over-driven fan to blow air across the top of the engine to remove heat, and was a mainstay of snowmobiles of the era. Other engines used a radial fan mounted on the end of the crankshaft to blow air across the engine, or simply had lots of extra cooling fin area with no fan at all, a technique commonly called free air (FA) and used mostly on the Modified pure racing sleds.

Rupp's first go at a Stock racer was successful. Numerous victories culminated with Bill Hepner's C Stock (340cc) win on a Nitro at the 1972 USSA World Series of Snowmobiling in Ironwood, Michigan.

The New, Improved 1973 Nitro

In 1972, Rupp rolled out its new, terrific-looking and considerably improved 1973 Nitro. Positioned specifically as a stock racer and described as the culmination of two seasons of racing development, the company had high hopes for its newest creation.

The Nitro's new, one-piece hood featured a flat black top that resembled the anti-glare panel on a fighter plane. Underneath was a new, high-energy capacitor discharge ignition (CDI) system with surface gap spark plugs, a greatly improved lighting system, self-adjusting disc brake and a new sound-reduction package.

The front end was heavily reworked for better handling with wider skis on a wider ski stance, new caster and camber angles on the spindles and new steering stops. A new adjustable aluminum slide rail suspension replaced the earlier steel slider unit. "It adjusts to any setting from all-out racing to all-out trail riding," boasted the brochure. "We've applied for a patent on it. Because there's nothing else like it."

Four engines were available, all axial fan twins built to Rupp specifications by Tohatsu in Japan. The 295, 340 and 400 engines fit the top three USSA Stock racing classes of the day, while the 440 was for the "outlaw" races and the trail riders, although all were legal and capable trail sleds.

Invitation To Snowmobiling magazine tested a prototype '73 Nitro 440 in the spring of 1972. Editors gave it a big thumbs up in the fun department, describing it as "an eye catcher, a mover and a handler;' and went on to say that it was "engineered to give you a great time – if you're man enough to ride it."

Editors pointed out that although it was very quick and agile, and the best-handling sled they tested that spring, it was also very noisy because part of the sound-deadening package was not installed in the prototype. They also found that the Rupp Rails suspension system was best suited for smooth trails, commenting that Rupp still had some work to do on the comfort and ride quality.

Slow Fade On The Track

The 1972-73 oval sprint race season started with promise. Nitros made an impressive three-win showing at the USSA Eastern Division opener at Redfield, New York. That performance included a one-two finish in Men's Stock B (295cc), a top-three sweep of Women's Class II (Stock 295cc) and a win in Junior II. Just days later, Janet Hempton, a Michigan Rupp dealer's wife, won Women's Stock 295 at the big Ironwood Snowmobile Olympus, the first major race of the season in the Midwest, with Janell Hempton taking Junior II.

Nitros saw numerous wins across the Snowbelt in the early going, mostly with the 295s and mostly at smaller events or on lower level race circuits.

But by the end of January, the hot new Arctic Cat, Ski-Doo and Polaris free air stock racers had pretty well pushed the fan-cooled Nitros out of the USSA class finals except in the less contested Women's and Junior brackets; and the Rupps were struggling there, too. There were a few late-season wins in local events, but it was pretty clear that the curtain was dropping fast on the fan-cooled stocker.

The lone exception was Eastern Division Junior Richard DeWitt who had been winning the Junior II class quite consistently with his Nitro, starting with the Redfield opener. He went on to take the class victory at the muddy 1973 World Series in Malone, New York. It would be the last time that a Rupp stocker, or any brand with a fan-cooled engine, would win a World Series title.

Finishing Out Of The Money

Rupp wasn't just falling behind on the racetrack, it was also losing ground in the showroom. Rupp's 1973 model year sales failed to meet expectations, and with the company facing bankruptcy, owner Mickey Rupp sold it on April, 1973, to a group of investors headed by Joseph Hrudka of the Mr. Gasket company.

The 1973 model year also marked the end of the line for Tohatsu engines in Rupps, as the company switched to Kohler power for 1974.

The Nitro would live on for several more years, but the 1973 version was the last successful fan-cooled racer that Rupp, or any other company, ever made.

1973 Rupp Nitro

MANUFACTURER
Rupp Industries Inc., Mansfield, Ohio

POWERTRAIN
Engine: Tohatsu-built Rupp axial fan twins with chrome plated cylinders
Displacement: 438cc/398cc/336cc/294cc
Carburetion: One Tillotson diaphragm pumper with ram tube
Compression Ratio: 7.47 to 7.8:1 depending on model
Ignition: Capacitor Discharge with surface gap spark plugs
Lubrication: Pre-mix at 20:1
Exhaust: Twin "tuned" pipes into one low-pressure muffler
Power Output: Claimed 40 hp @ 7,200 rpm (440)
Drive Clutch: Rupp lightweight centrifugal
Driven Clutch: Rupp "snow sensing" secondary

CHASSIS
Type: Hand-welded aluminum with steel sub-frame and chassis stirrups, chrome-plated forged steel skis and fiberglass cowl
Claimed Dry Weight: 385 pounds dry (440). Actual 447 pounds wet for prototype without sound deadening package as tested by *Invitation To Snowmobiling* magazine
Front Suspension: Multi-leaf springs with inboard-mounted chrome-plated hydraulic shocks
Ski Stance: 28.5-inches
Rear Suspension: Rupp Rails adjustable aluminum sliders with hydraulic shock on rear arm
Track: 15.5-inch steel and polyester-reinforced molded rubber
Brake: Self-adjusting mechanical disc on driven clutch
Fuel Capacity: 4.5 U.S. gallons
Standard Equipment: Speedometer/odometer, tachometer, dimmer switch, kill switch, snow flap, toolbox in rear of seat, passenger hand grips
Options: Gas gauge, electric start, cigar/cigarette lighter

Price: $1,450 (440), $1,350 (400), $1,250 (340), $1,150 (295)

1973 Rupp American
Performance For The Whole Family

Built to carry two adults in comfort, the Rupp American was a sporty sled that featured the extra stability and flotation of an 18-inch track, a popular width for premium models of the day.

Roots of the American begin with the 1971 line-leading Wide-Track 440. But according to Minnesota Rupp collector Tom Peterson, who worked for his uncle's Rupp dealership at the time, a limited number of Wide-Track 340s with American decals were also built as 1972 pre-production units. These first Americans were not included in Rupp sales literature, a common practice among many manufacturers in the fast-moving snowmobile industry of the day.

For 1972, the Wide-Track became an American. Available with a 30 hp 340, a 40 hp 440, and a rare 50 hp 650, the '72 American had electric start as standard equipment. But ski shocks, all instrumentation and even the snow flap were options. Described by *Snow Goer* editors as "an elegant looking machine," reviewers at the time concluded that the new American "lived up to (and surpassed) our expectations." They lauded the machine as fast, handsome, comfortable and well handling to make it "what an experienced snowmobiler would call a 'total' machine."

But the American didn't really hit its stride until 1973 when it got a substantial make over.

The Family Nitro

"Think of it as a family version of the Nitro," shouted the big black headline in the catalog. Bristling with new technology that was shared with the Nitro stock racer, but not always with the lower-priced Yankee and Sport, the new American was way ahead of the typical 1973 family sled.

All 1973 Rupp models got a new solid-state capacitor discharge (CD) ignition system that blasted 40,000-volts to the surface gap spark plugs for quicker starting, smoother running, longer plug life and better reliability than breaker points. CDI was just starting to take hold in snowmobiling, mostly on the emerging class of trail racers like the Nitro, and the 1973 *Popular Science Snowmobile Handbook* called this "an unusual step for a snowmobile builder."

An upgraded lighting system with a solid-state regulator provided 70 percent more wattage than the previous year. The new tuned exhaust improved low-speed torque and fuel economy while teaming up with more air silencing and insulation to cut noise emissions in half. Clutching was refined and a new flip-up center console improved engine access.

Underneath, the '73 American offered either traditional bogie wheels or new aluminum slide rails (previous Rupp sliders were steel) that were adapted from the Nitro exclusively for the American. Available for the first time in a Rupp trail sled, the lighter and simpler sliders eliminated link plate hassles, and the longer travel and adjustability greatly improved ride quality at a time when most family sleds still crawled along slowly on rough-riding bogies or hybrid suspensions that were no better.

A wider version of the Nitro track featured a more aggressive profile for better traction and was exclusive to these two models. And chrome ski shocks were now standard, but electric start became an option, allowing a $50 drop in the manufacturer's suggested retail price.

Limited Appeal

The American didn't get as much model-specific advertising support as the Nitro or the priceleading Sport. More expensive but not as well equipped as much of its direct competition, American sales were limited. But the bright red family sled won a following among Rupp fanatics who valued its looks and performance.

"They were a classy looking sled," remarked Peterson, who currently owns four Americans, including one that has been in the family since it was new and the one pictured here.

"I liked the American," he said. "That was always my favorite to ride. It was also the first one I worked on" at his uncle's dealership. One reason for the ride quality was the 18-inch track. "They were less tipsy," he explained, "and they stayed on top of the snow better." Also enjoyed the convenience of electric start.

Peterson didn't see any real difference in handling between the bogie and slide versions, but did say that in deep, wet snow, the slider skid frame would fill up more than the bogie wheel suspension.

The 1974 American was a left-over '73, underscoring the industry-wide inventory problem that was compounded by Rupp's change of ownership from founder Mickey Rupp to Joseph Hrudka of Mr. Gasket fame. "I've never seen a '74 American with a '74 serial number," Peterson said. "They're all '73s." The American hung on for one more season as the inventory was cleaned out while Rupp evolved into a low-volume, mostly high-performance sled specialist.

Conceived as a performance-oriented family sled, the Rupp American found an enthusiastic but limited fan base that it still retains to this day.

1973 Rupp American

MANUFACTURER
Rupp Industries, Inc., Mansfield, Ohio

POWERTRAIN
Engine: 438cc / 336cc Tohatsu axial-fan-cooled piston-port twin
Carburetion: One Tillotson diaphragm pumper
Compression Ratio: 8.14 to 1 / 7.8:1
Ignition: Capacitor Discharge (CD)
Lubrication: Pre-mix at 20:1
Exhaust: Single tuned pipe into muffler
Power Output: 40 hp @ 6,600 RPM/ 30 hp @ 6,800 RPM
Electrical Output: 128 watts
Clutches: Rupp

CHASSIS SPECS
Type: Hand-welded aluminum with steel subframe, stirrups, chrome-plated forged steel skis, forged spindles and polycarbonate hood
Dry Weight (claimed): Rupp didn't disclose but about 385 pounds.
Front Suspension: Multi-leaf springs with chrome hydraulic shocks
Ski Stance: 30.5 inches
Rear Suspension: Rupp Rails aluminum sliders with torsion springs and hydraulic shock on rear arm or 6-truck trailing bogie wheels with torsion springs
Track: 17.5- by-120-inch steel and polyester reinforced rubber
Brake: Self-adjusting mechanical disc
Fuel Capacity: 4.5 gallons
Standard Equipment: Adjustable handlebars, kill-switch, speedometer/odometer, dipstick gas gauge, passenger hand grips, tow hitch, snow flap, electric start
Optional Equipment: Speedometer/ odometer, tachometer, fuel gauge, kill switch, electric start, cigarette lighter, track cleat kit, snow flap, American tunnel decals

MSRP: $1,345 / $1,245

1973 Scorpion Super Stinger TK
The First TK Was Actually Yellow

In 1977 Scorpion unveiled its new '78 Whip TK premium trail sled, a machine of which many people are aware. But Scorpion's first TK was actually the 1973 Super Stinger TK.

Back then, the TK designation was only a production code to differentiate Super Stinger 400s with JLO piston port engines from Super Stinger 400 RVs with their CCW reed-valve engines.

But the big news was that the Super Stinger 400 TK was available not only in the company's well-established metal flake red, but also in an eye-catching sunshine yellow at no additional charge. This egregious disregard of the industry's well-established color code may have been due to the fact that the company's president at the time was former Ski-Doo distribution executive Warren Daoust. And the Super Stinger 440 was also available in an "immaculate white" as well as metal flake red.

These new hues were promoted with statements like "Who else but Scorpion would be first with colors?" Actually they were nowhere near first, as about a dozen smaller brands, including Viking, Swinger, Northway, Moto-Kometik and Ski-Zoom, had already offered color choices on their models, and several more including Ski-Doo, Arctic Cat and MTD Columbia broke the color code concurrently with Scorpion. But that didn't matter because the screaming yellow hood did its job exceptionally well by focusing many people's attention on Scorpion.

Evolution

The 1973 Scorpions really didn't look different from the 1972 models that had been nearly all new from the ground up, many of which were still piled up as unsold inventory from the 20,000 units produced for 1972. But there were many subtle changes.

In a major safety upgrade, ankle-breaker tunnel stirrups were history. A new version of the Power Thrust drive clutch was said to improve power delivery to the track by 20 percent. Polyurethane tracks replaced rubber ones, while the Para-Rail rear suspension rack was changed from steel to aluminum and got three more wheels on the internal cross shafts. Ski shock mounts were reworked, control upgrades improved operator comfort and more powerful headlamps met upgraded industry lighting standards.

Despite the aggressive sounding Super Stinger name, these sleds were anything but high-performance models. As *Popular Snowmobiling* magazine pointed out, "[Scorpion officials] never said they built a racing machine." And they certainly hadn't with the family oriented TK.

The PS reviewers rated comfort as the high point of the sled, commenting that "the rider (is) well protected," and noting that the engine housing insulated riders from engine noise but had large panels for effective access.

However, the reviewers did complain that the buckhorn handlebars were not shaped for maximum turning leverage, and handling was rated "slow and sluggish at lower speeds, but agile in lean and climbing tests."

Reviewers also noted that in aggressive handling tests, "the machine wanted to roll outward at inopportune times," common behavior of sleds with engines mounted on the tunnel. Other testers backed them up on this. "It goes over at 36 degrees," reported *Invitation To Snowmobiling* magazine. "We didn't test many tippier than that." *Popular Snowmobiling* also tried jumping the TK and had one word of advice afterward: "Don't!"

The final summation from *Popular Snowmobiling* was that the TK is "A good, reliable machine with a healthy engine that won't take too much high performance antics. Keep it on the ground and it should be ready whenever you are for a long ride."

Many buyers encountered reliability problems – notably ignition and clutching – with Scorpions from the early '70s. Braking distance was still poor despite increased brake surface, as noted by *Invitation To Snowmobiling*. And the Para-Rail was controversial to say the least. It worked well in low or no snow conditions, but did not deliver anywhere near the ride quality of a good slide rail system.

Encore & Exit

For 1974, the last year of the company's ownership by conglomerate Fuqua Industries, Scorpion did a modestly restyled version of these sleds as the swan song of the famous Stinger series, with the yellow replaced by gold metal flake.

The 1975 model year brought the virtually all-new Whip series that propelled Scorpion into modern engineering and construction methods, a series that would culminate with the Whip TK and TKX models a few years later.

The '73 Super Stinger 400 TK was the first and only yellow Scorpion ever produced. It contributed very significantly to the destruction of the industry's long held color code, and that makes it a historic sled for the entire sport, as well as a Scorpion fancier's delight.

1973 Scorpion Super Stinger 400 TK

MANUFACTURER
Scorpion Inc., Crosby, Minnesota, a Division of Fuqua Industries, Atlanta, Georgia

POWERTRAIN
Engine: 398cc Rockwell/JLO L-400/2 axial fan-cooled piston-port twin with one Walbro WDA diaphragm pumper carb, magneto and breaker point ignition, and single pipe into Donaldson muffler
Compression Ratio: 7.5:1
Lubrication: Pre-mix at 20:1
Power Output: 35 hp (estimated)
Clutches: Scorpion Power Thrust drive and torque sensing driven

CHASSIS
Type: Welded and painted steel with steel belly pan, pressed steel front bumper, chromed tube steel rear bumper and fiberglass hood
Claimed Dry Weight: 358 pounds
Front Suspension: Triple leaf springs with hydraulic shock absorbers
Ski Stance: 26 inches
Rear Suspension: Scorpion aluminum Para-Rail with 15 wheels, torsion springs and one hydraulic shock absorber on the rear arm
Track: 15-by-118-inch Power Bite molded polyurethane with dual internal drive; 54.5-inch footprint
Brake: Drum type on driven clutch
Fuel Capacity: 6 gallons
Standard Equipment: Speedometer/odometer, tachometer, Kelch fuel gauge, fuel primer, handlebar pad, kill switch, seat back storage compartment, chromed tube steel passenger grab handles, spill tray on gas tank

MSRP: $1,195

1973 Ski-Zoom Comet

Thinking Big, Crashing Bad

Conceived by engineer and racecar driver Francois Favreau, the Buzz snowmobile was introduced by Autotechnic Inc., of Montreal, Quebec, for the 1970 snow season. Built in St.-Pie-de-Bagot, Quebec, the Buzz had a riveted aircraft aluminum chassis, mid-mounted Sachs engine, disc brake and bogie wheel suspension, and was available in red, yellow, orange, blue or green.

But the Buzz didn't last. It was almost immediately rechristened as the Ski-Zoom. And a new Kohler-powered green and gold version called the Sno-Pack went into production for distribution in the United States by Leisure Mor, Inc., of Green Bay, Wisconsin. Private branding agreements like this were common, and Autotechnic was joining many other snowmobile companies in this process.

Meanwhile, Ski-Zoom was gaining acceptance by the Quebec snow machine press. "After driving other snowmobiles, getting into a Ski-Zoom is like going from a Chevrolet Impala to an Alfa-Romeo GTV," wrote Jaques Duval1 in the March 1970, issue of the French language *Vroum Motoneige* magazine.

Misreading The Tea Leaves

Under guidance of businessman President Simon Bedard, Autotechnic was a recreational manufacturer on the rise. Convinced that the booming snowmobile market was headed for the often-predicted sales of 1 million machines per year, and buoyed by the quick acceptance in the Quebec market, the company continued to invest in new products despite early signs of trouble.

Three new Ski-Zoom models were introduced for 1971, the entry-level Rebel, the mid-market Comet and the high-performance Fury. All sported a new hood design and were done in the orange over black that would become the brand's signature color scheme. But underneath nothing much had changed, and the 1971 lineup also included what were essentially left over 1970 models to use up the multi-colored hoods and excess Kohler engines from building the Sno-Pack.

That alternate brand deal was history as Leisure Mor had sold out to Farmington Engineering in Michigan, and that company was building its own sleds under the Sno-Pac label (note the spelling change). Ski-Zoom also entered the costly world of snowmobile competition with a short run (fewer than 100 units) of factory racers that accomplished essentially nothing.

However, like many other snow sled manufacturers, Autotechnic added a series of six mini bikes under the Mini-Zoom banner, and pressed ahead with sled development including consolidation of operations within a 100,000-square foot plant in Drummondville, Quebec, that was capable of building 60,000 vehicles per year.

The 1972 Ski-Zoom models were further upgraded with another new hood featuring a recessed headlight, a bigger gas tank and optional slide rail suspension. Promoted as the "sports car of snow machines" and carrying very competitive prices, these increasingly dated sleds failed to meet sales expectations. By late winter, Autotechnic's Manitoba distributor was closing out Ski-Zooms at its cost with a free 10-speed bicycle thrown in with every sale. And in Wisconsin, General Jobbing Corp. was liquidating Ski-Zooms at less than half of recommended retail prices.

For 1973, Ski-Zoom introduced its first engine-forward model, the G.T., as a replacement for the Fury series. Equipped with a 40 hp Sachs 440 engine in a fully enclosed engine compartment and a slide rail suspension, it was a thoroughly contemporary snow machine. However, the attractively priced but increasingly dated Rebel and Comet were still the mainstays. All models were further upgraded with a kill switch for safety and a dual drive track for better performance and reliability.

The Crash

Autotechnic showed up at *Snow Goer*'s 1972 spring tests with two incomplete '73 Comet prototypes instead of the new G.T. that was not yet ready, and the staff evaluated a 440 despite unfinished details everywhere. "The model we tested really only roughly responds to what you'll see in the showrooms this fall," the *Snow Goer* editors commented. The crew was impressed by the easy starting, power, climbing ability and rider comfort of the machine. They considered it a "good, basic, stylish trail machine," and also commented that it would be well suited "for farm or ranch work or other utility applications." But because the machine was really not representative of what a production 1973 Comet 440 would be, they could not be as conclusive about the machine as others they tested.

Ski-Zoom entered the 1973 selling season with great expectations for its now "low production, almost custom-made" sleds. But industry projections of a million machines per year were a mirage, with sales stalling out at roughly half that at the peak in 1972. The industry was producing far more sleds than there were buyers, so inventory problems were making sales increasingly difficult.

The bottom line was that Ski-Zoom just wasn't selling enough products to survive. Out of cash, out of credit and out of credibility, Autotechnic was forced to file bankruptcy in 1973 and no longer needed its huge plant in Drummondville.

1973 Ski-Zoom Comet 440

MANUFACTURER
Autotechnic Inc., Drummondville, Quebec, Canada

POWERTRAIN
Engine: 436cc Sachs SA-2 440 axial-fan-cooled piston-port twin with a Tillotson HD diaphragm pumper carburetor and single exhaust
Ignition: Magneto and breaker points
Power Output: 35 hp @ 6,500 rpm
Drive Clutch: St. Lawrence

CHASSIS SPECS
Type: Riveted aircraft aluminum with stirrups, chrome steel bumpers and fiberglass hood
Dry Weight (Claimed): 285 pounds
Front Suspension: Mono-leaf springs
Ski Stance: 27 inches (estimated)
Rear Suspension: Bogie wheels (12 on 3 trucks) with torsion springs
Track: 15-by-114-inch 3-ply nylon reinforced molded rubber with dual-sprocket drive
Brake: Mechanical disc

MSRP: $1,195

The Alouette Super Brute
Thinking Well Outside The Box

Most snowmobile manufacturers of the vintage era exhibited a follow-the-leader engineering mentality. But Alouette was definitely not one of them.

Maybe the first clue to that was the name of its originator, the Featherweight Aluminum Products Company of Montreal, Quebec.

Beginning with its first machines for the 1967 model year, the smallish Alouettes were usually the lightest sleds in their respective class. Moreover, Alouette was unafraid to push the engineering boundaries with features like Wankel rotary engines and its unique Ski-Sorber front suspension. Probably its most memorable creation was Gilles Villeneuve's controversial and crowd-pleasing IFS twin-track racers for the inaugural Sno Pro season in 1974.

However, the radical new trail sled that Alouette created for the 1974 season also introduced new ideas that foretold the future. Industry media immediately took notice of this startling new snow machine and reviewed it often and in detail. Alouette management was quoted in the *Sno-mobile Times 1973 Summer Yearbook* calling its new creation "the most promising sled in the industry." In some ways, Alouette was right.

"Une Bombe Originale"

"This is what engineering is all about," proclaimed the 1974 Alouette brochure. The lead machine was the all-new Super Brute. Visually distinctive and sophisticated under the skin, the Super Brute was described by Quebec's *Le Magazine L'Auto-Neige* (The Magazine of the Snowmobile) as "une bombe originale." Translated, that means a quite unexpected development. And they were certainly right about that.

Besides the sleek new styling that was a huge advancement from the nondescript earlier Alouettes, the immediately noticeable difference between the Super Brute and any other snowmobile was the control module on top of the handlebars. It grouped the instruments, headlight and wrap-around windshield together in a pod that rotated with the handlebars, allowing the light to illuminate the area where the skis were pointed. The brochure described this unique new feature as "a new high-power headlight that swivels to show you where you're going on curves."

Snow Goer Trade highlighted the directional headlight as one of the significant engineering improvements of 1974, declaring it the Super Brute's "outstanding unique feature." But there was a lot more to this new machine than the revolutionary handlebar pod.

More Than Skin-Deep Beauty

Under the aerodynamic new hood, Alouette engineers had done most everything possible to reduce weight. Most sleds with aluminum tunnels had a steel sub-frame to support the engine and front suspension, but not this new Alouette. The chassis was all aluminum, including the nose, tunnel, rear bumper, motor mounts and a new die-cast aluminum chaincase. A disc brake was mounted on the case, which contained a new, heavy-duty silent chain and was located on the clutch side to eliminate the weight and complexity of a torque-distributing jackshaft drive system. The front grab handles were heavy-duty rubber under a streamlined panel between the bumper and hood.

The sales brochure stressed its "race-proven front-end structure" and devoted a two-page spread to Villeneuve and his trio of Alouette Super racers. The shape of the highly successful professional race sleds had clearly inspired the beautifully clean lines of the Super Brute.

The all-new chassis also included built-in rear footholds for drag race starts and the back of the tunnel under the snow flap was open to eliminate clogging with snow. The new foam seat was built into a single-unit fiberglass mount, and the gas tank was a see-through polyethylene unit rather than the normal heavy steel tank. The design also abandoned the traditional under-seat storage compartment of earlier Alouettes for a small toolbox located in the center console above the gas tank.

Standard equipment also included a speedometer and temperature gauge, but a tachometer was an option.

Underneath it all, the new internal drive rubber track was quieter and more efficient mechanically than the usual system of toothed cogs engaging the reinforcing rods in the track. Inside the track lived a new adjustable slide rail system with dual springs but no shocks.

As with all performance-oriented Alouettes, Sachs power with Comet clutching was provided. Buyers had a choice of 295, 340 or 440 axial fan twins or a new Sachs 440 with a thermostatically controlled liquid cooling system. The only external differences were the engine-displacement decals on the hood.

The 440 fan seemed to be the most popular variant. It was rated at 42 hp, with a respectable 17.5 of it actually reaching the ground, according to chassis dyno tests. This was good for an 8.86-second, 58.6 mph pass in a tenth-mile drag, as tested at 48 degrees F on wet, granular snow by *Le Magazine L'AutoNeige*. This performance matched or beat similar 440 fans tested under much more advantageous conditions, so the Super Brute was definitely a runner.

Legacy Of The Super Brute

It was tough to sell snowmobiles in 1974. The previous year's oil crisis, a soft economy, a mild winter and mounting inventory of unsold sleds from industry-wide overproduction doomed Alouette and many other brands. The 1975 Alouettes were left over '74s without the water-burner model. The last Alouettes in 1976 were simply Rupps with different decals that were sold only in Canada.

But the innovative ideas in the Super Brute did not expire with the Alouette brand name.

For instance, the truly all-aluminum chassis later appeared in other models including the ground-breaking Arctic Cat Pantera free air introduced in 1976. The fairing over the space between the front bumper and the hood was seen again on the 1981 Scorpion Sidewinder.

The signature idea of the Super Brute, the handlebar pod with the headlight, windshield and instrumentation, reappeared 10 years later on what would become one of the hottest selling models of the 1980s, the Yamaha Phazer. Even the flat, square hood and slab sides of the Phazer echoed the Super Brute's styling, appropriately updated for the new decade. And the legacy of the Super Brute L/C was the later Yamaha Exciter II, essentially an improved and liquid-cooled Phazer.

The Super Brute was the last and best of the real Alouettes: The product of a company that was unafraid to think outside the box, the Super Brute's influence lived on decades after the sleds themselves had been thrown on the scrap heap of history.

1974 Alouette Super Brute 440

MANUFACTURER
Alouette Recreational Products Limited, a subsidiary of Coleco (Canada) Limited, Montreal, Quebec

POWERTRAIN
Engine: Sachs SA-2 440 axial fan twin
Displacement: 437cc
Carburetion: One Mikuni VM series
Compression Ratio: 10.6:1
Ignition: Bosch magneto and breaker points
Lubrication: 25:1 pre-mix
Exhaust: Single pipe with muffler
Power Output: 42 hp @ 6,750 rpm
Drive Clutch: Comet
Driven Clutch: Comet

CHASSIS
Type: Riveted aircraft aluminum tunnel and nose
Claimed Dry Weight: 325 pounds
Front Suspension: Alouette Ski-Sorber pivoting coil over hydraulic shock absorber
Ski Stance: 32 inches
Rear Suspension: Adjustable double slide rail with two horizontally mounted coil springs
Track: 15-inch polyester-reinforced molded rubber with internal drive
Brake: Mechanical disc
Fuel Capacity: 6 U.S. gallons

Price: $ 1,499

1974 Arctic Cat Panther VIP
A Technological Heavy Weight

In early 1972, I had the opportunity to ride a brand new Arctic Cat Panther 440 that looked externally just like any other '72 Panther. But under the hood, this Panther didn't have the usual clutches and drive belt. Instead it had a little automatic transmission—the same type found in automobiles—that used fluid to transmit energy within the device.

It was smooth, quiet and behaved just like any other Panther, seamlessly rolling off idle and cruising smoothly. I thought this was an interesting idea, as drive clutches and drive belts were notorious weak links in all the snowmobiles of the day. Maybe this was the key to power transmission reliability that the snowmobile industry desperately needed.

A few months later Arctic Cat was talking about a forthcoming new model, the 1973 Panther VIP. It would be a fully loaded, top-of-the-line luxury sled featuring the automatic transmission.

Something Special

Promoted as "a machine built only for the man who recognizes and appreciates unqualified excellence," the VIP was much more than just a 1973 Panther with a few add-ons.

The new Cat-A-Matic hydrostatic transmission was the centerpiece. Engineered by Kawasaki specifically for this application, the new fluid drive was said to virtually eliminate transmission service problems and provide constant torque to the track under all snow and terrain conditions. The fluid coupling isolated the driveshaft from the crankshaft, thereby eliminating a source of vibration. And with no exposed moving parts, it was also said to be-safer for users.

Power came from an upgraded Kawasaki 440 axial fan ("the D model") that featured oil injection, a huge convenience previously exclusive to Yamaha snowmobiles. The VIP also had capacitor discharge ignition (CDI) with surface gap spark plugs that were said to virtually eliminate fouling, another significant problem of the era. This ignition technology, which also eliminated the tuning and occasional problems with breaker points, was just starting to make inroads in the sport and was already available on other Cat models. Electric start was standard equipment on the VIP instead of a dealer-installed option for the first time on any Cat.

Full instrumentation including speedometer, odometer, tachometer and dual cylinder head temperature gauges was also included and space for an optional cigar and cigarette lighter was provided on the dash. The VIP retained all the normal 1973 Panther features like a kill switch, non-slip footrests, new fully enclosed hood for noise reduction and new internal drive 2/3-cleated track that promised to reduce cleat breakage as well as put more power on the ground. It was all topped off by Arctic's clearly superior and highly protective windshield, superb overall ergonomics and smooth-riding, slide rail suspension.

This engineering tour-de-force was wrapped in a new color and trim execution of the standard Panther exterior. A rich chocolate brown base color set the tone with a wood-grained dash and gold filigree trim decals on the hood. Even the traditional leopard print seat cover was discarded in favor of a simple brown one. Details like the color stripe in the front bumper and the handlebar pad were also design coordinated.

Finishing touches included chrome ski shocks instead of the black ones on the standard Panther and a personalized nameplate on the dash for owners who ordered their YIPs in advance.

Although six prototypes were built for the 1973 season, delays piled up upon delays. Eventually the 1973 Panther VIP became the 1974 Panther VIP. Nothing changed except the model year.

The Tail Of The Top Cat

Buyers receiving their VIPs began to discover some less-desirable aspects of the sled. They already knew it was really expensive. At a time when snowmobilers could still buy a decent snow machine for less than $1,000—few models topped the $1,500 mark—the VIP went for close to two grand, a ton of money for something frivolous like a snowmobile.

The brown Cat was also "Oh my God" heavy due to the weight of the transmission, electric start, oil injection and other extras piled onto what was already a big, hefty sled.

"It was a dog" said a dealer who must remain anonymous. The prodigious poundage overwhelmed the modest available power, restraining the VIP to fairly sedate performance on the trail. It wasn't as bad as the now-forgotten 1972 four-stroke Panther 305, but it wasn't going to give anybody whiplash, either. And many owners experienced fluid leakage problems with the automatic tranny, too.

Still, Arctic built and sold almost 4,000 of these big brown beasts in the one model year that it was available to the public.

Much of the relatively unique technology in the VIP was shelved, at least temporarily. The Cat-A-Matic fluid transmission never saw the light of day again. Too heavy and too expensive, advancements in clutch and belt technology rendered it unnecessary. Oil injection didn't appear again on another Arctic Cat until the 1979 Trail Cat, and it took even longer before another full-production Cat had electric start installed at the factory. CD ignition became an industry standard, but without the surface gap spark plugs. The brown color scheme re-appeared on some later Cat models like the Panteras and Cheetahs, but never really caught on with the snowmobiling public no matter how hard Arctic and some other manufacturers pushed it.

Many VIPs were stashed away in barns and sheds in good condition with relatively few miles on them. Due to relentless searches from vintage enthusiasts, they are now emerging more often at snowmobile shows as these collectors rediscover this unique and interesting Cat.

1974 Arctic Cat Panther VIP

MANUFACTURER
Arctic Enterprises, Inc., Thief River Falls, Minnesota

POWERTRAIN
Engine: Kawasaki T1B440D1A axial fan-cooled piston-port twin with chrome-lined cylinders
Displacement: 436cc
Carburetion: One Walbro diaphragm pumper
Compression Ratio: 6.8:1
Ignition: Capacitor Discharge (CD) with surface gap spark plugs
Lubrication: Oil injection
Power Output: 36 hp
Exhaust: Single pipe into Arctic muffler
Transmission: Kawasaki Cat-A-Matic hydrostatic drive

CHASSIS
Type: Riveted aluminum with welded steel sub-frame, aluminum belly pan and fiberglass hood
Weight: 430 pounds
Front Suspension: Single leaf springs with chromed hydraulic shock absorbers
Ski Stance: 26 inches
Rear Suspension: Aluminum slide rails with adjustable torsion springs and hydraulic shocks
Track: 17-inch wide internal drive fiberglass-reinforced tri-belt with 2/3-width hot-rolled steel cleats
Brake: Mechanical disc with parking brake
Fuel Capacity: 6.25 gallons
Standard Equipment: Personalized owner nameplate, electric start, speedometer with odometer, tachometer, dual cylinder head temperature gauges, wood grain dash, fuel gauge, model-specific handlebar pad and seat cover, kill switch, console storage compartment, tow hitch
Options: Cigarette lighter, rear view mirror, compass

Price: $1,895 MSRP

The 1974 Boa-Ski SS
Too Little Too Late To Save Two Companies

Boa-Ski had been building snowmobiles in La Guadaloupe, Quebec, since the 1968 model year. A solid second-tier brand, its bland Bombardier clones earned a reputation for reliability by that time that the company became part of Giffen Recreation, briefly the second largest snowmobile manufacturer in the world.

Alsport Inc. was a powersports manufacturer in southern Ohio who made a splash with its Tri-Sport three-wheelers. They subsequently purchased the Steen mini-cycle line, and late in 1972, acquired Boa-Ski from the disintegrating Giffen empire with the expressed intention of making it a major brand.

Alsport's forward-thinking corporate strategy was to offer dealers a "785-day selling season" for "365-day profit making" with its three product lines. The 785-day number came from selling Boa-Ski on a 180-day basis, Steen on a 210-day calendar and Tri-Sport year-round.

Part of this strategy was a sporty new top-of-the-line snowmobile with the distinctly unimaginative model name of SS that was carried over from a more traditional Boa-Ski of the previous model year. The new model would be built in Boa-Ski's spacious and modern Quebec production facility that opened in 1970.

Not Like Any Boa-Ski Before

The '74 SS certainly broke new ground for Boa-Ski with its lightweight riveted aluminum chassis, front-mounted engine and slide suspension. Additional advanced features including Mikuni carbs, CD ignition, hydraulic disc brake, aluminum skis, full instrumentation and a "full mitt grip" starter rope handle. The features raised this sled to a whole new level of engineering sophistication not found in any previous Boa-Ski.

But it was the styling that set it apart at first glance. Alsport management showed me the new SS prior to public introduction while I was touring its Norwalk, Ohio, facilities as part of its effort to hire me to manage its marketing communications.

It immediately reminded me of an armadillo, and I didn't think the Texas road kill critter was exactly a positive image for a performance machine. Under Giffen ownership, Boa-Ski had used snake imagery in an amateurish play on the brand name. Its old slogan of "Boa-Ski, the charmer" with a rising snake logo made no sense because Indian snake charmers use cobras, not boa constrictors. And as one of my reptilian-loathing lady friends put it, "Who'd want that anyway?" So maybe armadillo imagery really was a step in the right direction.

Nevertheless I departed Norwalk and went back to my existing job. Alsport put the new sled on the market and began to heavily promote the 785-day selling season concept in the powersports trade magazines.

The SS Performs

The radical new SS came with a choice of 440 or 340 axial fan-cooled power, and it began to win converts, at both the dealer and consumer levels. "I was 16 when I got my first SS," says Boa-Ski enthusiast Mike Golembiewski of Mosinee, Wisconsin, who grew up next door to a dealer. "I was used to Cats and Ski-Whizes." But the Boa-Ski SS made a very positive impression on him.

"It ran smooth, cornered good, turned really nice," Golembiewski says. He calls the cable activated mechanical brake "superb" and remembers coming to quick stops.

Three settings at each end of the skid frame allowed the owner to personalize the ride. The Mikuni carbs were fairly new to snowmobiles, and like virtually every other company, Boa-Ski jetted them conservatively. An update from Mikuni through Alsport suggested smaller pilot jets and main jets in the easily tuned carbs for better performance.

"It was quick out of the hole," Golembiewski remembers. "If it wasn't spinning, it was pulling the skis off the ground." And that led to some problems. The aluminum bulkhead had a steel cross-member for reinforcement, but slamming the ground coming down from ski lifts heavily stressed the whole assembly. Repeated pounding tended to crack the aluminum around the tie-rod holes, so later model year machines went to an all-steel bulkhead that could be retro-fitted to 1974 machines.

"The only thing I would have changed is the molded cleated track," Golembiewski says. "If [the cleats] broke and let loose, they'd tear up the bottom of the tunnel." A 1973 Arctic Cat El Tigré track was an easy drop-in solution to that problem.

Alsport dealers from New England to Minnesota and Iowa and even beyond were successfully selling the new SS models. But there just weren't a whole lot of Alsport dealers. The rest of the 1974 Boa-Ski-line-up was simply outdated machinery in attractive new livery. The mainstream Mark II and entry-level Mark I still had a tunnel-mounted engine with a diaphragm pumper carb and breaker point ignition, an all-steel chassis and bogie wheels. This was hardly the right stuff to appeal to gearhead snow riders in an increasingly sophisticated and competitive market.

Too Little Too Late

An outside factor also worked against Alsport: 1974 was a bad year to sell snowmobiles. The 1973 Arab oil embargo, a soft economy, a mild winter and industry-wide overproduction all contributed to a market where none of the dozens of manufacturers were making money on snowmobiles.

Alsport was pushing a trail performance machine with a fan-cooled engine that was seen by many as behind the times because almost all of the major players had gone to free air or even liquid cooling for their performance trail sleds.

Too few competitive models to sell through too few dealers eventually caught up with Alsport, and the company failed. Boa-Ski did continue in Canada, where the SS remained on the market with minimal changes through the 1977 model year, after which the brand expired, too.

The new SS was the first truly modern BoaSki. It was a good machine that broke the old mold. But it was too little, too late to save Alsport or Boa-Ski.

1974 Boa-Ski SS

MANUFACTURER
Alsport Inc. of Norwalk, Ohio, at La Guadalupe, Quebec, Canada

POWERTRAIN
Engine: Kohler 440 or 340 axial fan twin
Displacement: 436cc/338cc
Carburetion: Two Mikuni VM series
Compression Ratio: 7:1/7.5:1
Ignition: Capacitor discharge (CD)
Lubrication: Pre-mix at 40:1
Exhaust: Single pipe with muffler
Power Output: 42 hp/34 hp @ 7,250 rpm
Drive Clutch: Comet 100C
Driven Clutch: Boa-Ski

CHASSIS
Type: Riveted aluminum with steel reinforced aluminum bulkhead, aluminum skis, fiberglass belly pan, and ABS hood
Claimed Dry Weight: 330 pounds dry (440)/325 pounds dry (340)
Front Suspension: Multi-leaf springs with chromed hydraulic shock absorbers
Ski Stance: 28-inches
Rear Suspension: Easy Rider II adjustable aluminum slide rail skidframe with one hydraulic shock absorber
Track: 15.5-inch rubber with molded-in full-width steel cleats
Brake: Kelsey-Hayes hydraulic disc on chaincase
Fuel Capacity: 6 US gallons
Standard Equipment: Pop-up dual-beam headlight, speedometer, tachometer, engine temperature gauge, handlebar pad, passenger grab belt, snow flap, tool box, prewired for optional electric start

Price: $1,495/$1,395

1974 Chaparral Thunderbird

A Family Sled With Value And Flair

Many family snowmobiles of the early 1970s were frankly pretty dull, and just no fun compared to the emerging class of sporty single seaters and trail racers. But the 1974 Chaparral Thunderbird certainly wasn't an ordinary 2-up.

"The Thunderbird 440 is light, stable, responsive and quiet," summarized the *Snow Goer* review in fall 1973. What went unsaid in the review was how good a value the Thunderbird really was compared to other choices available at the time.

Brand New Big Bird

Like pretty much all 1973 snowmobiles, the '73 Chaparrals suffered their share of mechanical troubles. Introduction of safety equipment and noise emission standards by all the major brands had brought enclosed and insulated hoods that produced all too frequent sled-stopping vapor lock. Other industry-wide issues included drive clutch woes and ride quality shortcomings. So for 1974, Chaparral considerably reworked its family machine to increase its performance and overall appeal.

The most noticeable external change was a shift from Chaparral's traditional bright red hood to a classy deep maroon finish, with a significant upgrade of the trim decals. But there was a lot different under that new hood, too.

The five-port Fuji 440 engine got a Mikuni BNO "spill dam" carburetor to deal with the vapor lock issue. Like the more widely used Mikuni VM series, the BNO featured an enriching circuit rather than a traditional choke for easier cold starts. And a new 0.3-gallon reserve gas tank with a push-button activation switch increased the range on all '74 Chaparrals. Capacitor Discharge Ignition (CDI) replaced breaker points and combined with the new carb and a revised muffler to slightly bump the rated output from 39HP at 6,800 RPM to 40HP at 7,000 RPM. Finally, a new and more durable primary clutch increased drive train reliability.

In the tunnel, a new 15.5-inch wide rubber track with triple internal drive replaced the polyurethane 18-incher used on earlier Thunderbirds. The new adjustable slide rail suspension with rail wheels and 5 inches of travel was said to be 15 pounds lighter than the obsolete bogie wheel unit it replaced.

Other changes included reduction of the windshield tint to improve headlight reach by 35 percent and a redesigned throttle to improve operator comfort.

But the big seat was relatively unchanged. Five inches longer than the seat on other Chaparral models, it had slightly revised contours but retained the expansive under-seat storage compartment that had been popular on many brands back in the late 1960s. *Snow Goer* testers felt this seat did compromise rider comfort, stating a preference for thicker seat foam and less storage space, but still commented that "thanks to this [slide rail] suspension system, the Thunderbird rates above average in comfort."

To ensure buyer satisfaction, all 1974 Chaparrals were backed with the industry-first "No Downtime Protection Plan" that included a full one-year warranty (rare for this era), a parts and service "hot line" to the factory, and loaner sleds from participating dealerships.

A Performer
The new Thunderbird proved to be a performer on the snow. *Snow Goer* measured it as the fourth lightest 440 tested, with a 45-degree tip-over angle that made it the fourth most stable unit out of 17 440s. Steering was described as "quick and easy,' and top-end speed was rated as satisfactory despite an obviously out-of-adjustment clutch on the test unit.

The 1974 *Popular Science Snowmobile Handbook* backed up our predecessors' conclusions. "There's little doubt, in our opinion, that the Thunderbird is capable of lively performance on good snow," said the annual magazine, which tested it in heavy, wet snow that held down test results. The magazine also praised the excellent handling characteristics of the Thunderbird, which were certainly not typical for the era, especially with family sleds.

"It responded well to steering efforts and gave the driver a feeling of stability," the magazine testers said. "There was none of the squirrelly effect that some of the 15.5-inch tracks are prone to." What neither magazine pointed out was the Thunderbird's great value. Despite being one of the best performing family sleds of the year, it was also one of the least expensive with a suggested retail price as much as 20 percent less than most major brand competitors. And that advantage soared when the price was slashed to $850 during a factory-authorized, post-New Year's Day sale.

Stick A Fork In The Bird
The reason for the big sale soon became obvious. In February 1974, parent company Armco Steel announced that it would exit the recreation business immediately. Stung by the Arab oil embargo and skyrocketing gas prices as well as mounting industry overproduction, Armco was quick to kill a business unit that it probably should not have purchased in the first place.

Although the 1975 Chaparral line was ready to go, and American Motors Corporation and two other companies considered purchasing the Armco recreation group, it was fork time. The red bird was done. And few snowmobilers would ever know what a good sled or what an even better value the 1974 Chaparral Thunderbird really was.

1974 Chaparral Thunderbird

MANUFACTURER
Chaparral Division of Armco Recreational Products Inc. (Subsidiary of Armco Steel Corporation), Denver, Colorado

POWERTRAIN
Engine: 432cc Fuji Light Industries axial fan-cooled piston-port twin
Carburetion: One Mikuni BNO spill dam type
Compression Ratio: 12:1
Ignition: Capacitor Discharge
Lubrication: Pre-mix at 20:1
Exhaust: Single pipe with tuned muffler
Power Output: 40 hp @ 7,000 RPM
Drive Clutch: Salsbury 810

CHASSIS
Type: Riveted aluminum with extruded aluminum bumpers, sheet molding compound (SMC) hood & belly pan, and acrylonitrile butadiene styrene (ABS) dash panel
Dry Weight (claimed): 370 pounds; prototype weighed 431 pounds wet by *Snow Goer*
Front Suspension: Triple-leaf springs
Ski Stance: 28 inches
Rear Suspension: Adjustable aluminum slide rails with shock absorbers and rail wheels
Track: 15.5-inch steel-reinforced rubber with internal drive
Brake: Mechanical disc
Fuel Capacity: 5.0 gallons, with 0.3-gallon reserve
Standard Equipment: Speedometer/odometer, kill switch, vinyl padded dash, passenger grab handles, underseat storage, tow hitch, snow flap

MSRP: $1,295

1974 Johnson JX
New and non-conforming

The Johnson dealer ad in *Snow Goer Trade* magazine for May 1973 got right to the point. "In 1974, a lot of manufacturers will be asking you to sell a new paint job. Period. Not Johnson."

With weak winters and overproduction of sleds pushing unsold inventory to record levels, most manufacturers were not introducing significant new models, just changing graphics on existing ones.

But Outboard Marine Corporation (OMC) was bucking the trend. Its 1974 Evinrude and Johnson lines included all-new high performance sport models that were out of step with the industry in more ways than one.

New Everything

The Johnson JX and twin brother Evinrude Skimmer were significant upgrades over earlier OMC sport sleds. Virtually new from the ground up, these sleek, attractive machines broke with existing industry practice in some significant ways.

Under the hood, the venerable OMC opposed twin was history, replaced by a new alternate firing vertical twin with reed valve induction and axial-fan cooling. The upgrade actually brought the sleds in line with industry practice, but some of the engine's features did not.

Mounted low and well forward, the engine had cast iron sleeves in the aluminum cylinders and a one-piece crank instead of the common multi-part pressed crank. The carburetor was said to resist vapor lock, a common problem of the day. MagFlash CD ignition eliminated breaker points and used surface gap spark plugs that were said to last 10 times longer than conventional plugs.

The unique layout also placed the drive clutch, flywheel, electricals and fan drive all on the same side of the engine instead of splitting them as usual. The starter rope pulled a small pinion gear that meshed with the flywheel to provide a mechanical advantage for easier starting. Rubber engine mounts positioned at crankshaft level helped control vibration.

Plus, at a time when most manufacturers observed a voluntary displacement limit of 440cc for trail sleds, this engine was available as a 400, a 440 and a thumping 650 that was promoted as having "all the guts of a free air machine, but none of the headaches."

Despite OMC's heavy promotion of its quiet sleds, these models seemed above average for noise emissions, at least from the driver's ear.

The differences didn't stop there, either. Virtually the entire industry had recognized the benefits of slide rail suspension, and very few performance sleds were now being offered without them. But OMC had its own ideas.

"Johnson just thinks that bogies are the best type of suspension system for the best all-around snowmobile performance," the sales brochure stated. Called a "Controlled Ride" suspension, the bogie wheel unit included a damping system to limit wheel oscillation over rough terrain.

A new three-layer foam seat topped with a skid-resistant cover was also promoted as another part of the ride experience. It was roomy enough to handle two adults. The 1974 *Popular Science Snowmobile Handbook* did report that "the ride (is) comfortable."

Interestingly, the new-for-Johnson color scheme was very similar to the 1973 Rupp Nitro — black over red separated by a narrow white stripe, with the top of the hood black like the anti-glare panel on a fighter plane.

The overall package impressed the *Popular Science* crew, who said, "Johnson's JX 650 was the hottest of the new 1974 machines we tested." They went on to say, "Not surprisingly, its top speed was the fastest of all the sleds we rode this year." But the test was limited to 24 fan-cooled sleds with only one other more than 440cc. And the magazine completely ignored all of the numerous free air and liquid cooled performance models available.

The Kidd Endorsement
Oblivious to the fact that most snowmobilers didn't give a hoot about skiing, Johnson had retained Olympic ski racer Billy Kidd as its spokesman. He was all over the new JX series in trade ads, consumer ads and the sales brochure trying to focus attention on the new models. Speaking as a long-time marketing communications professional as well as a snowmobiler, I always felt this endorsement actually hurt Johnson more than it helped. After all, what did a professional skier really know about snow machines anyway?

Dealers and the public were generally indifferent to the nonconforming new OMC sleds and its spokesman.

Down The Stretch
OMC finally relented and offered slide rail suspension as an option on the otherwise little changed 1975 JX models. But as many other companies discovered, it was too little, too late.

Despite assuring customers Johnson was in the snowmobile business to stay, 1976 was its final season. And that made the nonconformist JX the last new model from the first big-name manufacturing company to enter the exploding snowmobile business more than a decade earlier.

1974 Johnson JX

MANUFACTURER
Outboard Marine Corp., Milwaukee, Wisconsin

POWERTRAIN
Engine: OMC axial fan-cooled, reed-valve twin
Displacement: 646cc/436cc/399cc
Carburetion: One Tillotson diaphragm pumper
Compression Ratio: 6.8:1
Ignition: Magflash Capacitor Discharge (CD)
Lubrication: Pre-mix at 50:1
Exhaust: Single pipe into muffler
Power Output: 50 hp @ 6750 rpm / 40 hp (440) / 35 hp (400)
Drive System: OMC torque-sensing centrifugal clutch system with neutral lockout

CHASSIS
Type: Welded and painted steel with aluminum bumpers
Weight: 448 pounds wet for JX650, as weighed by *Popular Science Snowmobile Handbook*
Front Suspension: Triple leafsprings
Ski Stance: 27 inches
Rear Suspension: Bogie wheels with dampened torsion springs
Track: 15.5 inches wide, molded rubber with internal drive
Brake: Mechanical disc with parking brake
Fuel Capacity: 6 gallons (US)
Standard Equipment: Choke, primer, kill switch, handlebar pad, passenger grab handles, rear seat storage compartment, snow flap
Options: Speedometer/odometer, tachometer, electric start, chrome ski shocks, tow hitch

Price: $1,495 (650), $1,350 (440), $1,225 (400}

1974 Northway Interceptor 15 440D

Forward-Looking, But Flawed

Right from the beginning, when established in 1968 with its first sleds designed to hit the market for model year 1970, Northway began to build a reputation for performance as well as "outside-the-box" thinking. Early features included completely enclosed engine compartments with automotive style rear-hinged hoods, a removable one-gallon reserve gas tank and the optional "Pioneer" high seat that provided significant open storage between the seat cushion and the tunnel. After testing the 1972 models, *Snow Goer* called Northway "the sleeper of the industry."

By 1974, snowmobile manufacturers were under a lot of pressure from rapidly rising gas prices, a stagnant economy and excess inventory across the industry. Northway was one of many companies that was still selling essentially the same machine that it had in 1972. But there were some very interesting upgrades and changes; particularly on the D (for Deluxe) versions of the Interceptor trail performance models. The number 15 or 18 on Northway models referred to the track width in inches.

Modifications For '74

Some of the changes on the 1974 Interceptors, like the substitution of St. Lawrence clutches for the previously used Salsbury, were the result of normal snowmobile component market activities. And others, like the use of silver on the Interceptor Deluxe models instead of Northway's signature lime green or candy apple red, were simply appearance moves for marketing purposes. But some of the updates were the result of more forward thinking.

For instance, '74 Northways were some of the first to offer height options for its "pop-out easy change" windshields.

Yet other changes were very important, like the all-new rear suspension introduced on the Interceptor Deluxe models. Most Northways still used bogie wheels, but the company dropped a slide rail option in favor or its new Super Cushion Ride (SCR) suspension. Similar to the earlier Scorpion Para-Rail and Roll-O-Flex Super-Flexion designs, the SCR mounted wheels on a rack of parallel rails with torsion springs and a single hydraulic shock. Using fewer wheels than the Para-Rail, the SCR was claimed to offer "the smoothest ride in the snowmobile industry." It worked OK in a straight line at slower speeds, but otherwise it was a disaster. "Handling was worse than we got from bogie wheels," stated the 1974 *Popular Science Snowmobile Handbook*. "To our test riders, it seemed difficult to turn and felt unstable in open field running."

The D models were also equipped with the innovative FasTrac from Stevens Molded Products Company in Easthampton, Massachusetts. Composed of multiple segments of steel-reinforced DuPont Hytrel polyurethane that were linked together with spring steel connecting rods, the FasTrac allowed replacement of damaged sections instead of replacing the entire track. The track was also very light and didn't stretch. Recognizing that one of the shortcomings of polyurethane as a track material was poor traction on ice, Stevens fitted the FasTrac with 96 tungsten carbide ministuds on top of the track lugs, the first appearance of this traction concept in the snowmobile industry. This made the Northway Interceptor Deluxe one of the very first sleds to be studded from the factory.

Fast, And Maybe Flammable
Magazine testers generally agreed that the Interceptor 15 440D was a hot sled worthy of consideration by performance-oriented riders.

Le Magazine de L'Auto-Neige ("The Snowmobile Magazine") summarized that, "The Northway Interceptor 440 is a very, very fast machine reserved for experienced riders accustomed to big engines mounted in the center of the chassis."

The *Popular Science Snowmobile Handbook* reported that, "it is a fast accelerating sled," but also pointed out that it could get hot in another way: "Fueling requires you to open the hood first, and there's a possibility that spilled fuel could come in contact with the muffler, which we feel could be potentially hazardous." Do ya' think?

Weighed down by industry-wide issues, Northway Snowmobiles Ltd. went bankrupt in the summer of 1973 while the '74 machines were under construction, and the bank locked the doors at the end of August. Only about 3,000 of the '74 Northways had been completed, roughly half the company's production at its peak in 1972. So the 1974 model year became Northway inventory clearance with the help of a Wisconsin-based liquidator.

Remaining assets were purchased by Barrie, Ontario, dealer Lewis Crowe, who continued to build and sell roughly 400 more units with Kohler power through 1979 when a fire wiped out what little was left of Northway.

Although late to the party, Northway had proved to be more of an innovator than most companies in the business, and it outlasted most of them, too. But despite the innovations, Northway was just one more company that was too small and insufficiently financed to weather the great manufacturer shakeout of the 1970s.

1974 Northway Interceptor 15 440D

MANUFACTURER
Northway Snowmobiles Ltd., Pointe Claire, Quebec, Canada

POWERTRAIN
Engine: 438cc Hirth 270R axial-fan-cooled piston-port twin with a Walbro WDA 33 diaphragm pumper carb
Ignition: Bosch magneto and breaker points
Power Output: 40 hp @ 7,000 rpm
Clutches: St. Lawrence drive and driven

CHASSIS SPECS
Type: Polished aircraft aluminum alloy with fiberglass hood and belly pan
Wet Weight (claimed): 413 pounds
Front Suspension: Multi-leaf springs with hydraulic shocks
Rear Suspension: Super Cushion Ride hybrid with 12 wheels on parallel rails, torsion springs and one hydraulic shock
Ski Stance: 30.75 inches
Track: 15-by-114-inch SMP FasTrac LS steel-reinforced polyurethane with 96 integral lug studs

MSRP: $1,400

1974 Roll-O-Flex Wild One

A Wild Ride In More Ways Than One

During the summer of 1973, Roll-O-Flex announced that it would produce a new and advanced high-performance model called the Wild One. First shown with a free air engine, the company intended to replace all existing Roll-O-Flex models with this new state-of-the-art product, so it was also to be built with fan-cooled power.

Sadly, the 1974 Wild One didn't get much of a chance to succeed. One of the most sophisticated sleds of its day, it had tremendous potential as a stock or modified racer as well as a high performance trail sled that could have easily adapted to cover other market segments. But overtaken by adverse circumstances, it was just too late arriving in the marketplace.

Betting The Company On Sleds

Saskatchewan-based Roll-O-Flex (ROF) was a deep-tillage farm machinery manufacturer that got into the snowmobile business in the 1960s as a distributor for Sno Jet and Boa-Ski. ROF General Manager Larry Fay had Boa-Ski build a private-brand sled called the Wild One, which became the first Roll-O-Flex snowmobile for model year 1969.

In September 1970, Roll-O-Flex received a funding grant from the provincial government to set up facilities to produce its own sleds. But the money came with conditions that included stopping manufacture of all current products. So ROF continued servicing its previously sold agricultural equipment, and bet the company on the booming snowmobile business.

By 1973, ROF had built a reputation for quick and fast sleds. A product development team led by Vice President Gene Glaze coaxed prodigious power from Yamaha fan-cooled engines through careful development and extensive dynamometer testing with exhaust system supplier ACS Ltd. of Toronto.

ROF also developed its own Super-Flexion hybrid track suspension. Similar to the Scorpion Para-Rail, the Super-Flexion had large wheels on and between two rails that were fixed to the front and rear arms. It transferred weight very well so it was ideal for drag racing, but despite long travel for the day (6.5 inches), some magazine testers rated the ride quality as no better than bogie wheels. And according to one *Snow Goer* reviewer, it exhibited a disconcerting sidestepping trait at speed. Nevertheless, the Super-Flexion suspension was licensed to Auto-Ski Inc. for use in its Auto-Ski and Pro-Am snowmobiles.

Meanwhile, financially constrained ROF expanded geographically, relying on local racing results and word-of-mouth rather than advertising and marketing programs to gain distribution to sell its sleds. By 1973 the company had sales coverage across most of the snowbelt.

The New Wild One
Unlike the previous tall, narrow, maroon Roll-O-Flex sleds with tunnel-mounted engines, the low, wide and sleek '74 Wild One was white, with the engine forward and a jackshaft drive, plus the shaft had a unique center support to eliminate flexing. A cast aluminum motor plate extended back and up to tie the engine to the jackshaft support, ensuring a constant center distance for the clutches. Outer ski edges were turned down for better bite in corners.

But a major last-minute problem arose. "Yamaha would not agree to sell us the free air engines for production sleds," Glaze said in a recent interview with *Snow Goer*. So Kohler power was substituted for both free air and fan blown Wild Ones, the latter with the 338cc K340-2AS axial fan-cooled engine. The last-minute change meant that carb jetting, exhausts and clutching were not fully calibrated, resulting in sub-par performance for the production machines.

That wasn't the only problem, either.

"We were using a lot of the same vendors as Arctic Cat and Polaris and a few others," Glaze said. "These vendors gave them delivery priorities. We were at some fault, too. We were making last minute design changes, which didn't go well with their tooling departments." These component delivery problems hampered efforts to ship sleds.

Two Wild Ones were built as featherweight Sno Pro racers with modified Kohler 340 and 440 free air power. They saw limited action as a series of events on and off the track took their toll.

But the biggest problem was increasingly difficult market conditions for smaller manufacturers like ROF. Declining snowfall in some parts of North America and tough competition from industry giants were compounded by the 1973 oil crisis that killed markets for anything that ran on gas.

ROF was about out of time and money. Sleds were completed and shipped as fast as possible, but no service manuals were produced for the Wild One. Total production for the 1974 season was only about 2,600 machines, including less than 400 Wild Ones, roughly half of 1973 total production. The bet on snow sleds had been lost, and Roll-O-Flex was liquidated in April of l974.

1974 Roll-O-Flex Wild One

MANUFACTURER
Roll-O-Flex Ltd., Regina, Saskatchewan

POWERTRAIN
Engine: 338cc Kohler K340-2RS "sunburst" free-air, piston-port twin with two Mikuni VM-34 slide valve carbs, breaker point ignition and single pipe into ACS muffler with internal tuned cone
Lubrication: Pre-mix at 20:1
Power Output: 43 hp
Clutches: Comet 100C drive and 90D driven

CHASSIS
Type: Aluminum with zinc-plated steel bulkhead aluminum bumpers, fiberglass hood and pan
Claimed Dry Weight: 320 pounds
Front Suspension: Triple-leaf springs with chromed hydraulic shock absorbers and three-position front ski mounts
Ski Stance: 34 inches
Rear Suspension: Super-Flexion hybrid with 12 wheels on parallel rails, torsion springs and one rear-mounted hydraulic shock
Track: 15-by-118-inch Bombardier nylon-reinforced molded rubber with internal drive
Brake: Kelsey-Hayes mechanical disc
Fuel Capacity: 5 gallons
Standard Equipment: Speedometer/odometer, tachometer, engine temp gauge, kill switch, tether switch, added knee protectors, non-slip footrests, passenger grab handles, snow flap

MSRP: $1,795

1974 Sno Jet Sabre Jet

Competition engineering on the trail

Growing rapidly from a modest beginning in 1965, Sno Jet became one of the most successful of the smaller manufacturers of the Vintage era. In 1968, the Quebec firm was acquired by Conroy Corporation of Texas, who made it a subsidiary of its Glastron Boat Company. Sno Jet production peaked out at a little over 31,000 machines for model year 1970, good enough to put the bright blue sleds on the market share leader board, although well behind the very top sellers.

Early Sno Jets were built in the classic Ski-Doo style. A European engine, usually a Hirth, was positioned on top of a steel tunnel with stirrups on the sides and a bogie wheel suspension underneath. Other than gradually migrating to Yamaha power (using pre-mix rather than oil injection) all Sno Jets for the trail used this basic format throughout the early 1970s.

But a new development project altered the way that Sno Jets for trail riding would be built. An independent racer named Jim Adema had revolutionized oval track competition in the early '70s with his Duane Aha-engineered Sno Jet Thunder Jet modified racers. These very successful oval sprint racing sleds used materials like aluminum and titanium to save weight, front-mounted engines for better handling and slide rail suspensions to put the power on the ground more efficiently.

The 1974 model year saw the debut of a sporty new Sno Jet trail sled that incorporated materials and engineering concepts from the Thunder Jet, and according to Calgary, Alberta-based Sno Jet expert Blake Read, this new machine was designed at least partly by Adema.

The Sabre Jet Takes Off

Sno Jet offered many trail sport models for 1974- probably too many- with the bogie wheel Astro Jet, the slide rail Astro SS, and the more powerful SST, each with three engine choices. But the Sabre Jet was the best looking, most powerful (along with the top SST) and technically most advanced Sno Jet of the season.

This almost all-new machine used the race sled approach of a stirrup-less aluminum chassis, slide rail suspension and a forward-tilted, front-mounted engine with a racer styling cue. The top of the Yamaha 440 powerplant stuck through the hood just like on Thunder Jet's and other free-air modified race sleds of the immediate past. But this engine had a fan for cooling instead of fins sticking up in the air stream, so the top shroud was chromed to make it more interesting visually.

New features on the Sabre Jet included the Positrack-Plus performance track that was said to allow the new model to match the climbing ability of any sled on the market, and the Ethafoam firm-flex seat for extra comfort. The skidframe was Sno Jet's unique Multiflex II slide rail suspension that allowed the steel rails to flex up and down.

Sno Jet claimed a "wide" ski stance, but at a fraction under 25 inches, it wasn't anything special. However, the Sabre Jet's lower center of gravity did make it a good deal more tip resistant than other Sno Jets and many competitive machines. Standard equipment included a fuel filler overflow guard on the large-for-the-day 7.5-gallon gas tank and a sleek, low, tinted windshield.

Heavily promoted with product publicity photo placements, in-store posters and magazine ads featuring a lumberjack-like character called Big Blue to embody the brand, the distinctive Sabre Jet quickly found a receptive audience.

Testers from snowmobile magazines of the day were favorably impressed with the Sabre Jet's appearance, performance, ride quality, stability, handling and low noise emissions. *Invitation To Snowmobiling* magazine lauded it as "the best pure-production sled yet from Big Blue," although they did have a few negative comments on safety because the machine lacked a handlebar pad and the engine kill switch was placed in a non-standard position.

Then in mid-season, Sno Jet upped the ante by announcing the Sabre Jet 650. Mounting a Hirth 281RO 650cc axial fan engine that delivered its 50 hp through a Comet 100 drive clutch, the big Sabre was visually very similar to the 39 hp, Yamaha-powered 440. The only giveaways were the Hirth's black engine cover, with the center section of the hood painted silver instead of black – just 281 of these super Sabres were constructed. They were quickly snapped up by enthusiasts back then and are greatly prized by collectors today.

Big Blue Gets The Blues
The Sabre Jet certainly wasn't the first model that featured racetrack engineering, which led to a better trail sled. Yet good as it was, it still became just one more of the industry's many one-year wonders when Glastron slashed its trailsled selection from 13 models to just 7 for the following season. But the Sabre Jet did usher in the aluminum chassis and front mounted engine for almost all subsequent Sno Jet trail sleds.

Big Blue's production was already falling annually by the time of the Sabre Jet's introduction. The company's marketing simply didn't match its major competitors' and despite some impressive models like the Sabre Jet and the Thunder Jet competition series, Sno Jet was just one more manufacturer being overwhelmed by market forces and bigger companies with greater resources.

Gross industry overproduction compounded by a lighter winter in 1973 had made it hard for any company to make a profit by selling snowmobiles. And Sno Jet's unsuccessful 1973 lawsuit against the United States Snowmobile Association (USSA) over Stock class racing rules had taken a financial and psychological toll, too. Then in November 1973, the Arab oil embargo put a major hurt on sales of anything that used gasoline.

Sno Jet sales slid to unsustainable levels in the following light winters, and in 1976 Conroy sold the brand to Kawasaki USA, Inc., which merely wanted the large Sno Jet dealer network as a quick entry into the snowmobile business.

1974 Sno Jet Sabre Jet 440

MANUFACTURER
Sno Jet division of Glastron Boat Company, a subsidiary of The Conroy Company Inc. of Quebec at Thetford Mines, QC
Engine: Yamaha Sport (S) series axial-fan-cooled reed-valve twin
Displacement: 433cc
Carburetion: One Keihin SD42 butterfly type with silencing air box
Compression Ratio: 6.5:1
Ignition: Magneto and breaker points
Lubrication: Pre-mix at 20:1
Exhaust: Single pipe into an ACS muffler
Power Output: 39 hp @ 6500 rpm
Drive Clutch: Yamaha
Driven Clutch: Sno Jet

CHASSIS
Type: Riveted aluminum with steel sub-frame and chromed bumpers, aluminum belly pan and fiberglass hood
Claimed Dry Weight: 390 pounds; pre-production model wet weight 450 pounds per *Invitation to Snowmobiling* magazine
Rear Suspension: Multiflex II flexible steel side rails with torsion springs and one center hydraulic shock absorber
Track: Positrak-Plus cog drive 15.5-inch nylon reinforced rubber with molded-in rubber cleats and 42.5-inch footprint
Brake: Borg-Warner self-adjusting mechanical disc
Fuel Capacity: 7.5 gallons
Standard Equipment: Speedometer, tachometer, Kelch gas gauge, under-hood tool bag, kill switch, tow hitch, snow flap

Price: $1.399

1974 Yamaha GPX

Hamamatsu's Hot Stocker

In spring 1972, the unveiling of Arctic Cat's new El Tigré sent other snowmobile companies scurrying back to their drawing boards in shock to engineer free-air engine stock racers to compete in the showroom and on the racetrack. Many of the new "hot stockers" were available for 1973, but it took Yamaha another year to get its response to market.

Born To Run

With no performance credentials at the time and sled models identified by letters that provided no clue to their purpose or market niche, Yamaha snowmobiles lacked sizzle. But the 1974 GPX changed all that. Building on the SR series of free air mod racers introduced in 1971, these new models created excitement that begins with the use of the sexy letter "X," supposedly for experimental, in the model designation.

The new five-port twins under the huge hood scoop were Yamaha's first free-air consumer sled engines as well as the company's first front-mounted mills. The 340 fit in the United States Snowmobile Association (USSA) Stock C class, but the 440 was too big for any USSA Stock class so it was restricted to Modified classes, "outlaw" racing and trail use.

The GPX twins were also two of the five 1974 Yamaha models equipped with the company's first-ever slide rail suspension, a requirement for a competitive race sled and another clear indication of performance intentions. "Yamaha Goes Slideways" promotional buttons from the introduction are now a serious collector's item.

A Genuine Yamaha Technology (GYT) high performance kit was available to upgrade the GPX for Modified class racing. Each GYT kit contained a fuel injection system, high compression heads with different head gaskets and race pipes to take horsepower figures into the mid-70s.

Sudden Success

Initially the GPX wasn't available to just anyone. "A dealership couldn't get one unless they had a race program," said Yamaha collector Jan Lesterhuis, who worked for an upstate New York dealer at the time. He also pointed out that the early-build '74s had magnesium sprockets, but that they reverted to less expensive steel as GPX production eventually soared into the thousands and purchase requirements were relaxed. Like most free airs, GPXs loved low temperatures. "The colder it was outside, the faster they went," recalls New York Yamaha racer and collector Tony Bellucco. The GPX won the 340 Stock oval sprint class at the Snowmobile Olympus in Ironwood, Michigan—the first major race of the 1974 season. It went on to compile a long list of C Stock wins at major events across North America, culminating with first, second, fourth and fifth in the class at the USSA World Series in Eagle River, Wisconsin.

The 1975 GPX looked the same but was definitely different. The 1974's XA jugs were replaced by more aggressively ported XB jugs with new pistons for more power. An improved CD ignition and a different track with different drive sprockets were used: skis, springs, seat and gas tank all had subtle changes, and the skid-frame was mounted differently. Plus the '75 was significantly lighter overall according to Lesterhuis.

Despite finishing first and second in the Sault Ste. Marie Soo I-500 enduro, and some GYT kitted GPX Mod wins in Alaska, overall success in 1975 was restrained by very intense competition. Although Stock GPXs did post wins in the East and Alaska, they ended the season as also-rans in both 340 and the new 440 Stock classes.

Nevertheless, the GPX was gaining popularity with the trail racer crowd. My buddy "Mr. Bill" bought one as his first Yammie, and that led to him and his business partner purchasing more Yamahas in years to come.

Soon Sidelined

Free air engines were maxed out for race sleds, and the GPX departed after just two seasons. But it had kicked the door open for Yamaha as a performance brand by generating an incredible amount of publicity from all those racing wins. And in doing so, it paved the way for popular models to come, like the legendary SRX and the popular Exciter, which was fundamentally a restyled and fan-cooled '75 GPX that was introduced for 1976.

And that makes the GPX the model that really put Yamaha into the mainstream for perfomance-minded North American snowmobilers.

1974 Yamaha GPX

MANUFACTURER
Yamaha Motor Company Ltd., Hamamatsu, Japan, for Yamaha Motor Company, USA, Buena Park, California

POWERTRAIN
Engine: 433cc/338cc Yamaha SX433/SX338 free-air-cooled piston-port twins
Carburetion: Two Keihin CDX 42-38 diaphragm pumpers/two Mikuni BN38-34
Compression Ratio: 7.5 to 1 / 7.75:1
Ignition: Capacitor Discharge (CD)
Lubrication: Autolube oil injection
Exhaust: Twin expansion chambers into a single muffler
Power Output: 55 hp/44 hp
Electrical Output: 128 watts
Clutches: Yamaha

CHASSIS SPECS
Type: Riveted and welded aluminum tunnel with steel bulkhead, stirrups, aluminum belly pan, chromed tube steel bumpers and fiberglass hood
Dry Weight (claimed): 350 pounds
Front Suspension: Three leaf springs with chromed hydraulic shock absorbers
Ski Stance: 34.5 inches
Rear Suspension: Slide rails with torsion springs and one mid-mount hydraulic shock
Track: 15-by-118-inch molded rubber with dual sprocket drive on steel cleats
Brake: Self-adjusting mechanical disc
Fuel Capacity: 6 gallons (high-octane required)
Oil Capacity: 2.4 quarts
Standard Equipment: Tachometer, tether switch, kill switch, parking brake, tube gas gauge, tube oil gauge, handlebar pad, non-slip foot rests, rear seat storage compartment, passenger grab strap, snow flap
Optional Equipment: Speedometer/ odometer, GYT kit

MSRP: $1,499/$1,399

The MTD Columbia
Another Me-Too Failure

The builders of several top-name brands, including Cub Cadet, Bolens, Troy-Bilt and Yard-Man, MTD also manufactures many other brands including several private labels. The metalworking giant has also successfully produced recreational equipment ranging from three-wheelers and trail bikes to bicycles and wagons.

Observing the crescendo of the snowmobile business at the beginning of the 1970s, the Cleveland-based company saw another opportunity. Snowmobiles could fill the gap for year-round sales as a counter-seasonal offering for its mower dealers in the Snowbelt.

Bombardier was the snowmobile industry sales leader, so MTD engineers did exactly what dozens of other companies had done. They used the classic Ski-Doo Olympique as their model, failing to comprehend that this template was already obsolete.

The Columbia Debuts

Introduced in 1971 for the 1972 model year, the all-new MTD Columbia snowmobile was launched with two distinct and visually different series: the premium SST with a slide rail suspension and the less costly Track Master with a bogie wheel suspension.

The snowmobile industry recorded another record sales season for model year 1972, but the new Columbia barely registered among the literally dozens of brands available. Despite demonstrating its reliability in the benchmark Winnipeg-to-St. Paul I-500 cross-country race, Columbia needed a sales hook, something to differentiate it from the crowd. The key word for Columbia became "choice."

"Choice" Performance

In 1973, Columbia introduced "Choice" performance as its marketing platform. Advertisements and sales literature explained it as "the power you need with the suspension you prefer and the colors you want."

The machines did get a superficial makeover. The two series were merged into one, with basic models designated C-340, C-400 and C-440 to match their respective engines. Upgrades included a much sleeker fiberglass hood, fully enclosed engine console, a redesigned rear bumper/hand hold for improved passenger comfort and additional safety reflectors. Horsepower ratings and claimed dry weights crept up a bit, too.

All three models could be purchased with either track suspension and either hood color, both at no extra cost. But ski shocks and instruments were now extra-charge options across the board.

Straddling the intense debate over track suspension types, Columbia continued to offer both the proven bogie wheels and the up-and-coming slide rails in all models. This was unusual, as the few companies that were using both types of suspensions generally offered only one or the other in any given model. The MTD slide suspension was a very primitive twin trailing arm in that it employed idler wheels fixed to a rail on each side. There were no shock absorbers or provisions for adding any. "You may even want both ... to adapt to any snow or trail conditions," the 1974 Columbia sales brochure counseled.

The hood color was an even bigger choice. In those days, every brand had its own signature color (like Ski-Doo yellow, Moto-Ski orange, Sno-Jet blue and Arctic Cat black) and it was almost unheard of for any model of any brand to be available in more than one color. Although Columbia wasn't actually the first to offer a color choice, it was the first company to widely promote it, thereby providing a long-lead preview of to day's color options.

The 1974 Columbia models were essentially 1973s with a hood scoop and revised graphics. The rated horsepower and claimed dry weight crept up again. Promoted as "a classic in its own time," and "quite simply the finest snowmobile ever built," the strategy of choice continued. But these old style sleds just weren't finding many buyers.

A joint venture with Kalamazoo Engineering, the leading traction supplier of the day, produced a handful of hand-built 1974 Kalamazoo Koyote Sno Pro oval sprint race sleds. Running free-air power in the face of new liquid-cooled engines from some of the major brands, the Koyotes were embarrassingly uncompetitive and failed to generate any new interest in Columbia snowmobiles.

MTD never did market matching apparel, but it did include an embroidered Columbia patch with each sled. The patch could be sewn onto an aftermarket snowmobile suit, another common practice of the era. In fact, the male model in the 1974 Columbia sales brochure wore a one-piece suit as he showed the choice of hood color, another telling point about Columbia's view of the sport, since one-piecers were pretty much passé by then, at least for the guys.

The 1975 season brought nothing significantly new.

Going Nowhere
As it turned out, the early 1970s was a bad time to introduce a new snowmobile. The 1973 Arab oil embargo sent shockwaves through the American economy and snowmobile sales dropped off sharply, reversing a decade-plus trend of new sales records almost every year. Light winters in 1974 and '75 compounded the problems and inventories of all brands began to pile up at dealerships.

Even worse, the Columbia was not being refined to catch up with rapidly advancing snowmobile technology. The styling stagnated. The tunnel was still steel, still had stirrups and the engine was still in the driver's lap. The primitive slide rail suspension had not been improved, and JLO stubbornly clung to breaker point ignition in the face of better performance from the new Capacitor Discharge Ignition (CDI) found on Japanese engines. In an intensely competitive world of high-tech Arctic Cats, increasingly sophisticated Ski-Doos, racy Rupps, seductive Skiroules and sporty Sno-Jets, the increasingly dated Columbia was about as sexy as an old maid school marm.

Embraced by few dealers, treated as an afterthought by the snowmobile press and generally ignored by the buying public, the Columbia snowmobile was going nowhere. After the 1975 sales season, MTD bowed to the inevitable and Columbia was one of a dozen or so brands that quietly slipped into history that spring.

Outdated engineering got the Columbia off on the wrong foot, and this problem was never addressed. The subsequent "choice" strategy did break new marketing ground in the snowmobile industry, but it just wasn't enough to save MTD's snow machine.

The 1975 MTD Columbia

MANUFACTURER
MTD Products Inc. Cleveland, Ohio

POWERTRAIN
Type: JLO axial-fan-cooled two-stroke twin
Displacement: 339cc (C-340), 398cc (C-400), or 428cc (C-440)
Carburetion: Walbro diaphragm pumper
Ignition: Magneto and breaker points
Lubrication: Pre-mix
Exhaust: Single pipe with Donaldson muffler
Power Output: 32 hp (C-340), 36 hp (C-400) or 40 HP (C-440)
Drive Clutch: RPM-sensing centrifugal type
Driven Clutch: Torque-sensing

CHASSIS
Type: Primed and painted welded steel
Rear Suspension: Trailing bogie wheel or torsion spring slide with 8 idler wheels (no shocks)
Front Suspension: Multi-leaf springs with optional shock absorbers
Ski Stance: 32 inches
Brake: Mechanical disc on driven clutch flange
Fuel Capacity: 6+ U.S. gallons
Listed Dry Weight: (dry, claimed): 376 pounds (C-340) or 378 pounds (C-400 & C-440)
Track: 15.5-inch wide molded polyurethane with dual sprocket internal drive

Price: $1,195 (C-340), $1,295 (C-400), $1,395 (C-440)

1975 John Deere 340/S
Deere Does It Differently

Like many other companies, John Deere entered the snowmobile market in 1971 by cloning market-leader Ski-Doo's traditional layout that placed the engine on top of a steel tunnel, with bogie wheels providing suspension. Early Deere sleds were solid and reliable, but ride and handling were constrained by the limitations of J. A. Bombardier's already outdated concept.

Deere's first real race sled, the limited edition 1974 295/S, was engineered for cross-country competition, specifically the huge Winnipeg-to-St. Paul International 500. Built on the obsolete existing chassis at the time, the additions of Mikuni slide valve carbs, CD ignition, optional slide rail suspension and optional rubber track just weren't anywhere near enough to make the 295/S competitive against the best from the industry leaders. It was clearly time to do something different.

New Ideas Take Shape
The 1975 John Deere 340/S was conceived with the help of two Arctic Cat racing legends who had defected to the Deere snowmobile team: 1969 Eagle River World Champion Roger Janssen and two-time Winnipeg winner Dale Cormican.

An all-new aluminum chassis put the engine down in front over the widened front end. An existing JD/Kioritz trail engine was warmed up with altered port timing, CD ignition with surface gap spark plugs and a more efficient exhaust system. A slide rail suspension with a cleated track resided in the tunnel.

Wider and lower than its predecessor, the 340/S also featured a more protective windshield. The new, larger gas tank was relocated to the center of the sled for better dynamic balance. The tank filler was on the driver's right side in the hood, immediately above the end of the exhaust system and in close proximity to the muffler, which some people thought was a safety hazard. Other key equipment included a hydraulic disc brake, quick-release hood pins and the racing-required tether switch.

A thousand or so of these new sleds were built in the late fall of 1974. The 340/S didn't appear in John Deere's full line snowmobile brochure, but the company did run an ad about them in some magazines to reinforce that these were stock sleds that supposedly anyone could purchase. This ad said they were limited-production machines but never explicitly stated that they were intended for cross-country racing, as Deere was also under pressure to get into oval racing at the time.

Deere also announced a substantial incentive program for 340/S racers, including a special bonus for winning the Winnipeg I-500. Some people felt Deere was trying to buy this high-profile race that had been dominated by Polaris and Arctic Cat. The Deere race school for teams entered in the '75 I-500 race attracted more than 125 people.

The Big Test
The 1975 Winnipeg race was certainly well contested. There were 373 starters from 14 states and six provinces on 13 different brands of sleds. Half the entries—187 to be exact—were Deeres. Serious factory competition came from Polaris and Arctic Cat, with a few factory-connected Ski-Doo, Mota-Ski and Scorpion entries rounding out the pro competition.

Attrition was very high, and only 37 sleds including 12 Deeres started the fourth and final day. In addition to the usual major mechanical failures and wrecks, many drivers were disqualified for violating the ditch running rules.

The 340/S didn't win. Ed Monsrud's factory Polaris TX 340 came in first, with Polaris' Burt Bassett second. But John Deere racers Jon Carlson and Roger Janssen finished just one second apart in third and fourth places. And Deere had 12 of the 22 finishers, although no more in the top 10.

Something To Build On
If nothing else, the new 340/S and the racer incentive program ensured that John Deere had a strong and competitive presence at every significant 1975 season cross-country race in the Midwest. Drivers didn't win much of anything, but the 340/S and the growing corps of Deere racers did lay the foundation for future success by showing Deere and Company how to build a competitive sled.

The new and very good 1976 Cyclone and Liquifire trail sleds were constructed on the same basic platform as the 340/S, although surprisingly few parts were actually carried over unchanged. The 340/S also evolved into the new Liquidator cross-country racer, again with surprisingly few parts going unchanged. Brian Nelson rode a Liquidator to victory in the 1976 Winnipeg I-500, as the wet-head Deere dominated terrain racing that season and for a couple more.

Even though it wasn't a winner in competition, the 340/S racer did generate the platform for later John Deere successes in terrain racing and the showroom. And that makes it a winner in a different sort of way.

1975 John Deere 340/S

MANUFACTURER
Deere & Company, Horicon, Wisconsin

POWERTRAIN
Engine: 339cc John Deere / Kioritz KEC 340RS/2 piston-port axial-fan-cooled twin
Carburetion: Two Mikuni VM-34 slide valve
Ignition: capacitor Discharge (CD)
Lubrication: Pre-mix at 50:1
Exhaust: Single expansion chamber with muffler
Power Output: 47 hp @ 8,000 RPM
Drive Clutch: John Deere/Comet 102C
Driven Clutch: John Deere/ Comet 90D (unique version)

CHASSIS
Type: Painted aluminum tunnel and belly pan with steel sub-frame and ABS hood
Dry Weight (claimed): 385 pounds
Front Suspension: Mono-leaf springs with hydraulic shock absorbers
Ski Stance: 32 inches
Rear Suspension: John Deere adjustable slide rail with twin, mid-mounted shock absorbers
Track: Goodyear 15.5-by-121-inch three-band with dual sprocket drive on full width grauser bars
Brake: Kelsey-Hayes 750HB hydraulic with 8-inch disc
Fuel Capacity: 9 gallons
Standard Equipment: Speedometer/ odometer, tachometer, fuel gauge, tether switch, kill switch, handlebar pad, rear seat storage compartment, snow flap, tow hitch, carbide ski runners

MSRP: N/A

The Rupp Nitro F/A
Rupp's Sole Free-Air Stocker

Maybe it's no coincidence that the words racy, red and Rupp all start with the same letter. The sanguine-hued sleds from Ohio were a prominent part of the performance scene for more than a decade in the heart of snowmobiling's golden era.

Few companies used racing to market sleds as well as did performance enthusiast Mickey Rupp's fun machine enterprise. Always outnumbered by the hordes of yellow, black and red-white-and-blue machines, and with additional competition from many other brands, Rupp still won more than its share of races, particularly on the grass.

One of my earliest memories in the snow machine business, from the days when "early season" meant September, is a Rupp district sales rep explaining the importance of winning grass drags. "They're really big for us," he emphasized.

Solving A Problem
By 1974, Rupp had a problem. The brand had done quite well in oval sprint and grass drag competition during the first years of the decade with its Magnum and Nitro racing models. Their Stock class success included domination of the 400 class in 1971, a 1972 World Series win in 340 and a 1973 World Series win in Junior II.

The Modified class Magnums had free-air engines like all its contemporaries, but the Stock-class Rupps all used engines cooled by axial fans.

The free-airs generally developed more initial horsepower with their extensively finned heads that dissipated heat into the passing air stream. But power output dropped off as they got hot from continuous running. This wasn't a big problem in a winter race, but it was definitely an issue in the summer and fall drags.

The axial fans eliminated most of the cooling fins in favor of an overdriven propeller that forced a high-velocity stream of cooling air through a shroud across small fins in the top of the cylinders. This system added a few pounds of weight for the fan, fan belt, pulleys and air ducting, plus the mechanical drag sucked up a few horsepower. But this also gave the fan-cooled engine a more consistent operating temperature- thus an advantage in longer races, especially in warm-weather grass drags. At least for a while.

In the summer of 1972, an almost overnight industry shift to free-air engines for the emerging 1973 hot stock racers left Rupp on the outside looking in. This shift was driven by many factors, including the increasing importance of Stock-class racing to snowmobile sales as well as improved engineering that allowed the free-airs to produce enough additional power to offset the advantage of consistent cooling of the fans. The racy image of the free-airs was a significant factor, too.

The big guys – Arctic Cat, Polaris and Bombardier – could afford to build Stock race sleds with free-air engines for winter-time oval track use without much regard for trail use or grass drags. Smaller companies like Rupp needed to sell its stock race sleds to trail riders to make it profitable to build. To Rupp's disadvantage, many people believed – wrongly, as it turned out – that free-air engines were no good on the trail. So Rupp engineers made a decision to stay with the fans, as they felt that fans best suited their needs on the grass.

Subsequently, Rupp's fan-cooled Nitros were generally blown into the weeds in 1974 when the free-air revolution really took hold, despite having done well overall on the race track in 1972 and managed to hang on in 1973. And this was particularly true on the oval track, which got most of the press coverage. Something had to be done, and that something became the 1975 Nitro F/A.

No Bones About It
Rupp sales literature and press releases made no bones about it: "The F/A stands for 'free air.' That should tell you a thing or two. Like maybe this sled isn't designed for casual cruising. Which it isn't."

This was a stock racer, pure and simple. No more worrying about the trail riders, because there were other Nitro models for them. No cooling fan to add weight and consume horsepower, either.

The Nitro F/A was new from the ground up. Sleek and aggressively styled like no Rupp before it, this machine was engineered to minimize weight. Unlike earlier Nitros, it didn't have a windshield, bumpers, tunnel stirrups or passenger hand holds. The slide rails and chaincase were made of lightweight magnesium. Short, aluminum racing skis were fitted. Gel-coated fiberglass side panels on the belly pan further reduced weight, and the 16-inch wide grauser bar track weighed just 31 pounds.

Standard equipment included a tether switch, a color-coded electrical panel and a tachometer, but no speedometer or odometer. The unpadded handlebars were height adjustable, and the left side of the seat had a snap-on pad to cushion the rider's leg against the tunnel during weight-shifting left turns. A tiny competition-style fuel tank precluded serious trail riding, but the headlight and taillight were part of the equipment necessary for Stock class racing under United States Snowmobile Association (USSA) rules.

The skis featured an unusual two-position, forward spring mount. Rearward weight transfer was said to improve when the front end of the spring was installed in the upper position, although this feature was more important for drag racing than oval use. The sled's 43-inch overall width was about 6 inches more than its widest contemporaries and allowed an unusually wide ski stance for better stability. It was a glimpse of things to come.

Kohler free-air power was employed. These were not the "Sunburst" radial-finned models that were used extensively in other race sleds, but rather a more traditional design in 340 and 440 sizes for the top two of the new 1975 USSA Stock classes. A special crankcase air duct helped with the cooling issues. Maybe more importantly, the engine was located low in the front of the sled instead of up in the rider's lap like in previous Nitros. Mikuni VM carbs and capacitor discharge ignition were fitted, and the exhaust system had twin-tuned pipes feeding a removable muffler.

In short, the rakishly good-looking Nitro F/A was a limited-edition machine suitable for racers only, and not just due to the engine.

Out-Manned, Not Out-Gunned
The 1975 winter oval racing season began with promise, as Vermont Rupp ace Keith Armstrong won two classes at the USSA Eastern opener in Jackman, Maine. If nothing else, this showed that the Nitro F/A was definitely a competitive sled.

But there weren't a lot of victories for the new Rupp stocker that winter, as Cat, Ski-Doo and a new rising force, Mercury, piled up the wins in probably the most competitive race season ever. A number of those firsts were taken by racers who had been Rupp riders just a couple of years before, but had defected to Merc or Cat when Rupp was struggling to stay competitive in the 1974 season.

Rupp was now out-manned, but not outgunned. The Rupp racing organization simply didn't have critical mass any more, and the red sleds ended up in eighth place among the 13 different brands that recorded at least one win in winter 1975 USSA competition. And although the Nitro F/A did take a few more sanctioned-circuit firsts in places like Greenville, Maine, and Okoboji, Iowa, many of Rupp's 1975 victories were with Modified- class sleds. The best the F/A could do at the USSA World Series in Weedsport, New York, was Ohio racer Ron Johnson's third in 440 Stock.

But all was not a loss. In a twist of fate, the Nitro F/A turned out to be an excellent drag sled. Light, powerful and with superior weight transfer from the suspension engineering, the F/A was well suited for grass racing, and it recorded many drag wins, particularly in the East. As reported in *Snow Week*, Dan Kneeskern's four firsts on a pair of Nitro F/As led Rupp domination of the air-cooled Stock classes at the October, 1976 Herkimer County Sno Sho drags in Frankfort, New York, which was a major race at the time.

A radical departure from previous Nitros, the sleek Nitro F/A remained a very competitive grass dragger, particularly at the smaller local events, for several more years even as the once red-hot Rupp snowmobile brand slowly faded to black.

1975 Rupp Nitro F/A

MANUFACTURER
Rupp Industries Inc. Mansfield, Ohio

POWERTRAIN
Type: Kohler free-air twin-cylinder
Displacement: 339cc / 436cc
Carburetion: Dual Mikuni VM-36 / VM-38
Ignition: Capacitor discharge with surface gap spark plugs
Lubrication: Pre-mix at 20:1
Exhaust: Twin tuned pipes with single muffler
Power Output: Claimed 65 hp / 75 hp
Clutch: Rupp "Friction Free" torque converter

CHASSIS
Type: Aluminum
Weight: Claimed 353 pounds dry
Front Suspension: Adjustable leaf springs with inboard-mounted chrome-plated hydraulic shocks
Ski Stance: 41 inches
Rear Suspension: Magnesium Rupp Rails adjustable slide rail
Track: 16-inch grauser-bar type with internal drive
Brake: Self-adjusting disc
Fuel Capacity: 3.2 U.S. gallons

Price: $1,749 (340) / $1,799 (440)

Scorpion Whip
The Last, Best, Real Scorpion

In 1973, the rapidly expanding snowmobile industry started to experience severe problems. Massive industry-wide overproduction of sleds, the relatively light winter of 1972-73 and the national energy crisis spawned by the Arab oil embargo combined to turn the snow machine business from a cash cow into an ocean of red ink almost overnight. Companies started bailing out right and left.

Fuqua Industries, the company that purchased industry pioneer Scorpion (originally Trail-A-Sled) in 1969, sold the Iron Range sled builder to a management group headed by Harvey V. Paulson at the end of calendar year 1973.

Paulson, who had joined the business just a few months earlier, knew the company needed to improve its products and product quality to have any chance to survive. The cornerstone of that effort was the new Whip, a breakthrough model for the company that was introduced in 1974 for the 1975 model year.

Breaking With Tradition
Positioned as a comfortable and powerful family sled, the Whip was about as big a break with traditional Scorpion product as possible. The almost all-new model featured an aluminum chassis with a forward-mounted engine, a float type carburetor, wider track, expanded ski stance, sleek new styling and a new blue hood instead of the familiar Scorpion red and black. It was well-equipped with ski shocks, instrumentation mounted in a wood-grained dash panel, and a primer. But the Whip retained older technology that bordered on obsolescence including breaker point ignition on the JLO engines, a drum brake and buckhorn handlebars.

Scorpion's patented Para-Rail suspension, introduced on 1973 models, was standard equipment. This unique undercarriage, said to combine the best features of bogie wheels and slide rails into one unit, had multiple wheels mounted on a pair of solid rails that moved together. It did provide the low-snow or no snow capability of bogie wheels with a considerably improved ride, but it never came close to providing the ride quality of any of the better slide rail systems. Despite that, the overall ergonomics of the Whip were very good. It was a comfortable and enjoyable sled.

The company claimed that the Whip was the lightest sport sled in the industry, and spring prototype tests for the *Popular Science Snowmobile Handbook* did reveal the lightest wet weight of anything the magazine evaluated with a 340 or larger engine. It was also one of the quietest machines tested that spring.

Snow Goer predecessors liked the Whip very much saying, "test riders ranked it at or near the top in the important categories of comfort, handling and gas economy." They went on to say, "the Whip is the culmination of the best of Scorpion engineering and a breakthrough that has put the company into the 'bests in all categories' league."

Impressive Accomplishments
Over the next few seasons, the Whip was upgraded with a slightly wider front end, optional slide rail suspensions and cosmetic changes that included a new but similarly styled hood and belly pan. Model extensions like the

Range Whip, the Whip TK/TKX and the Sting were added to the line. And the Whip would compile a list of significant accomplishments along the way.

In 1975, Roger Ebert rode a stock 340 Whip to become one of only 22 racers from a field of 377 starters to complete the prestigious Winnipeg-to-St. Paul I-500 cross country race.

In 1977, a group of snowmobilers from four clubs in the Grand Rapids, Michigan, area established a new 24-hour world endurance record, shattering a six-year-old mark by recording 1,172 miles on one stock Whip and 1,108 on another one. And they got better than 15 mpg while doing it.

And during the winter of 1977-78, Fritz Sprandel rode his stock Whip more than 5,000 miles from Westport, Washington, to Eastport, Maine.

But despite the sales and impressive accomplishments of the Whip, profitable operation continued to elude Scorpion Inc. The company had purchased Brutanza Engirneering and sold its Brut snowmobile as a Scorpion model for a couple of seasons. It also purchased the JLO two-cycle engine factory from Rockwell International and moved it from Germany to Minnesota, re-christening the power plants as Cuyuna engines for their exclusive-to Scorpion service.

A deal to produce badge-engineered snowmobiles for Massey-Ferguson helped some, but Massey departed the sled biz after the 1977 season. More money was sunk into development of a line of Scorpion mopeds with new Cuyuna engines for 1978. But it just wasn't working out on the accounting ledgers. So, Scorpion Inc. was sold to Arctic Enterprises in March, 1978.

End Of The Line
Continuing as the mainstay of the Scorpion line under Arctic Enterprises ownership, further changes to the Whip were mostly limited to cosmetics. Although the Whip was, at the time, a very good value for the money, sales of all Scorpion models continued to slow.

The last Whips were manufactured in 1979 for the 1980 model year. Enough were left over that they remained on the market unchanged for the 1981 model year. And in spring 1981, the financially over-extended Arctic Enterprises was forced into bankruptcy, due in part to purchasing Scorpion.

The Whip family of sleds turned out to be the last and definitely the best sleds engineered by this industry pioneer. (The awesome 1981 Scorpion Sidewinder was an Arctic Cat El Tigré in drag.) Solid, competitive product despite a few outdated features, the Whip was a giant step forward for Scorpion. But good as it was, it just wasn't enough to make the company profitable. It's questionable if Scorpion, or any of the other smaller snowmobile brands of the day, was actually salvageable. Still, Paulson and his people made a great try with the Whip at the heart of the attempt.

And to this day, the Whip remains a personal favorite sled of the entire Vintage era. I still love those buckhorn handlebars.

1975 Scorpion Whip

MANUFACTURER
Scorpion Inc., Crosby, Minnesota

POWERTRAIN
Engine: Rockwell JLO axial fan-cooled piston-port twins
Displacement: 428cc/ 399cc/ 338cc
Carburetion: One Walbro WF float type
Compression Ratio: 12:1
Ignition: Magneto and breaker points
Lubrication: Pre-mix at 40:1
Exhaust: Single pipe into muffler
Power Output: 40 hp [440]/ 32 hp (340) @ 7,000 rpm
Electrical Output: 150 watts
Drive Clutch: Scorpion Power Thrust
Driven Clutch: Scorpion

CHASSIS
Type: Welded and riveted all-aluminum with extruded aluminum front bumper and tubular steel rear bumper
Weight: Claimed 372 pounds dry; weighed 418 pounds wet by *Popular Science Snowmobile Handbook*
Front Suspension: Mono-leaf springs with hydraulic shock absorbers
Ski Stance: 28 inches
Rear Suspension: Scorpion Para-Rail with torsion springs and one hydraulic shock absorber
Track: 16-by-118-inches polyurethane with fiberglass rod reinforcements
Brake: Drum type on driven clutch
Fuel Capacity: 6 gallons [US]
Standard Equipment: Speedometer/odometer, tachometer, fuel gauge, fuel primer, handlebar pad, kill switch, passenger grab strap, under-hood storage compartment
Options: Electric start

Price: $1,595 (440)/ $1,495 (399)/ $1,345 (340) MSRP

1976 Arctic Cat Pantera

Birth Of The Catillac

In 1966 Arctic Cat revolutionized the snowmobile with the original Panther. A decade later, in 1976, the Pantera redrew the Cat blueprint to create a cross-country race sled for the trail.

The Pantera name had been introduced in 1975 on a machine that was little more than a Panther with a mid-mounted gas tank and orange trim instead of purple. However, the 1976 Pantera was virtually all new and definitely different from the ground up, sort of a cross between a Panther and an El Tigré.

A Winnipeg Racer For The Trail

Some manufacturers, including Arctic Cat, Polaris and Viking, had been building low volume specials for the famed Winnipeg-to-St. Paul International 500 cross country race for several years. These specials were typically longer two-seat family sleds with a competition-style free-air engine poking out of the hood and an auxiliary fuel tank on the back end. The new 1976 Pantera turned this basic formula into a full production model, but it was built on a whole new frame with some substantial differences.

The new chassis was all-aluminum instead of including the usual steel front end. To reduce vibration, the engine was suspended in the frame rather than being bolted down onto it. Instead of locating the driven clutch on the chain case as in the Panther and Cheetah, the jack shaft drive system from the El Tigré was used to better distribute stresses in the chassis.

Although this was a single-seater, it was five inches longer than the two-up Panther and had more track on the ground than any solo sled in the industry. And for the first time, the track featured DuPont Fiber B (Kevlar) reinforcement. New arched skis were said to make turning easier. And new slide rails allowed the hyfax to be slid on and off through the track windows instead of removing the skid frame and laboriously drilling out numerous hyfax rivets, a truly monumental maintenance improvement at the time.

The engine itself was part of the brand new Suzuki-built Spirit series ("The Spirit's goin' to move ya") that replaced Kawasaki power in all full-sized 1976 Cats. Larger than the usual 440s by design, the Pantera's 500 free air produced more torque and power at lower RPMs for better performance, less noise and longer engine life. In an Arctic promotional video, former Cat Sno Pro racer Charlie Lofton revealed that the machine delivered 24 foot-pounds of torque to the track, probably the most of any production machine available that season.

In the rear, a high-back seat cushioned the auxiliary 3.5-gallon gas tank that drained down first. When it was empty, the fuel system automatically switched to the 7.1-gallon, mid-mounted tank. This 10.6-gallon total capacity was completely unprecedented in a stock snowmobile. Unfortunately the tiny storage compartment on top of the rear tank wouldn't hold much more than a spare set of spark plugs.

A tall windshield and some orange and yellow pin striping topped off this impressive package that was dubbed the "Catillac" in the sales brochures. It became Cat's most-produced model for the 1976 season, with 7,501 of these awesome but pricey machines being manufactured and sold.

"Good Times Are Comin' On The Cat"

Catillac was certainly a good nickname for this Pantera because it was a huge sled that set new ride standards for a single-seater. Fast and smooth, and lighter than most people believed, the powerful Pantera was embraced by riders who wanted a performance sled with extra range and real comfort for those long days in the saddle. The relatively light weight and large track area gave it good acceleration and deep snow performance. And the free air Suzuki engine started very easily and was rock-solid reliable, even in well above-freezing weather.

The Catillac wasn't perfect, though. Handling was definitely not a strong point of this long, narrow sled. Cargo capacity for spare parts and ride necessities was just about non-existent. The little plastic tether switch wasn't up to race sled standards and tended to break off so easily that most people didn't bother using it. And the plastic rear compartment door was also easily broken off by any good whack from a snowmobile boot being slung over the seat.

Still, this was an impressive overall package that definitely raised the bar for serious performance trail riding.

The Pantera Goes Racing

The International Cross Country Snowmobile Federation (ICCSF), a sanctioning body created specifically for this type of competition, was also new for 1976. For the first time, Arctic Cat fielded a full factory-sponsored cross-country team instead of leaving this activity to the field test crew. Managed by race rider/engineer Doug Dehnert, the seven racers were mounted on the new Cross Country Cat, a '76 Pantera variant fitted with the Suzuki Spirit AB34F3 340cc engine to meet ICCSF race rules. Cat green trim instead of orange and yellow made this batch of 625 sleds easy to identify.

Although the team was definitely competitive and made several solid showings, only independent racer Guy Useldinger actually won with the sled by taking the Stock class at the Mille Lacs 300 to close the ICCSF season. However, an updated Cross Country Cat carried XC Team Arctic's Chet Bowman to the ICCSF season points title the following winter.

Legacy

The Pantera continued to be built on this platform with relatively few changes through the 1979 model year. Additional variants included a long-seater that swapped the rear gas tank for passenger space, and a 500 fan with upgraded trim decals and optional electric start.

Although free-air power was on the way out, the Pantera did give us a peak at the future in several ways. The big Cat was definitely the next major step in the continuing enlargement of the snowmobile. The 121-inch track under it gradually replaced the 114 and 116-inchers used on contemporary single-seaters, and combined with the overall sled length and superb skid frame to raise the bar on ride quality and deep snow capability. Innovative engine mounting, slide-off hyfax and increased gas capacity also previewed later construction.

Although thousands of these unique sleds were built and sold over the four years it was produced, they are rarely seen and even less appreciated today. And that's a shame because the Catillac is one of the more prominent mileposts on the way to the modern performance sled.

1976 Arctic Cat Pantera

MANUFACTURER
Arctic Enterprises, Inc., Thief River Falls, Minnesota

POWERTRAIN
Engine: Suzuki Spirit AC50F2 Series 5000 free-air-cooled piston-port twin
Displacement: 500cc
Carburetion: Two Mikuni VM-32 slide valve with single air intake silencer
Compression Ratio: 6.9:1
Ignition: Capacitor Discharge (CD)
Lubrication: Pre-mix at 20:1
Exhaust: Single pipe into Arctictron muffler
Power Output: 55 hp @ 7,200 rpm
Electrical Output: 120 watts
Drive Clutch: Arctic hex drive
Driven Clutch: Arctic die-cast aluminum

CHASSIS
Type: Riveted aluminum with extruded aluminum front and chrome tube steel rear bumpers, fiberglass hood and belly pan
Claimed Dry Weight: 381 pounds
Front Suspension: Mono-leaf springs with chromed hydraulic shock absorbers
Ski Stance: 30 inches
Rear Suspension: Aluminum slide rails with 4-position adjustable torsion springs and one hydraulic shock absorber on rear arm
Track: 16-by-121-inch internal drive molded rubber logo dropper with Fiber B (Kevlar) reinforcement and molded-in 2/3 width steel cleats, 40.5 inches on the ground
Brake: Manually-adjustable mechanical disc
Fuel Capacity: 10.6 gallons
Standard Equipment: Wood grained dashboard, Kelch fuel gauge on front tank, kill switch, tether switch, halogen headlight, resistor spark plugs, snow flap

MSRP: $1,995

1976 Polaris Colt S/S
Frisky Free-Air Favorite

The Colt had been a staple of the Polaris lineup ever since Herb Howe rode one to victory in the inaugural Winnipeg-to-St. Paul I-500 cross-country race in 1966. Conceived as a lighter, more agile and low-cost alternative to the wide-track Mustang, the Colt rapidly gained favor with Polaris enthusiasts. With the Polaris emphasis on competition, the Colt always had more of a performance image than any other low-priced sled, and that went double for the hotter S/S models that were added in 1972.

Perhaps the best example of the Colt S/S is the 1976 version. Done in traditional Polaris red, white and blue that was supremely appropriate for America's bicentennial year, this was the last and most powerful of the Colt S/S variants with the racy free air engines, a spunky 250 and an upgraded 340.

Style And Substance

Polaris snowmobiles had never been real head turners like the racy red Rupps, sexy Skiroule RTX or Arctic's El Tigré, but the mid-1970s Colts were a notable exception. "One of the prettiest sleds you'll see on the snow, the Colt S/S takes a back seat to nobody in the styling department; enthused the *Popular Science Snowmobile Handbook*. They were actually talking about the 1975 Colt S/S, but this basic body style was built largely unchanged from 1974 through 1978.

However, the 1976 Colt S/S 340 had a whole lot more going for it than just good looks. At its heart, the revised twin-carb Star free-air engine pumped out 32 HP, up 3 Bobs from the 1975 version. Like most fins-in-the-air powerplants, it started very easily. It also ran more quietly than earlier versions thanks to improved air box induction, additional foam under the hood and a fiberglass-packed Polartone muffler. And unlike the fan-free ashtray makers from Austria, the Fuji-built free air was as reliable as the day was long, even in warm spring weather and heavy, wet snow.

Coupled with the highly efficient Polaris clutches, this warmed over twin allowed the Colt S/S to show its signature twin-bulb taillight to most other sleds with similar sized engines, and a lot of them with bigger motors, too. At the *Snow Goer* spring evaluations, the '76's outran every other 340 family sled, only bowing to a trio of 340 trail racers.

Maintaining motion through soft, wet snow by staying up on top when heavier machines sunk in and got stuck, the Colt S/S could also use its cleated track to out-climb many other machines of the era, allowing it to go where a lot of other sleds simply wouldn't.

It was considerably better equipped than most of the directly competitive machines, too, starting with the Polaris hydraulic disc brake that was unmatched at any price point by other brands. Full instrumentation included a tach, something seldom seen on anything other than trail-racers. Chrome ski shocks added to the good looks, while twin headlights and a handlebar pad added safety when others scrimped on it.

Two separate storage compartments provided ample carrying space when many competitive machines had none. With seating space so limited on this small sled, the passenger handgrips were more useful for kids than adults, but they were there.

However, it wasn't all sweetness and light. In some ways, the Colt could be compared to a Pepsi truck- same red, white and blue color scheme, same rough ride. Some also said it steered like a truck, although that was certainly less than a universally held opinion. Many riders valued the ability to toss this loveable lightweight around with body English, and *Snow Goer* testers complimented the machine's "excellent handling." Some riders didn't care for the short, sporty windshield, either.

Still, customer satisfaction with the sled was generally good, and die-hard Polaris partisans absolutely loved it. When *Snow Sports* magazine did an owner's survey at the end of the winter, overall dependability and ease of starting were rated as the 1976 version's best features. "This is my second Colt," said one West Coast owner. "Wouldn't trade with anyone we ride with."

A *Snow Goer* tester nicely summarized the 1976 Colt S/S 340 as "a good, dependable snowmobile that is an awful lot of fun."

Out To Pasture

The Colt S/S was built for two more years with more mundane axial fan-cooled power in an otherwise mostly unchanged form. Finally put out to pasture after more than a decade, the Colt quietly slipped into history as one of the industry's best-known and longest running model names.

And like Polaris itself, the Colt is and always has been a survivor. They're still around today, more of them banging around the back trails than on exhibit at vintage shows. As such, those old Colts become a pleasant reminder of a time when our sport was more about inexpensive fun than meeting government-mandated emissions regulations or re-mortgaging your house to buy a new sled.

Maybe those retro riders are on to something.

1976 Polaris Colt S/S

MANUFACTURER
Polaris division of Textron Inc. at Roseau, Minnesota

POWERTRAIN
Engine: 336cc Polaris Star/ Fuji Heavy Industries free air piston-port twin
Carburetion: Two Mikuni VM-26 slide-valves
Compression Ratio: 11.6:1
Ignition: Magneto and breaker points
Lubrication: Pre-mix at 40:1
Exhaust: Single pipe into Polartone muffler
Power Output: 32 HP
Clutches: Polaris Torque Balanced drive and driven

CHASSIS
Type: Welded and painted steel with steel bumpers, fiberglass hood and polycarbonate console
Dry Weight (claimed): 358.5 pounds; 390 wet measured by *Snow Goer*
Front Suspension: Triple leaf springs with chromed hydraulic shock absorbers
Ski Stance: 28 inches
Rear Suspension: Steel slide rails with torsion springs and one hydraulic shock on rear arm
Track: 15-inch three-band reinforced rubber with steel cleats and molded rubber grousers
Brake: Hydraulic disc
Fuel Capacity: 5 gallons
Standard Equipment: Speedometer with odometer, tachometer, gas gauge, kill switch, handlebar pad, passenger hand grips, glove box above dash, rear seat storage compartment, twin 30-watt sealed beam headlamps, snow flap

MSRP: $1,499

1976 Ski-Doo T'NT RV

A new day dawns

The pale light of the early morning sun illuminated the new machine on the full-page color brochure photo. The message was unmistakable. The 1976 Ski-Doo T'NT RV was the beginning of a new day for Ski-Doo performance trail sleds. The promotional flyers were more direct, bluntly stating, "Look at our get-serious T'NT R/V for '76." (But they weren't consistent about the RV designation, showing it both with and without the slash that was later dropped.)

Since essentially inventing the performance trail sled category in the late 1960s with the T'NT, Bombardier had surrendered leadership of this rapidly growing market segment to other companies. But it managed to stay competitive in Stock class racing, and the virtually new from-the-ground-up 1975 T'NT RV 245 had won more sanctioned Stock races than anything else in its class. Now there was a winning Stock racer as a serious trail sled for performance-oriented recreational riders, too.

Changes For The Trail

The 1976 T'NT RV had substantial changes from the prior year's Stock racer, but within the same basic concept. Beyond the color and trim, the most obvious changes were moving the headlight from inside the front scoop to the top of the hood, and the addition of a low windshield. A 114-inch, internal-drive, molded-rubber track on a longer suspension replaced the 102-inch cleated track on the racer. Mounted nearly 7 inches farther back in the chassis for better ride and stability, the longer track added five inches to the overall length of the machine. Fuel capacity was more than doubled to 5.5 gallons, and these changes added roughly 20 pounds to the machine.

Two free-air Rotax engines were offered: the over-achieving Type 247 of the race sled in the T'NT RV 250 and the more powerful Type 345 in the RV 340. Both used the unique rotary valve induction concept that added some complexity and weight but allowed the engines to make more power than contemporaries of similar displacement, although both required premium gasoline to do it.

These engines also introduced Mikuni VM series float carburetors with external fuel pumps to Ski-Doo trail sleds. Besides allowing better performance, they eliminated the vapor lock that had always plagued the diaphragm pumper carbs used previously. Power was delivered through a new square shaft clutch with a wider ratio than found on previous T'NTs.

And unlike earlier T'NTs, this was a single-seater with no provision for carrying passenger. This completed the metamorphosis of the snowmobile from a two-place utility to a strictly personal recreation device, a change that started with the original Ski-Doo T'NT in 1968 and '69.

Performance And Problems

The new lightweight performance trail machine was received with praise.

"For a sled that is bred as a racer, the RV has made the transition from track to trail quite nicely," reported *Snow Sports* magazine.

Acceptance by trail riders was quick, but not without consequences. The expansive-for-the-day 34-inch ski stance and 41.75-inch overall width forced snowmobile clubs to widen their bridges.

Very maneuverable due to sharp, precise steering with a tight 40-degree turning radius, Snow Sports commented that the wide, low slung machine had "excellent close quarters handling." Editors were also impressed with the performance, noting, "In our speed runs, the 340 kept up with many machines 100ccs larger."

I can say from personal experience that the lightweight and responsive RV was an absolute blast to ride and I liked it better than almost anything else on the trail at the time. That's while it was running. Unfortunately, the Rotax free air engines were already gaining a reputation for being unreliable, and that reputation would unfairly sully the image of all free airs in the eyes of many.

Nevertheless, the trail model RV sold well and stayed in the line more or less unchanged, except for twin pipes on subsequent models, through 1978.

That year the free air RV was joined by a heavier but more powerful and definitely more reliable liquid cooled variant called the Blizzard 6500 Plus. Set apart by a black hood, the 6500 also had a more reliable ignition system, greater gas capacity and a 16.5-inch wide track. Tweaked up a little more, this became the 1979 Blizzard 7500, the last trail development of the RV chassis.

Most of these models also had very similar but not identical Moto-Ski versions in orange and navy blue livery.

Returning To The Racing Roots

One very notable variant was the 1977 and '78 RV Cross Country, a terrain racer with a 75 hp Type 354 free air 340 engine, twin fuel tanks carrying more than 10 gallons of gas and a tall windshield. The 1977 model also had twin pipes and a massive seat back but the '78 reverted to the single pipe and straight seat back of the trail sleds. RV CC production was only 125 for 1977 and 250 for 1978, but in the very capable hands of Gerard Karpik, these models became consistent winners.

The 1979 Blizzard Cross Country, a terrain racer version of the liquid cooled Blizzard 7500, was the final variant, and it continued to win as the leaf spring era was drawing to a close.

Star of the oval track, terrain racing and spirited trail riding, the RV remains as one of the best and most versatile Bombardier performance sleds of all time. And the 1976 T'NT RV was the first version available to the average trail rider, making it an outstanding collectible for today's vintage enthusiasts.

1976 Ski-Doo T'NT RV 340

MANUFACTURER
Bombardier Inc., Valcourt, Quebec, Canada

POWERTRAIN
Engine: Rotax Type 345 rotary-valve free-air cooled twin
Displacement: 336.7cc
Carburetion: Two Mikuni VM-38 slide-valve float type
Compression Ratio: 12.5:1
Ignition: Bosch Polar Fire capacitor discharge
Lubrication: Pre-mix at 40:1
Power Output: 48 hp @ 8,200 rpm
Electrical Output: 100 watts
Exhaust: Single pipe into double-wall tuned muffler
Drive Clutch: Bombardier "Instant Torque" square shaft
Driven Clutch: Bombardier cam action

CHASSIS
Type: Riveted all-aluminum with steel rear bumper, steel skis and fiberglass belly pan and hood
Weight: 345 pounds (dry claimed)
Front Suspension: Mono-leaf springs with hydraulic shock absorbers
Ski Stance: 34 inches
Rear Suspension: Torque Reaction aluminum slide rails with hydraulic shock on rear arm
Track: 15-by-114-inch fiberglass-reinforced molded rubber with internal drive
Brake: Self-adjusting mechanical disc
Fuel Capacity: 5.5 gallons
Standard Equipment: Handlebar pad, tether switch, primer, tachometer, carbide ski runners, snow flap
Options: Speedometer, halogen headlight bulb, rear view mirror, tow hitch

MSRP: $1,995

The First Yamaha Exciter
Hamamatsu Breakthrough

An excellent example of the track-to-trail technology transfer that drove snowmobile development hard and fast during the vintage era, the new 1976 Exciter was basically a '75 GPX Stock-class racer with a fan-cooled engine to appeal to the many riders who didn't believe in free-air power for trail use.

And as one of the first Yamaha sleds to carry a memorable model name rather than alphabetic gibberish nomenclature, the Exciter helped break new ground in Yamaha snowmobile marketing to become one of the most important models in the brand's long history.

Excitement Begins

The Exciter burst onto the scene during the evolution of snowmobiles from family utility machines that could play a little bit to pricey personal recreation devices. Although equipped with passenger grab handles, it was really a fairly large single-seater that was intended to provide lively entertainment for one person.

Initially offered with a choice of 340 or 440 engines, both of which were stronger than average for their displacement, the Exciter was also well equipped for the day. Full instrumentation, parking brake, tether switch, chrome ski shocks, CD ignition and especially Yamaha's Autolube oil injection, a huge convenience not found on any other brand in the industry at the time, combined to make this a premium trail performance sled in every respect.

And the Exciter was also one of the first snowmobiles to be fitted with a shock absorber charged with compressed nitrogen over oil instead of the usual air over oil, resulting in better rear suspension performance. This Yamaha development began the move toward the huge variety of better performing gas shocks that we enjoy on today's snow machines.

Sales of the appropriately named Exciter took off immediately, expanding what the GPX had done to establish a trail performance identity for Yamaha, a new image that was critical for success in the increasingly performance-driven snowmobile industry of the 1970s.

Snow Goer evaluators were really pleased with the new model, saying that "all we had to write about (previously) was Yamaha's durability and consistently strong engine. But that's all over." They went on to say that the Exciter was "fast and super quick," but also noted clutch problems with the test unit.

According to an owner's survey published the following season in *Snow Sports* magazine, first year Exciter buyers were generally happy with their new ride, praising its handling and stability, overall performance and oil injection. But on the other hand, many did not like the fuel economy or the grabby clutching that quickly wore belts and required frequent lubrication. As one owner put it, "It has bugs. But for a first year model, it's great."

The Exciter really hit stride with the 1977 model. Revised porting provided a modest power increase. But the real improvement resulted from another racetrack technology transfer, the drive clutch from the SRX suitably retuned for the fanner's power band. The new clutch improved efficiency to deliver about 5 more horsepower to the track while improving belt life and gas mileage at the same time.

Excitement Continues

The Exciter was continually improved in typical Yamaha fashion. The 1978 model brought a new Keihin carb that increased fuel economy, new bearing materials in the drive clutch for better reliability, a more tapered tunnel, new seat and footrests, an 8-gallon gas tank and relocated larger instruments for better readability. And the 1979 version changed hood color to black with red trim. It was also the last year for the 340 version. The 1980 models are very distinctive with their gold tunnels and a return to gold trim on the hood.

The Exciter lasted through the 1981 model year when the sleeker SS 440 functionally replaced it, but the name was resurrected a few years later for a new water-burner pogo stick model.

By the end of its initial six-year run, the original Exciter had been a huge asset for Yamaha in weathering the final stages of the great manufacturer shake-out. It had significantly helped to establish the company as a builder of performance-oriented trail sleds that people actually wanted to buy, and helped vault Yamaha over other manufacturers into a position where it would soon assume snowmobile industry sales leadership.

My buddy Tony "Yammiegod" Bellucco sums up the Exciter as "One of the best Yammies of all time, saying, "I've seen some of these sleds with over 9,000 miles and they still run like new."

1976 YAMAHA EXCITER 440

MANUFACTURER
Yamaha Motor Company Ltd., Hamamatsu, Japan

POWERTRAIN
Engine: 433cc Yamaha reed valve 7-port Torque-Induction axial fan-cooled twin with one Keihin PW42-38 slide valve carb
Ignition: Hitachi CD
Power Output: 48 hp @ 7,500 rpm
Drive & Driven Clutches: Yamaha

CHASSIS SPECS
Type: Riveted and welded aluminum tunnel with steel bulkhead, aluminum belly pan and chromed tube steel bumpers
Dry Weight (estimated): 380 pounds
Front Suspension: Four-leaf springs with chromed hydraulic shock absorbers
Ski Stance: 35.5 inches
Rear Suspension: Slide rails with torsion springs and one mid-mount gas shock
Track: 15-by-116-inch fiberglass-reinforced molded rubber
Brake: Self-adjusting mechanical disc

MSRP: $1,799

Arctic Cat Jag
Thumbs Up For Charlie's Cat

A direct derivative of the incredibly successful 1972 EXT racer, the Jag (not Jaguar) began as essentially a budget version of the first El Tigré. Introduced on a limited basis in 1975 with a Kawasaki free air engine, the first Jag was not shown in the 1975 sales brochure.

For 1976, the Jag switched to Suzuki power, along with the rest of the full-sized Cats, and became a full production model, with Arctic building about 15,000 of them – more than any other Cat for that season. And that set it on a path to become one of the most popular Cats of the leaf spring era.

Going Green
The Jag really hit stride in 1977 when the trim color was switched from a lackluster light gray to eye-catching Cat green. This was also the year that Arctic Enterprises began to use retired Team Arctic racer Charlie Lofton as the spokesman for the Jag. Known as the fastest man on snow from his speed runs in the famous Boss Cat II, Lofton appeared in all kinds of advertising and sales promotion materials.

"I gave up racing," he was quoted as saying, "but I'll never give up performance."

Shown riding the Jag in Cat videos and discussing its capabilities in sales brochures and magazine articles, Lofton lent the sporty lightweight a lot of credibility as a performance sled that anyone could afford. And as an evolved race sled, it did have a lot of performance attributes, from its jackshaft drive and low center of gravity to its lightweight design and excellent handling.

Half a dozen 1977 Jags with unique Charlie Cat identification were used in a major promotion for Revlon's Charlie and Chaz fragrances for women and men, respectively. Actress and future television star Shelly Hack (Jack in the "Jack & Mike" TV show) became the human face of the promotion when it was continued the following season. Hack appeared with Charlie Cats in fashion magazine ads and on point-of-purchase material in hundreds of major department stores coast-to-coast all winter. This totally unprecedented and very unique two-winter promotion exposed snowmobiling and Arctic Cat to a whole new audience, helping move the sport further upscale.

Accolades Accumulate
The media and the buying public also received the Jag very well.

Then United States Snowmobile Association President Tom Putnam lauded his new Jag in *SnoTrack* magazine, describing how it incorporated concepts and features that had been tested and proven on the race track. *Snow Goer* praised its handling and ergonomics, and noted that the 340 Jag outran five 440s at the spring tests. SG testers also found that the machine averaged 23 mpg in a high-energy 20-mile trail ride over a variety of trails, and stated emphatically that the Suzuki Spirit engine absolutely ended all the myths about free airs being unreliable. Meanwhile, *Snow Sports* magazine concluded, "there are some other machines you could buy for considerably more bucks that aren't a lick better."

Rank and file snowmobilers agreed. *Snow Sports* consumer surveys confirmed that owners were pleased with the machine's great value and unusually high dependability.

On a personal basis, the '77 was easily my favorite of the three leaf spring Jags that served our household. Inexpensive to purchase and operate, this sporty Jag had excellent ergonomics, was an absolute blast to ride, rock-solid reliable and dirt simple to maintain. The free air Suzuki was easy to start yet provided enough power to move the featherweight chassis with authority at typical trail speeds of the day. And a huge list of options allowed tailoring the machine to personal tastes.

The only shortcomings were lack of storage and a buckboard ride.

All-Timer

The Jag continued evolving further in 1978 with a new hood and a fan-cooled engine option, and cemented its status as Arctic Cat's best-selling model. A 1979 Jag with the Series 2000 275cc free air engine set a gas mileage mark of 42 mpg in an industry-wide fuel economy test. All Jags were built on the original chassis through 1981 when Arctic Enterprises died.

A heavily redesigned Arctco Jag appeared in 1985, was reworked again to handle the AFS ski suspension for 1989, and remained a solid seller all the way through the 1990s, making it one of Cat's longest running model names. Unlike many inexpensive trail models, the Jag cashed in on its performance ancestry to become a huge success in the marketplace. Built in large quantities, many still survive and they make great retro-riders or easy low-budget restorations.

So, besides being the fastest man on snow, Charlie Lofton really knew how to pick a winner in the showroom and on the trail.

1977 Arctic Cat Jag 3000

MANUFACTURER
Arctic Enterprises Inc., Thief River Falls, Minnesota

POWERTRAIN
Engine: 339cc Suzuki Spirit AA34F2 Series 3000 free-air-cooled piston-port twin with one Mikuni VM-30 slide valve carb, Capacitor Discharge (CD) ignition, and single pipe into Arctictron muffler
Compression Ratio: 6.5:1
Power Output: 30 HP @ 6,000 rpm
Clutches: Arctic hex drive and die-cast reverse cam aluminum driven

CHASSIS
Type: Riveted aluminum with steel subframe, extruded aluminum front and chrome tube tube steel rear bumpers, fiberglass hood and belly pan
Claimed Dry Weight: 337
Front Suspension: Mono-leaf springs with hydraulic shock absorbers
Rear Suspension: Aluminum slide rails with four-position adjustable torsion springs and one hydraulic shock absorber
Ski Stance: 28 inches
Track: 15-by-116-inch Fiber B (Kevlar) reinforced 3-brand logo dropper with molded-in 2/3rds steel cleats and quadruple internal drive
Brake: Manually adjustable mechanical disc
Fuel Capacity: 6.1 gallons
Standard Equipment: Kelch fuel gauge, kill switch, resistor spark plugs, pre-wired accessory terminals, passenger grab strap, snow flap

MSRP: $1.425

1977 Kawasaki Sno Jet SST

The "strange bedfellows" sled

Things can get strange when one company buys another one, and nothing in the snowmobile world was ever any stranger than the transitional 1977 Kawasaki Sno Jet SST series. These two first-year Kawasaki snowmobile models brought together no less than four of the big names in the industry in one product.

Essentially a carry-over Sno Jet design that was significantly improved by Kawasaki engineers, these sleds used Yamaha engines and were assembled by Arctic Enterprises with Cat drive clutches. And these first and only American-made Sno Jets actually worked very well despite their mongrel origins.

How It Happened

The SST had been one of Sno Jet's best selling models in the early 1970s, and it got a major redesign for the 1975 model year. But Big Blue was simply melting away from the withering heat of relentless competition, with sales declining to unsustainable levels.

Meanwhile, Kawasaki made no secret of the fact that it was planning on entering the snowmobile market as a full-fledged manufacturer. In fact, the company's desire to do so was a major reason that Arctic Cat dropped the green streak guys as its near-exclusive snow machine engine supplier when the contract expired following the 1975 model year.

Not yet quite ready to introduce its own designs, Kawasaki purchased the failing Sno Jet business from Conroy Corporation in 1976. This gave the Japanese company an instant network of more than a thousand experienced snowmobile dealerships across the North American Snowbelt. Sno Jet operations at Thetford Mines, Quebec, and Winooski, Vermont, were shut down and Kawasaki set up its snowmobile division headquarters in Grand Rapids, Michigan.

Besides the dealer organization, Kawasaki also got preliminary engineering for the 1977 Sno Jet models and stocks of components ranging from Sno Jet-manufactured parts to purchased assemblies including engines from arch-rival Yamaha. Over time, Yamaha had pushed out Hirth and Sachs to become Sno Jet's exclusive power plant supplier, although these engines lacked the Autolube oil injection system used on otherwise identical motors in Yamaha's own snow sleds.

As Kawasaki was not ready to start building snowmobiles at its Lincoln, Nebraska, motorcycle plant, the company contracted its old partner Arctic Enterprises to assemble the new Kawasaki Sno Jets in Cat's relatively new, modern plant in northern Minnesota. Arctic was actively seeking assembly work to fill its excess production capacity, and Cat's ability to supply a proven drive clutch was an added plus

Definitely Not The Same Old Sled
Kawasaki engineers made 60 detail upgrades in the 1977 SST. They started with a new hood, new color scheme, new controls and a new and more protective windshield. Inside the sleds got upgraded brakes, improved engine and exhaust system mounts to reduce vibration, an all-new aluminum chaincase with stronger internals, new cowl hinges and better soundproofing. Down underneath were stronger ski spindles and improved steering gear with redesigned tie-rods for easier toe adjustment, new skis for better bite, longer travel ski shocks with improved calibration, a strengthened track suspension and a new lighter weight track and drive sprockets.

Snow Goer testers at the time were impressed with the new SSTs.

"Performance with the SST is such that you must keep reminding yourself that the sled is family oriented with speed being a secondary concern" editors said. "The SST out-ran every other fan-cooled or free air in both family and high performance categories ... Only the liquid-cooled trail racers could out-pull the SST fan down the quarter- and eighth-mile runs." The writers complimented the SST's comfort and precise steering, although one editor felt the steering effort was very high due to the new Kawasaki-designed skis. The editors also noted the much-copied tapered tunnel allowed the track and suspension to clear out snow build-up in the deep powder.

Snow Sports magazine concurred, commenting very positively on top speed, acceleration, climbing ability, handling and deep snow ride quality. They concluded that, "it would be a big mistake to overlook the '77 Kawasaki Sno Jet."

One And Done
Kawasaki introduced its new snowmobile designs for 1978, including the popular Invader and fan-cooled Intruder. To no one's surprise, the Yamaha-powered SST vanished while the similar Kawasaki-powered '77 Astro was redone as the Inviter 340 to serve as the entry-level model. (The Inviter was renamed Drifter for 1979 and subsequent seasons.)

The book was closed on the Kawasaki Sno Jet, but this "strange bedfellows" sled had done its job and helped establish Kawasaki as a serious player in the North American snowmobile market, a task that could have otherwise taken years to accomplish.

1977 Kawasaki Sno Jet SST

MANUFACTURER
Kawasaki Motors Corp. U.S.A., Snowmobile Division, Grand Rapids, Michigan; assembled under contract by Arctic Enterprises, Inc., at Thief River Falls, MN

POWERTRAIN
Engine: 433cc or 338cc Yamaha, axial-fan-cooled reed-valve twins
Carburetion: One Mikuni VM 36 / VM 34 with induction baffle tube
Compression Ratio: 7:1 / 6.4:1
Ignition: Capacitor Discharge (CD)
Lubrication: Pre-mix at 25:1
Exhaust: Single pipe into an ACS canister muffler
Power Output: 47 hp @ 6,800 rpm / 36 hp @ 7,000 rpm
Electrical Output: 100 watts
Drive Clutch: Arctic hex shaft
Driven Clutch: Sno Jet

CHASSIS
Type: Riveted aluminum with steel sub-frame, aluminum belly pan and fiberglass hood
Weight: 360 pounds (440) / 350 pounds / (340) dry (claimed)
Front Suspension: Multi- leaf springs with inboard-mounted chrome-plated hydraulic shocks
Ski Stance: 30 inches
Rear Suspension: Slide rails with torsion springs and one hydraulic shock absorber
Track: 15-by-116-inch fiberglass-reinforced molded rubber with internal drive
Brake: Mechanical disc
Fuel Capacity: 6.5 gallons
Standard Equipment: Speedometer/odometer, tachometer, fuel gauge, kill switch, adjustable padded handlebars, non-slip footrests, passenger grab handles, snow flap, under-hood tool pouch

MSRP: $1,895 for the 440: $1,745 for the 340

1977 Polaris TX-L
The power package of the future

"The TX-L is not the only liquid-cooled snowmobile on the market" read the 1977 Polaris full-line brochure. "But it's the only one with the name Polaris on it. And that makes a difference."

The difference was simply this: Polaris was an industry pioneer, a well-established major brand and one of the strongest supporters of racing when it was infinitely more important then than it is now. With this machine, Polaris became the first of the big three to endorse this emerging engine technology for consumer use.

And although the new Fuji engine set the TX-L apart from the other 1977 TX models, it wasn't the only engineering breakthrough in this very significant machine.

Building On Success

The Polaris TX had been around a long time, and it had put more than a few trophies on the shelf. The 1971 TX modified racers had dominated the oval tracks. The 1973 and later TX stockers had done well on the ovals and cross-country venues, and gained favor on the trails. But they were all powered by the old technology free-air powerplants with their trademark heavily-finned heads. And the 1976 TX racers had been overwhelmed by competitive product. "Free-air engines have a certain amount of heat sag in them," explained Don Erickson, then General Sales Manager of Polaris. "That means they start tightening up when they get warm and can slow down a sled as much as 6 to 8 mph. It's most noticeable when temperatures are up in the 20s and 30s."

Closer tolerances possible in a liquid-cooled engine allowed greater power output with better fuel mileage over a wider range of temperatures, plus improved reliability, longer life and reduced noise. The thermostatically controlled cooling system used a water pump on the engine to move coolant out and through extruded aluminum heat exchangers mounted underneath the running boards where they would be sprayed by snow. A side benefit of this setup was warmer feet. A radiator was not provided.

Developed over an extended period beginning with the 1974 Sno Pro oval racing season, the new Fuji liquid-cooled engine had been further refined in cross-country competition. Available on a very limited basis in kit form for the 1976 season, Bob Przekwas showed that it was ready for release by winning the modified class easily at the Mille Lacs 300 lake enduro in Minnesota, the last major cross-country race of the winter.

But the new engine wasn't the only major advancement in the 1977 TX-L. Underneath, a new all-rubber molded track with internal drive required less power to turn and allowed higher top speeds than the old drive-on-the-cleat track. Seven inches longer than the track on the free-air TX models, the new TX-L rubber track also provided better deep snow performance and improved ride quality.

A new mostly aluminum skidframe featured dual rear shocks that were mounted outboard of the rails but still inside the tunnel. Larger diameter ski spindles added durability to the TX-L, and there was also a new console and new handlebars with upgraded handgrips.

The "water burner" was differentiated visually from free-air TX models by a large "TXL 340" decal on the rear of each side of the tunnel, and by a row of white stars in the red stripe on each side of the white hood. The stripe was solid red on air-cooled models.

The down side of all this hot new technology was cost. At $2,495, the TX-L was several hundred dollars more than an air-cooled TX, and was actually one of the most expensive sleds of the year from any brand. And high-octane premium gas was recommended for the engine to avoid detonation problems.

A Winning Effort
Available to the public in limited numbers, the 1977 TX-L delivered exceptional performance.

In a September 1976 *Snow Goer* preview, editors commented, "the TX-L just plain outperforms any other production sled we have ridden - any size, any color." They went on to say that "the acceleration is impressive, even at 50-60 mph," and "high-speed stability was absolutely superb," concluding that "the TX-L 340 is one of the most sophisticated and refined models available."

The new Polaris quickly became a cross country racing sensation. Competing against several factory teams and many independents, 18-year old privateer Archie Simonson led a TX-L sweep of the top nine places in the Winnipeg-to-St. Paul I-500, arguably the single most important race of the era. Overall, the new Polaris machines took 15 of the top 20 positions, and fully half of the sleds that finished the grueling marathon were TX-Ls.

TX-L racers also took seven of the top 10 positions — including the first three, and also won the Pro Stock 340 class at the Regina-Minot I-250. Simonson led a one-two TX-L finish at the Balsam Lake Classic in Wisconsin, and TX-Ls also ran one-two at two Minnesota events: the Eagles Heartland Grand Prix and the Detroit Lakes Grand Cup 200. Although a factory team racer on another brand managed to win the South Dakota Governor's Cup, TX-Ls ran very strong to finish second through sixth in that event, too.

It was the same story at many of the other big cross-country events that winter. The TX-Ls were the sleds to beat. By the following season, the TX-L was an unquestioned success and it became a fixture in the Polaris line up.

One More Step
By combining a liquid-cooled engine with its already efficient clutching and an all-rubber track, Polaris had its drive train of the future. This generic combination of components would become the standard power train of the entire industry, and most popular models from all manufacturers use this same basic package to this day.

The aluminum chassis needed one more major change, a better front end than the traditional, but limited, leaf springs. The absolute superiority of the sprint car style coil-overshock ski suspension had already been demonstrated by Chaparral, Alouette and Skiroule modified racers. When Polaris put the independent front end its 1977 RXL oval race sleds, it forced everyone in the industry to follow suit or abandon the oval track.

After development work that lasted another three seasons, the combination of the TX-L power train and track in the RXL-type chassis emerged as the 1980 Polaris TX-L Indy. This basic package would evolve and come to dominate the sport, allowing the company that had once led the industry in sales to lead it again.

1977 Polaris TX-L

MANUFACTURER
Polaris Industries, Minneapolis, Minnesota, at Roseau, Minnesota

POWERTRAIN
Engine: Fuji Heavy Industries SuperStar liquid-cooled piston-port twin cylinder
Displacement: 333cc
Carburetion: Two Mikuni VM-38
Compression Ratio: 12:1
Ignition: Capacitor discharge
Lubrication: Pre-mix 40:1
Exhaust: Single tuned pipe with Polartone muffler
Power Output: 56 hp
Clutching: Polaris "Sno Pro Torque-Balanced"

CHASSIS
Type: Aluminum with steel and aluminum bumpers, die-cast aluminum chaincase and fiberglass belly pan and hood
Weight: Claimed 405 pounds dry; *Snow Goer* spring prototype test: 380.5 pounds dry and 412 pounds wet.
Front Suspension: Mono-leaf springs with hydraulic shocks
Ski Stance: 31-inches
Rear Suspension: Extruded aluminum slide rails with torsion springs and cantilevered dual rear shock absorbers
Track: 15-inch internal drive directional molded rubber with fiberglass reinforcement
Brake: Hydraulic disc
Fuel Capacity: 5 U.S. gallons
Standard Equipment: Speedometer with odometer, tachometer, engine temperature gauge, gas gauge, kill switch, low windshield

Price: $2,495

The Sno-Runner Saga

Chrysler Couldn't Conquer The Sled Biz

Before the current wave of snow bikes, there was a major effort from what some would consider an unlikely source.

Like many durable goods manufacturers of the post-WWII era, Chrysler Corporation exhibited great interest in the rapidly emerging snowmobile industry. Chrysler Marine purchased the West Bend engine business in the 1960s and sold the engines for use in several brands of snowmobiles including Hus-Ski, Sno Pony and its numerous derivatives, Snowbug and Swinger. Near the end of the decade the company considered purchasing the Silverline snowmobile operation (EsKee-Mo, T-Bird and Yukon King) from Moorehead Plastics, but decided not to do so.

When Chrysler finally did announce its own snow machine in 1979, it was something quite out of the ordinary.

Genesis

The tandem-ski snow bike with chain driven paddle track propulsion was patented in the 1970s by Illinois inventor Royce H. Husted after a decade of work. The machine featured the first stock plastic skis on a snow vehicle, using a new nylon-elastomer blend material, DuPont Zytel FE-8015, that allowed the skis to flex when crossing bumps.

Quick-release pins at strategic frame points allowed breaking the snow bike down into as many as five sub-assemblies to fit into the trunk of an automobile for easy transportation. No lighting was included. With many manufacturers searching for a breakthrough vehicle that would revolutionize snowmobiling like the Honda 50 and 90 had revolutionized motorcycling, the snow bike was a very appealing idea.

Husted's design firm, Saroy Inc., licensed three major corporations to build his bike. The Echo Division of Kioritz built a few thousand bikes with Echo engines and graphics that were otherwise pretty much unchanged from the original design. But Kioritz soon exited the business, allegedly under threat of legal action for insufficient safety equipment from major North American snowmobile manufacturers of the day, and dumped most of its bikes in Japan and Europe.

Roper Corporation spent 1977 to 1981 developing its considerably different version, the Sno-Cycle XS22, for Sears, Roebuck and Company. Built only in development quantities,

102

it never entered mass production. Some of both the Echo and Roper versions have survived to this day to confound collectors who are only familiar with the widely known Chrysler version of Husted's snow bike.

Chrysler started working on what became the Sno-Runner in 1975, reportedly in an attempt to generate cash flow for the financially troubled corporation, and it put far more effort into it than either of the other two licensees. Chrysler engineers gave it a snappy West Bend engine with a 90-watt alternator to power full lighting, plus side reflectors and a handlebar-mounted kill switch to comply with snowmobile industry safety requirements.

Unfortunately the exhaust system chosen was not well suited to the engine and restricted performance to about 25 mph, and a lot less at higher altitudes. And at some point during the development phase Chrysler tried unsuccessfully to sell the Sno-Runner to the U.S. military.

The first production Sno-Runners rolled off the assembly line in May of 1979, and the search for dealer representation was on. Prospective dealers were advised that the Sno-Runner would be packed and shipped only in lots of six bikes. Suggested list price was $645 plus freight. The minimum order was 12 units at a 20 percent dealer discount plus at least one spare parts kit costing $463.44, all plus freight, for a total minimum investment approaching $7,000. The dealer discount rose to 25 percent for more than 24 units.

Underlining Chrysler's dire financial situation at the time, the Sno-Runner did not qualify for any Chrysler supported dealer acceptance program, and terms of sale were limited to cash, sight draft/bill of lading or floor plan through the dealer's bank. Marketing communications support positioned the Sno-Runner as a lightweight, low cost, breakthrough vehicle. It was promoted with high quality full-color sales literature with a running rabbit as part of the Sno-Runner logo, press releases to numerous publications, full-page color national magazine advertising and industry magazine test articles.

"Unique, inexpensive, simple to operate, and fun," concluded *Snow Goer* testers at the time.

Personally I was very skeptical when shown an early production Sno-Runner in the trunk of a Chrysler sales rep's automobile. I really didn't think it would even support my weight, let alone go in the snow. Apparently I wasn't the only doubter.

Exodus

Chrysler tried to sell the Sno-Runner for two seasons but didn't find anywhere near enough takers at either the dealer or retail level. The tiny, underpowered bike simply didn't work in most snow conditions, so it was restricted to groomed trails. And even then some said it was tricky to ride. An optional high performance kit that kicked the horsepower up to 10 made no difference.

Supposedly about 28,000 Sno-Runners were built, but a significant percentage of them were not sold. So Chrysler dumped the remaining inventory to C.O.M.B. Liquidators of Minneapolis, which removed the Chrysler identification and blew out the balance of production as Sno-Rabbits at $288. And that ended Chrysler Corporation's time in the snowmobile business.

1980 Chrysler Sno-Runner

MANUFACTURER
Chrysler Marine Division, Hartford and Beaver Dam, Wisconsin

POWERTRAIN
Engine: 134cc Chrysler West Bend Power Bee 820 fan-cooled reed-valve single with chrome-plated bore, Tillotson 320A diaphragm pumper carb and breakerless magneto ignition
Lubrication: Pre-mix at 24:1
Power Output: 6.25 hp
Drive Clutch: Automatic centrifugal

CHASSIS
Type: Welded and painted aluminum alloy with steel fittings and plastic track guard and skis
Claimed Dry Weight: 72 pounds
Front Suspension: Flexible plastic ski
Rear Suspension: Flexible plastic ski and foam filled seat
Track: 63-inch nickel-plated chain with 3.125-inch wide molded polyurethane cleats
Brake: Band type on clutch
Fuel Capacity: 1.3 gallons
Standard Equipment: Manual choke, twist throttle, kill switch, four-position footrests, sealed beam headlight, taillight with brake light, side safety reflectors

MSRP: $645

1980 Kawasaki Invader LTD 4/6
Confusing Collectable

When Kawasaki introduced its new-for-1980 Invader LTD 4/6, there was some confusion over whether it was a performance sled or a luxury sled – or if it was some of both. No matter, Kawasaki made it clear that it regarded this model as "the most advanced snowmobile ever made," and that it would be built in limited numbers, so the LTD nomenclature would be appropriate.

A Technological Tour de Force
When the original Kawasaki Invader appeared for 1978, it was almost the last gasp of a dying breed, a performance sled that still had some basic passenger capability like a family sled. This sort of ambiguity continued with the new Invader LTD, starting with an extra-plush version of the "king and queen" seat that was used in various forms on all Invaders and Intruders.

The LTD certainly looked like a performance sled under the hood. Power came from a standard Invader engine that had been upgraded to breathe better with new jugs featuring four transfer ports feeding six cylinder-wall intake ports (thus the 4/6 in its name), slightly different pistons and a twin pipe exhaust system with individual mufflers instead of the usual single pipe.

This engine also featured two spark plugs per cylinder, something that Kawasaki had done on some engines it had previously built for Arctic Cat. The extra plug is supposed to provide a faster and more complete fuel burn that theoretically results in more power. I remember a top Kawasaki snowmobile executive commenting off-hand that "one of our engineers wrote a paper on it (dual plugs per cylinder) once."

A Mikuni-engineered automatic fuel shut off kept gas out of the crankcase if the sled was parked facing downhill, so no manual shut-off was needed unlike on other machines. This feature was also standard on all 1980 Invaders and Intruders. Kawasaki's dual cooling system included heat exchangers in the tunnel, but the cross-flow radiator under the hood of the LTD was repositioned for better efficiency, and warm air exited behind the windshield to improve operator comfort.

Externally, the unique LTD hood featured an asymmetrical raised section on the rider's right side, just above the radiator, with an Invader 4/6 logo on the front end of the bulge. Consequently it required a different windshield. The classy looking glacier green and silver color scheme with gold pin striping looked really sharp and further differentiated the LTD from the rest of the line.

Underneath, the new Vari-Ride variable rate skid frame improved ride quality. Oil injection, full instrumentation, adjustable handlebars and two storage compartments were also included. But electric start was optional and other luxury touches available on competitive models – like mirrors and heated handgrips – were not included.

On the other hand, the twin pipes, dual ignition, hood bulge and complete instrumentation added up to a claimed 15 pounds more than a standard Invader that had the same basic engine, though the single-piped version was officially rated at 10 fewer horsepower. And almost all competitive, serious performance sleds were still running pre-mix engines, too, which allowed operators to theoretically optimize their oil mixture for their particular needs.

Neither Fish Nor Fowl

On the snow, the big bad Kawi received mixed reviews, which is somehow appropriate. When *Snow Goer* tested the LTD 4/6, the riders were impressed with the power, calling it "consistently one of the fastest machines" at the spring Shoot-Out. They also praised the overall handling but disliked the heavy steering effort that was required, particularly at low speeds.

Out in the fields across North America, Kawasaki fans loved its performance, but many riders of competitive performance sleds considered it easy pickings in impromptu drag races. Personally I was not impressed by the only LTD that I ever rode, a non-current '82 that handled like an old school bus with binding king pins, but I have to believe that it could have been set up a lot better than it was.

So was the LTD a performance sled or a luxury sled, or both? In the end it really didn't matter. With a very stiff price for the day, the technologically advanced LTD was intended to be a brand flagship, not a high-volume seller. Initial demand failed to meet even the limited supply, so some 4/6s went unsold and were offered with a $200 factory rebate the following season.

Meanwhile, the 4/6 engine was a one year wonder, replaced by a new eight port engine with Keihin butterfly carbs and two-stage ignition in the 1981 Invader LTD that was offered in both manual and electric start models. For 1982, the company introduced the single-seat Interceptor as its serious performance sled and discontinued the base Invader, making the LTD the only Invader model that year. But Kawasaki corporate had pulled the plug on snowmobiles and was simply clearing out inventory, so the LTD never had a chance to evolve into either a full-blown luxury touring sled, an all-out performance sled or arguably even into a fully developed hybrid of both. So the identity crisis of this technology demonstrator was never really resolved, but the brand flagship LTD remains popular with Kawasaki fans to this day.

1980 Kawasaki Invader LTD 4/6

MANUFACTURER
Kawasaki Motors Corp. U.S.A., Grand Rapids, Michigan, at Lincoln, Nebraska

POWERTRAIN
Engine: 436cc Kawasaki TC440C-A201 piston-port liquid-cooled twin with two Mikuni VM-36 slide valve carbs, capacitor discharge (CD) ignition and twin exhaust pipes
Lubrication: Oil injection from 2.5-quart reservoir
Power Output: 77 hp @ 8,300 rpm
Clutches: Kawasaki drive and driven

CHASSIS
Type: High Strength Low Alloy (HSLA) steel and aluminum with stainless steel rivets, extruded aluminum bumpers and sheet molding compound (SMC) hood
Claimed Dry Weight: 430 pounds
Front Suspension: Mono-leaf springs with hydraulic shock absorbers
Ski Stance: 31 inches
Rear Suspension: Vari-Ride slide rail with torsion springs, rail wheels and one hydraulic shock absorber
Track: 15-by-121-inch, Kevlar-reinforced molded rubber with dual internal drive
Brake: Mechanical disc
Fuel Capacity: 8 gallons
Standard Equipment: Speedometer/odometer, tachometer, fuel gauge, oil gauge, engine temp gauge, kill switch, adjustable handlebars, passenger grab handles, pop-up headlight, two storage compartments

MSRP: $3,499

The Vintage SRX
Racetrack Rarity To Trail Performance Standout

The first Yamaha to carry the SRX model designation was the company's 1974 Sno Pro racer, with a very few units handcrafted for the fledgling professional racing circuit. They weren't big winners or the most publicized Sno Pro sleds and most snowmobilers never even saw one.

The SRX designation was not used in 1975. It returned in 1976 and '77 for Yamaha's race-ready oval sprint sleds that were offered in limited numbers to qualified independents for the "Stock" class competition of the day. Built to go fast and turn left until there was no more hundred-plus octane aviation gas remaining in the tiny 2.6-gallon fuel tank, the sleds had aluminum skis, a tachometer (a speedometer was optional), no windshield and only a pretense of trailability.

Ed Schubitzke electrified the snowmobile world by winning the 1976 Eagle River World Championship on a slightly modified SRX – a truly incredible performance for a stock snowmobile that would run with the best of the modified race sleds from the other brands. "Fast Eddie," Bobby Donahue, Dick Trickle, Bob Hulsebus, Oscar St. Onge and numerous others went on to compile an enviable competition record with the '76 and '77 SRX racers. In addition, factory driver/engineer Morio Ito and his mechanic Tom Marks used an SRX as their test mule for coil-over-shock suspension development for the forthcoming SSR oval racer.

From The Track To The Trails
In 1978, the SRX became a trail model available to anyone who wanted to purchase one. Positioned as a lake runner, this first liquid-cooled Yamaha trail sled retained the basic appearance of the earlier stock racers but in many details it was a different machine.

Numerous components were strengthened including the jackshaft, the driveshaft and the skid frame, which was beefed up with more travel. Skis were steel. Engine cooling was accomplished with the same system of a small radiator and heat exchangers, but the tunnel-mounted exchangers were lengthened for increased cooling capacity. Belly pan vents also helped cooling. Steel cleats were deleted from the molded rubber track. The seat looked the same but was actually a new design. Full instrumentation was provided and a 7-gallon gas tank was fitted, as was a short windshield.

The new 440 engine was engineered to run longer than what was needed for oval sprint racing. Using the 1977 SRX engine base and crankshaft with different cylinders that featured less aggressive port timing, the new engine had smaller Mikuni VM series carbs, a lower 7.7 to 1 compression ratio and a less aggressive ignition curve. It produced about 80 hp on premium pump gas instead of hard-to-find aviation fuel and it could be built up to crank out lots more power. But unlike all the other

Yamaha trail sled motors, this engine retained the pre-mix lubrication system of its racetrack predecessors.

With the basic formula established, the SRX quickly became a favorite of the serious go-fast crowd on tracks, lakes and trails.

The 1979 version was quite similar to the '78, but there were some significant powertrain changes. The engine was reconfigured to run on regular gas while retaining the 80 hp output by reworking the pistons and further reducing the compression ratio to 7 to 1. But unlike other Yamaha trail sleds, it still required pre-mixed oil and gas. Heat exchanger capacity was expanded again and the new YP drive clutch was fitted. The hood color changed from the traditional Yamaha white to jet-black.

"Beat Thy Neighbor"

For 1980, Yamaha decided it could have its cake and eat it, too, by making the SRX more palatable to the average trail rider. It was promoted as the sled to keep up with "the Joneses, or the Johanssens, or the Jovanoviches"

Addition of Yamaha's Autolube oil injection eliminated the fuss and mess of pre-mixed fuel, but also reduced user control of the gas-oil mix. Easier-pulling Mikuni butterfly carbs replaced the traditional VM-series units. The drive clutch was upgraded, new nitrogen-charged shock absorbers were used and the belly pan vents were eliminated even though pre-production photos showed them. The race-required tether switch was an option. Gold was introduced as a trim color, with the tunnel and belly pan gold-anodized for an unmistakable new appearance.

Some felt the previous pre-mix version ran stronger. "When I bought mine, my dealer told me that knowing what I was going to use it for, he thought I'd be happier with a left over '79," recalled New York ice drag racer Tony Bellucco.

However, the 1980 model was definitely a sales success and Yamaha continued to build market share with the SRX as its trail performance image leader. Autolube gave it a convenience advantage over every other hot trail sled on the market and it's appearance and actual performance ensured that Yamaha was taken very seriously in the increasingly important trail racer market.

1980 Yamaha SRX

MANUFACTURER
Yamaha Motor Company Limited at Hamamatsu, Shizuoka Prefecture, Japan

POWERTRAIN
Engine: Yamaha RT 439 liquid-cooled piston-port twin
Displacement: 439cc
Carburetion: Two 36mm Mikuni B (butterfly) series
Compression Ratio: 7.0:1
Ignition: Capacitor Discharge (CD)
Lubrication: Autolube oil injection
Exhaust: Twin tuned pipes into a single muffler
Power Output: 80 hp @ 9,000 rpm
Electrical Output: 75 watts
Drive Clutch: Yamaha YP
Driven Clutch: Yamaha

CHASSIS
Type: Riveted and welded aluminum tunnel and belly pan with steel bulkhead, rubber boots over steering gear and fiberglass hood
Weight: Claimed 399 pounds dry
Front Suspension: Mono-leaf springs with KYB hydraulic shock absorbers
Ski Stance: 35 inches
Rear Suspension: Slide rails with torsion springs and 2 nitrogen/oil shocks
Track: 15-by-116-inch fiberglass-reinforced molded rubber with internal drive
Brake: Self-adjusting mechanical disc
Fuel Capacity: 7 gallons (US)
Oil Capacity: 2.6-quarts (US)
Standard Equipment: Speedometer, tachometer, engine temperature gauge, oil gauge, quartz-halogen headlight, under hood storage pouch
Key Option: Tether switch for competition use

Price: $2,895

1981 Arctic Cat El Tigré 6000

Last licks from the original Cat

Fast on the race track, smooth on the trail. That was the story of the El Tigré 6000, a transition model between the new and old Arctic Cat.

The last of the major manufacturers to make the move to liquid-cooled trail sleds, Arctic Enterprises Inc. (AEI) began offering the El Tigré 6000 for the 1978 season with a 440 engine. The Suzuki-built twin delivered power through the proven and popular Arctic hex drive clutch that was pushed to the limit by the power of the new Suzuki water burner.

The El Tigré 6000 was, fundamentally, a liquid-cooled version of the well-established free-air El Tigré 5000. The "Six" employed a dual cooling system with tunnel-mounted heat exchangers augmented by a small radiator under the windshield for lake running and other low-snow conditions. It was also the first consumer Cat to be fitted with an all-rubber track for better top-end performance.

Powertrain upgrades came annually, with a 500 engine in 1979, a Comet drive clutch to handle the additional power in 1980, and a new Arctic reverse-cam driven clutch and wider 1-3/8-inch drive belt for 1981. The reverse-cam design made belt changing easier, and the wider belt handled the power better. The '81 version also got an extruded aluminum rear bumper in place of the chrome steel tube with rubber grips found on earlier models.

Flying Tigers

A pre-production 1981 6000 claimed the title of the World's Fastest Snowmobile at the *Snow Goer* Shoot Out in February 1980. But critics contended that straightline lake racing wasn't all there was to snowmobile performance.

The critics were silenced in December 1980 when retired Arctic Sno Pro racer Larry Coltom rode a 6000 to victory in the industry's first-ever major snocross, the Dayco Holiday Spectacular Muscle Machine Shoot-Out in Alexandria, Minnesota. Cat opened by winning two of the three qualifying motos. In the feature, Coltom defeated 11 other muscle sleds — half of them IFS machines — representing the best from the seven other brands available. Doug Oster's 6000 challenged for the lead until he broke a ski near the end. Dan Oostdyk's Scorpion Sidewinder, essentially the same sled with the older 440 engine, finished third overall, and the Arctic Enterprises contingent took four of the top seven positions.

However, 6000s reaching customers just weren't all that impressive. Like many snowmobiles of the day, they were jetted rich at the factory to prevent burn downs. But proper rejetting of the mains and needle jets for local altitude and temperatures turned them into real flying tigers.

Maybe the most impressive thing about the 6000's trail performance was that it was a very docile and comfortable sled at normal trail speeds. You could win lake races with the guys on Saturday, but still loaf it around with the kids during the Sunday club ride. The "Six" simply rode better than most competitive machines, and its low center of gravity and wide ski stance made it a solid, predictable handler. It really did fly well, too, with what seemed like unusually good pitch and roll control when it was off the ground, which was a lot more common in those days of relatively limited suspension travel.

Ergonomically, it put everything else on the trailer with very comfortable controls and seating, secure footrests, full instrumentation, easy starting and an effective windshield. It was relatively quiet, too, due to the liquid-cooled engine.

I recall fondly how owners of directly competitive sleds were always grinning ear to ear when they got off my "Six" — it didn't matter what other brand they rode, they loved that fast Cat. One, whose father was a big wheel in a competitive company, begged me not to tell her dad how much she liked it.

Shortcomings were minor, such as a tendency for collected snow to block the headlight in some conditions; a brake that required periodic manual adjustment and a need to rebuild the drive clutch every 1,000 miles or so to maintain top performance.

In isolated cases, the water pump drive belt would fail. This happened to a member of my club when his recoil broke and the spring sliced right through the belt. Naturally they were out in the middle of nowhere. But amazingly, one of the other guys had a spare belt in his sled, and they changed it on the side of the trail.

If nothing else, this illustrates the value of you and your riding buddies all having the same sled. In our case, it was six guys in our club who rode 6000 tigers. We were known as, what else, the Cat Six. One of the guys even had Cat Six caps made for us.

Down The Trail

Over-extended financially from ·a multipronged entrance to the marine business and the acquisition of Scorpion, Arctic Enterprises went bankrupt and was forced into liquidation early in 1981. The future of this awesome sled was uncertain as AEI melted away with the winter snow under the warm spring sun.

But the "Six" wasn't dead yet. It returned as a transition model for 1984 when a new company, Arctco, picked up the pieces and got on with Arctic Cat's next life. These models can be easily identified by the addition of gold trim to the color scheme, but are otherwise essentially indistinguishable. The 1985 model ushered in the first coil spring El Tigré.

The 1981 El Tigré 6000 was the last and best Cat from the original company, and in this rider's opinion, the best snowmobile of the entire leaf spring era. I had mine for eight years, and I wish I had it back today.

1981 Arctic Cat El Tigré 6000

MANUFACTURER
Arctic Enterprises Inc., Thief River Falls, Minnesota

POWERTRAIN
Engine: Suzuki Spirit AH50L2 liquid-cooled twin
Displacement: 500cc
Carburetion: Two Mikuni VM-38
Compression Ratio: 6.8:1
Ignition: Capacitor Discharge (CD). Normally Closed Ignition (NCI)
Lubrication: Pre-mix at 20:1 (Arctic Cat Purple Powerlube or equivalent)
Exhaust: Single expansion chamber into muffler
Power Output: 85 hp @ 8,250 rpm, 20 pound-feet at 4,000 rpm
Alternator Output: 120 watts
Drive Clutch: Comet 102C
Driven Clutch: Arctic reverse-cam die-cast aluminum

CHASSIS
Type: Riveted aluminum with welded steel subframe, extruded aluminum bumpers, aluminum belly pan and fiberglass hood
Weight: Claimed dry weight 415-pounds / 474 pounds ready to ride
Front Suspension: Tapered mono-leaf springs with hydraulic shock absorbers
Ski Stance: 32 inches
Rear Suspension: Aluminum slide rails with four-position adjustable torsion springs and one hydraulic shock absorber on each suspension arm
Track: 15-inch internal drive molded rubber with Fiber B (Kevlar) reinforcement, 116-inch circumference, 37 inches on the ground
Brake: Manually adjustable mechanical disc with parking brake
Fuel Capacity: 7 gallons (US]
Standard Equipment: Adjustable handlebars, speedometer with odometer and resettable trip meter, tachometer, coolant temperature gauge, Kelch fuel gauge, seat back storage compartment
Options: Handlebar heaters, tow hitch

Price: $4,199

1981 Yamaha SRX
The Radical Rocket

"If Darth Vader rode a snowmobile, it would be an '81 SRX," asserts Tony Bellucco, a Yamaha-focused collector, restorer and former racer.

Maybe one of the most intimidating production snowmobiles ever built, the first pogo stick SRX was awesomely fast but very demanding to ride, and that was just the start of the problems.

A total departure from the previous, popular leaf spring SRX models, the 1981 SRX 440E was conceived as a lake racer and built around a radical engine that originated in Yamaha's road bike program. The single-head, five-port twin used Mikuni butterfly carbs and dual expansion chambers to produce exceptional output.

"It had a power band like a chain saw," Bellucco recalls. "This motor did nothing from idle to 5,900 rpm but puke, bog, foul plugs and cough. But once it hit 6,000 rpm, it was like a turbo kicked in." A dual cooling system with both a radiator and a tunnel-mounted heat exchanger was used, as was fairly common at the time. Up front, the Yamaha TSS strut suspension that had been introduced the year before on the SR-V made the '81 SRX one of the first coil-over muscle sleds.

Other notable features included the Yamaha YPZ drive clutch, closed-top skis, instruments located in the handlebar pod behind a vestigial windshield, and a hideaway headlight.

Everything on the angular body style was done in solid black with minimal trim. It looked fast and imposing, even when standing still. And when it ran right, it was a very tough sled to beat as I can attest from personal experience informally racing against them.

But the 1981 SRX was mechanically troublesome from the start, especially when ridden as a trail sled because it wanted to be raced, not trail ridden. And it hated warm weather, running its best when the mercury was deeply buried. Ice drag racer Bellucco reports that his '81 SRX clocked 102 mph on radar at minus 2 degrees F, an excellent speed for the era with a 440.

The Mikuni butterfly carbs were difficult to adjust properly. The sled's tech manual listed 21 separate updates, including the Fast Trail update with 18 separate items covering everything from electricals to clutching, jetting, motor mounts, even the seat storage box latch and more.

The drive clutch was a key issue. The original YPZ pulley just couldn't handle the high revving power. Replacement with the Comet 102C was a big step in the right direction, but belt wear problems persisted and the primary spring recommendation was changed later. Crankshaft life was an issue on some machines. And the list of problems continued from there.

Owner comments reflected the promise and problems. "What a pig it was! Always breaking down. When it ran, it would run like a bat out of hell," one owner said. He wasn't alone. "Owned one for one season," said another former '81 SRX rider. "This machine put on more miles being towed. Went like a rocket, but it was always a slow walk home. Couldn't keep pistons in it."

The pogo stick SRX was also very squirrelly to ride, juking and feinting constantly making it a real handful at speed. Although the sled ate bumps very well in a straight line, overall handling was mediocre. And when run hard, it guzzled gas so range was also a significant issue.

Lesson Learned

Warranty claims skyrocketed, so something had to be done to impove reliability. Yamaha tried to correct the problems with a radical rocket for 1982 that had an updated 500-class engine, but that model had so many teething problems that it was never released to the public. A handful of field-test, pre-production 1982 SRX units that escaped destruction and are still in existence.

The lesson had been learned. High-strung radical race sleds just didn't make sense for performance-minded trail riders who would buy these sleds even if they weren't really suited for the trail.

A new and thoroughly de-bugged version with a bigger but less high-strung engine was released in 1983 as the Vmax 540, and that well-sorted-out machine carried the Yamaha trail performance banner through 1987 when it was superseded by the similar but further improved Exciter II.

Still, nothing ever matched the looks and performance of a dialed-in and thoroughly tuned '81 SRX. As Bellucco says, "After it knocks your eyes out, it will blow your socks off."

1981 Yamaha SRX 440E

MANUFACTURER
Yamaha Motor Company USA, Cypress, California, by Yamaha Motor Company Limited at Hamamatsu, Japan

POWERTRAIN
Engine: 437cc Yamaha RT 437 piston-ported liquid-cooled twin with two Mikuni 40-38 butterfly carbs, capacitor discharge (CD) ignition, and twin tuned pipes into a single muffler
Compression Ratio: 6.7:1
Power Output: 88 hp @ 9,250 rpm
Clutches: Yamaha YPZ or Comet 102C drive with Yamaha driven

CHASSIS
Type: Riveted and welded aluminum tunnel and belly pan with steel bulkhead, fiberglass hood
Claimed Dry Weight: 425 pounds
Front Suspension: Telescopic Strut Suspension (TSS) integrated coil-over-shock
Ski Stance: 34.6 inches
Rear Suspension: Slide rails with torsion springs and one nitrogen-charged shock
Track: 15- by-121-inch fiberglass-reinforced molded rubber with internal drive
Brake: Self-adjusting mechanical disc
Fuel Capacity: 5 gallons
Standard Equipment: Speedometer/odometer, trip meter, tachometer, engine temperature gauge, oil gauge, kill switch, tether switch, handlebar pad

MSRP: $3,899

1983 John Deere Sprintfire
Innovation At The Industry Low Point

The absolute low point of the modern snowmobile industry was 1982. Cat and Scorpion were recently deceased, Kawasaki's snowmobile division was in liquidation, and Polaris was essentially starting all over again after being sold by Textron. Ski-Doo was preoccupied with the Quebec market, Moto-Ski was on its last legs and Yamaha was scrambling to recover from its pogo stick SRX disaster, so there just wasn't anything really new. Except from John Deere.

Deere's 1982 mid-season introduction of its new Sprintfire and Snowfire models showed that despite the woes afflicting the snowmobile sport and industry, one company was still trying to improve the state of the art. These successors to the Spitfire were light in weight but heavy on innovation. The Sprintfire was the world's first liquid-cooled, direct-drive snowmobile, and both it and the free air-powered Snowfire became full production models for 1983.

Technology Takeover

Deere had introduced direct-drive in 1977 on the 1978 Spitfire. This new technology eliminated the weight and cost of roughly 40 heavy parts, including the chaincase, by mounting the driven clutch directly to the drive axle. This lowered the center of gravity and improved driveline efficiency and reliability but it also degraded performance, particularly when the machine was required to pull hard in deep snow. Nevertheless, it made a lot of sense for family trail sleds. Polaris adopted this innovation for its Cutlass chassis, and Arctic Cat did, too, but went out of business before its direct-drive Jags and Pumas made it to market.

Always pushing ahead with materials technology, Deere also kept the new direct-drive twins light by using a full H-34 aluminum alloy chassis with only a small plate of high-tech Ultra Form 80 alloy steel to protect the steering gear. The lightweight steel alloy was also used for the driven clutch. The chassis was welded together because Deere felt it was more reliable than riveting. A thermoplastic rubber (TPR) belly pan was light and dent-proof.

The Kawasaki-built Fireburst engine in the Sprintfire was cooled by a tunnel-mounted heat exchanger without the added weight of a radiator. Engineered to provide the benefits of liquid cooling including fuel efficiency, noise reduction and extended engine life, it was clutched for a maximum of 6,000 rpm and therefore lacked any serious performance pretentious. Factory dynamometer testing predicted that the machine would deliver about 28 mpg on the trail.

Equipped with a bench seat for two and a passenger hold-on strap, the

Sprintfire was positioned as a value-oriented family trail sled, and perhaps a semi-luxurious yet relatively economical first snowmobile in the household.

Heavily promoted in advertising, it was also on the cover of Deere's full line snowmobile brochures for 1983 and '84. The 1983 models were further backed with limited no-interest financing, and later a $175 factory rebate.

Real World Reaction
In a 100-mile *Snow Goer*/Quaker State fuel economy test, the Sprintfire recorded 37.03 mpg overall, finishing second to a John Deere Trailfire LX (at 38.48 mpg) among 10 models from 1982 and '83 with engines ranging from 244cc to 463cc. It tied with the Trailfire LX at 40.46 mpg for the best score on a 30-mile econo-tour at a steady 35 mph, and actually did better than some machines with smaller engines.

When *Snow Week* newspaper evaluated it over a full winter, the writers noted that the Sprintfire was predictable and reliable, required minimal maintenance and that the smooth clutch engagement was popular with women riders. Real world gas mileage was consistently in the 20s during use by a variety of riders in a variety of conditions. The reviewers concluded that it did everything pretty well, except that its light weight compromised ride quality. Other reviewers were similarly unimpressed with the ride, and sometimes with the handling, but were otherwise generally rather pleased with the machine.

But sleds weren't selling very well for any manufacturer as low-snow winters and an economy in recession took the snowmobile market to a historic low point in 1982-83. The Sprintfire never really caught on with the public, and only slightly more than 2,800 were built, starting with about 150 pre-production units for late-season introduction in model year 1982. The only full-production model was the 1983 version. Deere and Company sold its snowmobile business to Polaris in fall 1983, with less than 300 of the 1984 Sprintfires built before production ceased.

Today, this unique machine from John Deere is rarely seen.

1983 John Deere Sprintfire

MANUFACTURER
Deere & Company, Horicon, Wisconsin

POWERTRAIN
Engine: 339cc Kawasaki Heavy Industries Fireburst TC-340E liquid-cooled, piston-port twin with one Mikuni VM-32 slide valve carb, Kokusan capacitor discharge (CD) ignition and a tuned pipe
Lubrication: Oil injection from 1.25-quart reservoir
Power Output: 35 hp @ 6,000 rpm
Electrical Output: 160 watts
Clutches: JD/Comet 102C drive and JD reverse cam (outside helix) driven

CHASSIS
Type: Welded aluminum with steel steering protection plate, TPR belly pan and sheet molding compound (SMC) hood
Claimed Dry Weight: 334 pounds
Front Suspension: Mono-leaf high arch springs with hydraulic shock absorbers
Rear Suspension: Adjustable aluminum slide rails with torsion springs and a shock absorber on rear arm
Ski Stance: 32 inches
Track: 15-by-116-inch molded rubber with riveted steel cleats and internal drive
Brake: Mechanical disc
Fuel Capacity: 5.5 gallons
Standard Equipment: Adjustable handlebars, speedometer/ odometer, Kelch fuel gauge, oil level indicator, temp light, glovebox, passenger grab strap
Optional Equipment: Tachometer, handlebar heaters, backrest, helper springs, halogen headlight, spare belt clip, tow hitch

MSRP: $3,099

Moto-Ski Mirage III
The last of many orange sleds

The 2010 season marks the 25th anniversary of the passing of a long-running and popular brand in snowmobile history. Begun in 1962 in Sainte-Anne-de-la-Pocatiere, Quebec, Moto-Ski rose to become number three in sales as the snowmobile industry peaked in the early 1970s, but then began a long slow fade out that ended in 1985. Along the way the company sold more sleds for more years than any brand that didn't make it.

Ups And Downs
The orange sleds from the south shore of the St. Lawrence River were famous for their landmark "Tougher Seven Ways" advertising campaign, a gritty racing effort and a series of rugged and reliable family trail sleds that found considerable favor on both sides of the border.

Operating against giants like Bombardier, Outboard Marine and AMF, plus other industry pioneers like Polaris, Scorpion and Arctic Cat, Les Industries Bouchard built Moto-Ski sales and market share before selling out to Miami, Florida-based Giffen Industries in 1968. The momentum continued under the new ownership.

By the end of the 1971 season, Moto-Ski's 840 employees were building about 50,000 sleds a year and selling them through a network of about 1,200 dealers. This made Moto-Ski the third most popular brand out of nearly 100 on the market, and second only to Ski-Doo in Canada. But the brand was simultaneously done in by Giffen's financial failure near the end of calendar year 1970. Bombardier acquired the brand in early 1971, apparently, because Giffen owed it a lot of money for component purchases.

Initially Bombardier operated Moto-Ski as a separate business, but with the post-energy crisis collapse of the industry in the mid 1970s, Moto-Ski business operations were fully integrated into Bombardier at Valcourt, Quebec. Meanwhile the sleds evolved into Ski-Doos with some minor differences like color scheme, track choice and sometimes the engine. Orange fanatics claimed that the meaning of the BSE label on Moto-Ski engines had changed from "Bouchard Snowmobile Engine" to "Bombardier Surplus Equipment"

However, separate dealer organizations and marketing programs were maintained, and Moto-Ski was kept current with contemporary technology including liquid-cooled engines and coil spring front suspensions. Formula One star and legendary snowmobile racer Gilles Villeneuve, who got his competition start by racing his father's Moto-Ski, was the brand's highly visible spokesman for a few seasons until his untimely death in 1982.

But Moto-Ski sales and market share continued to shrink, and Bombardier ultimately offered Moto-Skis to any Ski-Doo dealer who wanted to sell them. Still, weak as it had become, Moto-Ski had outlived more than 100 rivals, including big names like Evinrude and Johnson, AMF and Harley-Davidson, Mercury, Suzuki, and Kawasaki as well as many other industry pioneers like Arctic Cat, Scorpion, and Skiroule — although Cat, of course, resurfaced.

The Mirage Appears
Introduced in 1979 as a Moto-Ski version of the Ski-Doo Safari, the Mirage was positioned above the price-leader Elan-clone Moto-Ski Spirit. Initially just one model, the Mirage was quickly expanded to a three-model series. These

family oriented mid-range sleds featured fan-cooled engines and modest levels of standard equipment to keep prices reasonable.

But by 1985, the Mirage series had been trimmed back to just one model again, and all the other Moto-Ski models had been discontinued, so this was the last of the famous brand. Bombardier presented it as a sort of a touring sled. "Designed for long distance travel, Mirage III opens new horizons" said the sales flyer. But with just about zero marketing support, it was totally ignored by the media and pretty much ignored by everyone else.

That was a shame because this racy-looking trail sled was actually docile enough for just about anyone to operate. Stable and a good handler, it would turn inside most other sleds on the trail at the time. The skid frame and ski shocks on the increasingly outdated leaf spring ski suspension provided a reasonably comfortable ride on a good trail, and the Rotax fan twin had enough power to haul one or two people at a modest rate of speed. Range was pretty good because the small-bore engine just didn't use all that much gas and a full-sized tank was provided. The low windshield was more for looks than protection.

People with small hands tended to complain about the reach to the brake lever, but that was the machine's only other real ergonomic faux pas. Otherwise the Mirage III was a good basic snow machine with excellent visual appeal that would provide hours of entertainment for the non-performance crowd. In other words, a worthy successor to the venerable Capri and Zephyr models that had built Moto-Ski's reputation for solid, dependable family sleds.

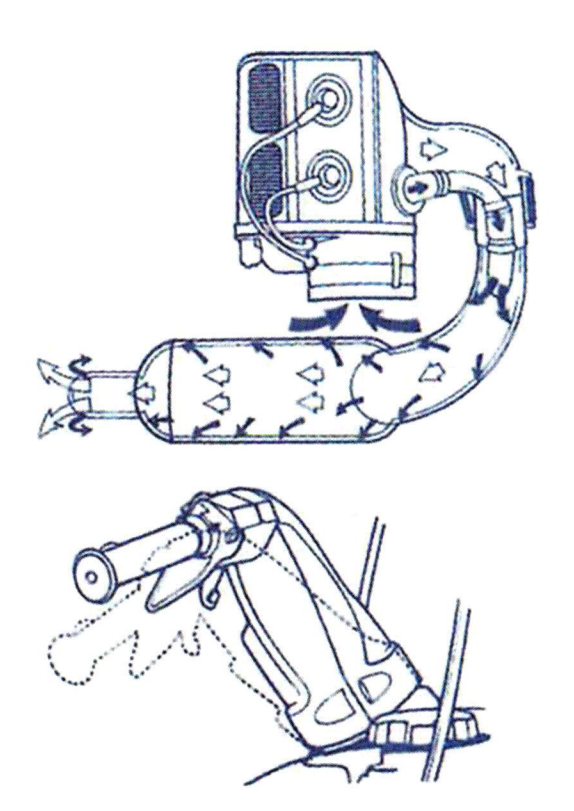

But soon it was over. With a vanishing customer base, little dealer support and no marketing behind it, the Mirage faded out and Moto-Ski become a memory.

1985 Moto-Ski Mirage III

MANUFACTURER
Bombardier Inc. Valcourt. Quebec

POWERTRAIN
Engine: Rotax Type 377 axial-fan-cooled piston-port twin
Displacement: 368.3 cc
Carburetion: One Mikuni VM-34 slide valve type
Ignition: Capacitor Discharge (CD)
Lubrication: oil injection
Exhaust: Single pipe into forced flow muffler
Power Output: 38 hp @ 7,000 rpm
Electrical Output: 160 watts
Drive Clutch: Bombardier Instant Torque square-shaft 2 roller
Driven Clutch: Bombardier

CHASSIS
Type: Aluminum with steel sub-frame, reaction injection molded (RIM) urethane belly pan, fiberglass hood, and tubular steel rear bumper
Claimed Dry Weight: 390 pounds
Front Suspension: Mono-leaf springs with hydraulic shock absorbers
Rear Suspension: TRS 6 Torque Reaction adjustable aluminum slide rail with torsion springs and one hydraulic shock absorber
Ski Stance: 32.25 inches
Track: 15-by-114-inch fiberglass reinforced molded rubber
Brake: Self-adjusting mechanical disc
Fuel Capacity: 8.4 gallons
Oil Capacity: 2.7 quarts
Standard Equipment: Adjustable handlebars, passenger grab strap, tinted windshield
Optional Equipment: Speedometer/odometer, tachometer, electric start, halogen headlight, mirrors, carbide runners, tow hitch

MSRP: $2,349

1986 Ski-Doo Formula SP

The Last Leaf Spring Performance Sled

As the 1985 snowmobile pre-season got underway in spring '84, whispers from my contacts at big yellow indicated that they had something special coming later on. And sure enough, in the fall Bombardier announced a new model aimed at performance-oriented trail riders who wanted the ultimate in comfort and ride quality.

The White Sled, as it was known in Ski-Doo-speak, turned out to essentially be a 1985 Formula SS with a plush-riding long-travel rear suspension. And because it followed the introduction of Arctic Cat's 1985 Pantera by several months, the new Ski-Doo Formula SP became the industry's very last leaf spring performance sled.

Evolution

The leaf spring ski suspension had ruled snowmobiling for well over two decades. However, by the mid-1980s, it was obvious that the coil-over shock front end was the future of the sport. Each of the four remaining snowmobile manufacturers had its own version of a coil-over ski out on the trails, but Bombardier continued cranking out less expensive leaf spring sleds for use on all those wide, smooth trails in Quebec.

The White Sled had its origin in the 1984 SS-25, a sleek, new, low-profile performance sled for Ski-Doo's 25th anniversary season that was slotted below the Blizzard 9700 lake racer. In 1985, the SS-25 returned pretty much unchanged as the Formula SS. Essentially a Safari with Bombardier's low-end, liquid-cooled engine, the SS was a good looking and solid trail sled that ran pretty well. It was positioned at the low-end of the new 1985 Formula performance sled family that was otherwise equipped with Ski-Doo's Progressive Reaction Suspension (PRS) coil-over-shock design in the front.

The new 1985-and-a-half Formula SP slid right in between the leaf spring Formula SS and the coil spring Formula MX. This mid-season entry utilized a skid frame with external coil-over shock springing similar to that on the discontinued Blizzard 5500 MX, although it failed to match the 10-inch travel of the Blizzard MX. But the new suspension did increase total slide rail travel from 6 inches on the SS to a solid 8 inches on the SP, a big improvement in those days. Track width was also increased from 15 to 16.5 inches for more stability and better deep snow performance. Color was the only other significant change.

The plush-riding SP outsold the SS in 1985, so it was retained in the lineup for 1986 while the SS was discontinued. The only changes on the 1986 SP were revised shock damping, a new voltage regulator, a slightly taller windshield and different trim graphics.

Boulevard Ride

When the *Snow Week* test team tested the 1986 Formula SP, the ride quality made a big impression. "Maximum bump absorption with a minimum of trade-off in the handling area," was the key comment. "On the trail, the leaf spring front end seems to be a perfect match-up for the compliant track suspension as the SP has easy steering and the kind of predictable handling that assures rider comfort and confidence"

The review also noted that the engine got good fuel mileage on regular or unleaded gas, and that the sled was good in deep snow due to the leaf springs and wider track. The reviewers concluded that, at $500 and a few horsepower less than the Formula MX, the Formula SP was a good lower-cost, high-performance machine.

Having spent an afternoon pounding an SP over some badly beaten Adirondack trails, I absolutely concur with the *Snow Week* testers. The externally sprung skid frame did a great job of absorbing the bumps. It was easy to bounce the front end into the air and ride it on the rear suspension a good deal of the time. In fact, I rate it as the best riding leaf spring sled I've ever been on, and I've tried a whole lot of them.

Short Life Span

The Formula SP was a lot of fun with decent ergonomics, more-than-adequate power for trail use and no handling issues. It was also fairly well equipped for the day. My only real complaint was the lack of a front bumper that would have made it a lot easier to pick up and tie down. But the increasing popularity of coil-over shock front ends meant that there just wasn't much of a market left for leaf spring performance sleds. Almost all go fast buyers were willing to pony up the extra bucks for the improved ride and handling of the coil-over models, so the short-lived Formula SP disappeared after the 1986 model year.

Nevertheless, this relatively rare machine retains the distinction of being the last leaf spring performance machine to make it to the marketplace, and that makes it a very collectable snowmobile.

1986 Ski-Doo Formula SP

MANUFACTURER
Bombardier Ltd., Valcourt, Quebec

POWERTRAIN
Engine: 463cc Rotax Type 462 rotary-valve liquid-cooled twin
Carburetion: One Mikuni VM-34 slide-valve float type
Compression Ratio: 6.7:1
Ignition: Capacitor discharge (CD)
Lubrication: Oil injection
Power Output: 56 hp @ 6,750 RPM
Electrical Output: 160 watts
Exhaust: Single pipe into free flow calibrated muffler
Drive Clutch: Bombardier "Instant Torque" three-roller square shaft
Driven Clutch: Bombardier cam action

CHASSIS SPECS
Type: Painted aluminum and steel, painted tube steel rear bumper, Reaction Injection Molded (RIM) urethane belly pan, fiberglass hood
Dry Weight (claimed): 434 pounds
Front Suspension: Mono-leaf springs with hydraulic shock absorbers
Ski Stance: 32.25-inches
Rear Suspension: Torque Reaction aluminum slide rails with outboard coil-over, dual-rate shocks
Track: 16.5-by-114-inch fiberglass-reinforced molded rubber
Brake: Self-adjusting mechanical disc
Fuel Capacity: 8.4 gallons
Standard Equipment: Speedometer/odometer, tachometer, temperature gauge, fuel gauge, oil level indicator, high beam indicator, kill switch, handlebar pad

MSRP: $3,499

Snow Bikes
Wobbling Through The Years

A snow bike always looks like such a fun idea. After all, if people enjoy riding dirt bikes and street bikes they should absolutely love riding snow bikes, right? Well, maybe, or maybe not.

Snow bikes go back a long way and have come in many forms, but commercial success with them remains elusive.

Bicycle Beginning

Harold Neitzke is one of the forgotten pioneers of snow travel. In the post-WWII era, the Wausau, Wisconsin-area inventor was creating snow bikes by mating a modified Schwinn bicycle frame, front fork and handlebars to a cleated track and a low-power four-cycle engine. Wooden skis attached to the front fork supported the rider's feet.

Called the Sno-Bi-Kin, this early snow machine reportedly went pretty well in soft deep snow, but handled poorly. However they were apparently the first snow machines used by the Wisconsin Department of Natural Resources. With only 11 built, the Sno-Bi-Kin concept stalled out and Neitzke went on to Merit Gear, where he helped engineer the more conventional Bear Cat snowmobile, not to be confused with the later United Snow Sports Bear Cat, but that's getting off track.

Motorcycles & Mini-Bikes On Snow

If putting tracks and motors on bicycles was a little off the wall, putting tracks on motorcycles seemed like a much more logical idea. The conversion kit concept blossomed during the snowmobile boom of the late 1960s and early '70s when numerous companies produced kits that would let a rider convert a motorcycle for use on snow.

Small bike kits like the 1968 Shrew from Nepelo Inc., of Garfield, Washington, would convert a ride like a Honda 90 street bike by replacing the front wheel with a ski and the rear wheel with a narrow track that extended forward under the engine.

Further up the motorcycle powerband, the 1973-74 Snow Job from Advanced Recreational Equipment of Mountain View, California, required at least a 250cc engine. Also a single ski kit, this one used twin tracks but the rider could still lean the bike into turns to preserve the motorcycle feel. It sold for $780, much more than the snow bikes built by the mainstream snowmobile industry, and more than an entry-level conventional sled of the day.

Motorcycle conversion kits like these are still on the market today, but remain a niche product sold to a mostly western market. Some of the new designs are quite capable and interesting.

Mini-bike manufacturers gave it a try, too, with products adapted from the wheeled vehicles that they were already producing. The Trakcycle from Tri-Rod ATV builder BGW Industries of Mansfield, Ohio, was pretty typical.

Powered by a 4-hp Tecumseh four-cycle engine, the Trakcycle used a narrow track and a ski that bolted over the front wheel. Awkward and underpowered, it was slow and not very reliable. The sparse Clinton All Terrain Bike (ATB) was a similar product that used interchangeable forks to mount a wheel or ski up front. And there were others, none of which went anywhere, literally or figuratively.

The Scandinavian Slant

The Larven was one of the strangest snow bikes ever marketed, yet one of the longer lived ones, too. Built by Firma Lemko in Ostersund, Sweden, from the mid-1960s into the early '70s, the Larven put the rider astride the tall, thin, lengthy enclosed machine. Handlebars herded the unit along while skis supported the rider's feet and helped in

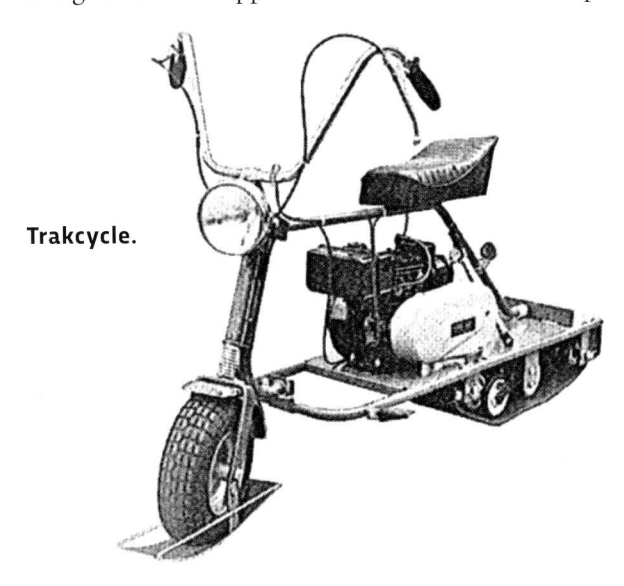

Snow Job.

Trakcycle.

directing the travel of this odd Husqvarna-powered sled.

Reportedly very useful in the soft Scandanavian snow, the Larven was never anything more than a curiosity in North America.

Snowmobile Industry Attempts

The first snow bike from the mainstream snowmobile industry was the Ski-Jet from multi-line manufacturer Lionel Enterprises of Princeville, Quebec. Appearing in prototype form in the mid-60s, it became a production model for 1967. The Ski-Jet had a tall seat like a minibike, a protective curved front shield like a moped, a 180cc Hirth two-cycle engine that made 8-hp a 15.5-inch wide track and a single ski. The 1968 model was badged as a Sno Prince Ski-Jet and sold alongside the new Sno Prince conventional sleds, but it was discontinued at the end of that snow season.

The 1972 Sno-Byke was said to "combine the fun of snowmobiles with the easy handling features of a mini-bike." This 97-pound machine from a Minneapolis manufacturer had a lot more eye appeal than previous mini-bike based efforts – or the Ski-Jet for that matter.

A nicely shaped body was offered in red or yellow, while an 8-hp Chrysler two-stroke used a single sprocket to drive an 8-inch wide track and allowed the machine to do a claimed 30-mph. "Two Sno-Bykes cost less than one average snowmobile," advised the company's dealer recruitment ad in *Snow Sports Dealer News* of October, 1971. But only 13 units were built before Sno-Byke fell over dead.

The 1973 Sno-Blazer from Minneapolis-based Fun Seasons was bigger and better. This 225-pound snow bike used a 15.5-hp JLO 230 or a 20-hp Hirth 292 to power a 10.75-inchwide dual-sprocket-driven rubber track at trail speeds in excess of 50-mph. Promoted at major shows and in sled magazines for $895, it found few takers and the asking price dropped like a rock as this one-year wonder also failed to sell.

Sno-Blazer.

Ski Trike.

Chrysler Corporation had sold engines to power many brands of mini-sleds and had also considered purchasing the Silverline snowmobile operation (T-Bird and Yukon King) from Moorehead Plastics in the late 1960s. Chrysler introduced its own original product, the Sno-Runner, in 1980. Built in Hartford, Wisconsin, this bantam-weight (72 pounds) snow bike used a 134cc Chrysler two-stroke controlled by a twist grip throttle with a centrifugal clutch driving a 3.125-inch-wide, 63-inch-long track to a claimed 25-mph. Two skis were mounted in tandem, the front one to steer and the rear one supporting the rider's feet, and they were the first factory stock plastic skis in the snowmobile industry.

Suitable only for packed snow and small people, the tiny, easily transportable but tricky handling $699 Sno-Runner was backed with serious marketing efforts but simply didn't sell well. C.O.M.B. Liquidators bought the remaining inventory in 1982, stripped off the Sno-Runner decals, and blew them out cheap as Sno-Rabbits.

Snowmobile suspension innovator A.D. Boivin of Levis, Quebec, introduced the Snow Hawk in 2000, and it has become the most successful snow bike yet. Powered by a variety of Rotax snowmobile engines, the fast and sophisticated Snow Hawk has a small but enthusiastic fan base scattered across North America. However, in June, 2011, Boivin sold the complete Snow Hawk business to Motorsport Thibault of St. Samuel-de-Horton, Quebec, which is now responsible for support of existing machines.

Success Is Still Elusive

Sixty years of snow bikes have now slipped into the past. A.D. Boivin is the only company that has even approached commercial success with a snow bike, but even it finally gave up and sold its product to another company.

This leads to one inescapable conclusion. They may be a lot of fun, but there simply isn't enough of a market to support a snow bike as anything more than an obscure niche product at best.

Rebadged & Rejected
Badge Engineering's Long History In The Snowmobile Market

The graphics on the sled say it's a Sears Sportster, a Montgomery Ward's Riverside or a Snow Cruiser, but do you *really* know who built that classic sled you spotted at the local vintage snowmobile show?

Badge engineering, or rebadging for short, is the practice of selling essentially the same product concurrently under more than one brand name, usually through different sales channels. Rebadging has been around for many decades with automobiles, commercial trucks, lawn mowers, mini-bikes, ATVs, bicycles, outboard motors, canoes and farm tractors, among other products. But it has almost never been seen on the scale that it was done in the snowmobile industry.

Virtually every big name in the industry, along with many smaller players, has been involved with it in some way. Snowmobile badge engineering has ranged from simply changing exterior colors and decals to slightly altering the product by using a different engine, a different hood or other easy changes, to a whole new exterior appearance to conceal the same sled underneath.

And now rebadging returns with the alliance between Arctic Cat and Yamaha. That makes this a great time to look back at some of the other examples that intermix brands in the history of the sport. Our story name-checks 69 brands, and we know it's not the complete list.

Snowmobile Rebadging Gets Rolling
There are many reasons for rebadging. Sometimes manufacturers with low brand recognition will rebadge their products for distributors who supply them to an existing dealer network. Attractive to undercapitalized manufacturers because it helps spread the financial requirements and risk, and to under-distributed manufacturers because it quickly adds many retail outlets, this practice restricts the ability of the manufacturer to build up its own brand name so it is generally only done in early stages of a manufacturer's existence.

During their early years, Polaris supplied yellow Sno-Travelers to H.C. Paul Ltd. of Winnipeg, Manitoba, for sale in Canada as Autoboggans. Likewise, Arctic Cat iron dogs were assembled and sold in French Canada by the Roy Skimobil Division of Eugene Roy Enterprises in L'Assomption, Quebec. Only the Roy decals set them apart from other red Arctic Cats. Both of these badge engineered Canadian brands expired as the iron dog era began coasting to a close in the mid-1960s. Likewise, Sno-Ro started life as a Scorpion clone, complete with the ill-conceived and short-lived fiberglass chassis, but also failed to survive the '60s.

Autotechnic, of Montreal, Quebec, provides an example of cross-border badge engineering going the other way. Its Buzz snowmobile, soon re-named Ski-Zoom, was also sold for the 1970 season as the green and gold Sno-Pack by Leisure-Mor, Inc. of Green Bay, Wisconsin. Autotechnic did use a different engine brand in the Sno-Pack, but other differences were strictly cosmetic. Later Sno-Pac sleds (note spelling change) were a different design built by Farmington Engineering.

Polaris was actually one of snowmobiling's most prolific practitioners of rebadging, selling sleds under numerous brand names with various business agreements in the 1960s and early '70s. Polaris designed and built sleds were offered

The ever-so-fashionable Starcraft snowmobiles were just rebadged Alouette snowmobiles.

Later, Alouette was on the other side of this turn, as models like this 1976 Sno Brute were merely a rebadged Rupp Rally.

under the Homelite, Larson, Montgomery Ward's Riverside and Sears Sportster names in the U.S., and under Autoboggan, Eaton, Marshall-Wells and McLeod Hardware's Hiawatha brands in Canada. Most were short lived. For the last two years of production for Eaton, 1968 and '69, the sleds were simply a standard Polaris with a different hood, seat riser and color and trim that was known as a Viking. This should not be confused with the very different Viking snowmobile built by Ashland Industries in Wisconsin and later in Minnesota. The American Viking was also sold for the 1969 season as the Wildcat by Leisure Industries of Minneapolis, Minnesota. But Leisure did a poor job of marketing, leaving Viking to dispose of much of the Wildcat production through its own dealer network. Today's Viking enthusiasts embrace the Wildcat brand as their own.

Lionel Industries of Princeville, Quebec, was Canada's most prolific rebadging manufacturer, building small volumes of many similar sleds under numerous brand names between 1968 and 1972 to gain economies of scale. Boa-Ski, Sno Prince, Moto-Mower's Snow Commander, Sparton (note altered spelling), Sno-King, Ski-King, Trail King (sold by Woolco Stores) and Voyager (for Hudson's Bay Company) were among them. But Lionel failed financially and assets were liquidated, so all but Boa Ski and Sno Prince quickly vanished.

Another reason for rebadging is to clear out excess parts inventory. One-year wonders like the Messelt Sno King, a rebadged Polaris sold by a used car dealer in Roseau that is not to be confused with the Lionel Sno King, the Lionel Sno Job built from Sno Prince leftovers and the all-but-forgotten MSC kit sleds utilizing remaining Trade Winds parts are good examples of these seldom-seen very low production brands.

Private Brands

One big reason for badge engineering is to supply a major retailer who has no engineering or manufacturing capability but wants its own brand name product in a particular product category. This is called a private brand or private labeling, with chain stores and retail catalogs as the typical customers.

During the 1960s and early 70s, Sears, J.C. Penney's, Montgomery Ward's, and Agway, as well as several Canadian retailers including Hudson's Bay Company, The T. Eaton Company, Marshall-Wells, McLeod's Hardware and others sold private brand snowmobiles. Manufacturers who supplied thinly-disguised product to them included Polaris, Larson, Arctic Cat, Scorpion, AMF, OMC's Trade Winds Division, Robin-Nodwell, Gilson Brothers, Dauphin, Somovex (Chimo), Lionel Industries, Yard Man, Northern Manufacturing (Ice Skeeter) and even Sno-Tric from Sweden. It would take a sizeable book to cover this aspect of badge engineering in any detail.

Arctic Cat's arrangement with Yamaha isn't their first trip to the rebadging rodeo. The 1962 Roy Skimobile was assembled in Quebec from Arctic Cat parts with the vehicle name the only difference. Another example was this 1966 Penney's Foremost which had only a few minor differences from the Cat it was based on. This nice example was spotted at Arctic Cat's 50th anniversary event in the summer of 2012.

Hey Ski-Doo fans, does this Moto-Ski Sonic MX look familiar? It should — it's just a Ski-Doo Blizzard 5500 MX with a different hood and color scheme.

OMC had multiple snowmobile brands back in the day, all of which were the same sleds other than colors and graphics. These two Johnson and Evinrude models were both sold by both divisions.

Rebadging for this type of customer is difficult because they typically buy on annual competitive bids and change suppliers frequently, making it difficult for manufacturers to make a profit. Constant supplier turnover insures that post-sale parts and service are continuing issues. These retailers typically have minimal pre-delivery capability, too, so all this adds up to mostly one-time buyers who frequently end up as unhappy customers.

Few of the numerous chain store or catalog brands survived more than a couple of seasons, none had any real impact on the snowmobile market, and none made it past the industry's big shakeout of the mid-70s. Today, accurate restoration of any of these can be a major challenge.

Multiple Dealer Networks

Another common reason for badge engineering is to supply multiple dealer networks for the same company, theoretically providing an increase for the manufacturer's sales. Outboard Marine Corporation (OMC) maintained two identical but distinct outboard motor brands, Evinrude and Johnson, that were sold through two different dealer organizations in one of the most successful badge engineering efforts of all time.

When OMC entered the snowmobile business in 1964, they took this practice even further by establishing the OMC Snow Cruiser brand for their Canadian dealers. All three brands were identical other than colors and graphics. Snow Cruiser was terminated in 1971, but Evinrude and Johnson sleds were sold through the 1976 season placing them the among longest lived and most successful badge engineered brands in snowmobile history.

OMC wasn't the only company to try this tactic, either. Moorhead Plastics, later known as Silverline, Inc., built quite similar sleds under the T-Bird, Es-Kee-Mo, and Yukon King names for a few years in the late 1960's. And the 1974 and '75 Pro-Am snowmobile was an Auto-Ski in a different color scheme intended for a second dealer network. But that effort died quickly in the rapidly contracting snowmobile market of the day. And there were others.

The last badge engineered sled until now was Moto-Ski. Acquired by Bombardier in early 1971 from bankrupt Giffen Industries, the Canadian giant attempted to operate an independent Moto-Ski dealer network for a few seasons. But the contracting snowmobile market doomed the attempt. By the late 1970's, Moto-Ski was essentially an orange Ski-Doo that often shared space in 'Doo dealerships. The proud old brand that sold more sleds than any nameplate that didn't make it to the present day quietly slipped away following the 1985 season.

Two-Way Streets

Sometimes badge engineering can be a two-way street. When Buffalo, New York, ATV manufacturer Recreatives, Inc., wanted to enter the snowmobile business in the early 1970s, they found a willing partner in Northway Snowmobiles of Pointe Claire, Quebec, Canada.

the smooth, speedy, sassy ones for '69!

HOMELITE SNOWMOBILES

After Textron purchased Polaris, it sold three different rebadged Polaris sleds under its Homelite division: the Ranger, the Forester and the Explorer.

Recreatives shipped parts for their three-wheeler and Max 6-wheeler products to Pointe Claire for Northway to assemble as their Explorer brand summer vehicles for sale in Canada. In return, Northway built Sabre snowmobiles for Recreatives to sell stateside. Essentially a Northway with JLO power (the only non-captive major European engine brand that Northway didn't use in their own sleds), the Sabre had different body colors and less standard equipment, but contributed a sleeker hood design for later Northways.

Recreatives was unsuccessful marketing Sabres for 1972 and 73, and withdrew from the sport before it killed their ATV business. Meanwhile, Northway Snowmobiles Limited went bankrupt in August, 1973, so this two-way street turned out to be a dead end in both directions.

Alouette was badge engineered both ways. Original manufacturer Featherweight Corp. of Montreal, Canada, also built Arlberg sleds for Alcock, Laight, and Westwood of Bramlea, Ontario. Pure Alouette underneath, an Arlberg was disguised with a different hood, console, seat, and graphics, but a single parts manual covered both brands. However Arlbergs sold poorly and were only produced for 1969 and 70, with the left-overs closed out cheap in 1971.

Industrial conglomerate Bangor Punta Corp. already owned Starcraft Campers when they acquired Alouette in 1970, and they decided to put the camper company into the snowmobile business as well. Essentially yellow and black Alouettes with slightly different hoods and seats, the Starcraft snowmobile line went nowhere fast, so Bangor Punta terminated that program after two unsuccessful seasons. Following the big snowmobile market crash of the mid-70's, Alouette ended life in 1976 as a badge engineered Rupp differentiated only by decals.

Roll-O-Flex was also badge engineered both ways. The rare 1971-72 Smith-Roles was a yellow Roll-O-Flex with new decals, which is only fitting because the first Roll-O-Flex in 1970 was basically a Boa-Ski.

And They Kept Trying

Many more examples of badge engineering existed. Fox Tracs were built under license in Canada for the McCulloch and Sno-Trek brand names, and were also marketed briefly under the Ski-Ram label. The C.F. Struck Corporation of Cederburg, WI, sold their compact sled kit as both the Sno-Skat and the Sno-Skoot through the same direct marketing channel for reasons that remain unclear. Harley-Davidson snowmobiles were badge-engineered AMFs that lingered on after the AMF snowmobile died. The 1975 Suzuki Fury and 1981 Scorpion Sidewinder were Arctic Cat El Tigrés in drag, which wasn't a bad thing at all. Late model (1976 & 77) Massey Fergusons were Scorpions with an extra headlight, including the Cyclone which was a Brut that was then owned by Scorpion, and so on.

And then there's one that never made it to market. If Polaris had carried through with producing John Deere snowmobiles after purchasing that business in 1984, the 1985 Deeres would have been rebadged Polaris sleds. But Polaris cancelled production after discovering that there was only minimal demand for snowmobiles from Deere Consumer Products dealers.

The New Twist

In the end, all of the rebadged brands from the Vintage era had one thing in common. They were all rejected by the marketplace, most of them pretty quickly.

Could this time be different? There is one significant new twist to the current badge engineering agreement between Arctic Cat and Yamaha. For the first time in the snowmobile industry, both partners are significantly participating in the effort by contributing in their specific areas of expertise. The engines are from Yamaha, the chassis from Cat, and each company is using its own clutches, tracks and other components in addition to different cosmetics. How successful with this latest effort be? We'll see what happens over the next few seasons.

The Great Stock Racing War

It lasted just five years, but those few seasons redefined the snowmobile and reshaped the industry that built them. It was the Great Stock Racing War of the 1970s.

The Way It Was
Snowmobile racing was booming in the late 1960s. Literally thousands of races were running on fairgrounds and farm fields from coast to coast. Each weekend, hundreds of hopeful racers would gather from far and wide to cluster in the pits with those wearing the same colors: Ski-Doo yellow, Moto-Ski orange, Rupp red, Sno*Jet blue, Skiroule green, Arctic Cat black, and so on. A class winner at a big race could more than pay for his sled with his victory check.

The unmistakable scent of two-stroke racing oil filled the air while the grandstands filled with spectators. At most races, crowds stood atop the banks around the tracks outside of whatever minimal safety provisions had been made, and watched while racing went on from early morning until dark. The noise was deafening. Literally.

Big events like Eagle River, Wisconsin; Ironwood, Michigan; Peterborough, Ontario; and Boonville, New York, drew 40,000 to 50,0000 spectators for a weekend. On Monday after a race, Boonville merchants put a half million dollars in the bank, and that was when gas was under 30 cents a gallon, a new car was three grand, and $15,000 would buy you a brand new house in a nice suburb.

The other thing that happened on Monday was that dealers of winning brands sold more sleds. Race track victories had helped make Ski-Doo the top selling brand in the business, and were propelling Arctic Cat towards the top, while Polaris, Moto-Ski, Rupp, Scorpion and many others fought for positions to round out the top tier in sales volume.

Rule Change Inception
During the vintage era, the United States Snowmobile Association (USSA) was the sport's leading race organization. With four divisions — East, Central, West, and Alaska — it was our only nationwide sanctioning body. As the '70s dawned, their Stock classes were 250cc, 295cc, 340cc and 400cc, designated Stock A, B, C and D respectively. Four Women's and three Junior Stock classes had the same displacement limits.

In spring 1971, USSA decided that all sanctioned oval sprint racing events would offer all classes. Previously many events, including virtually all the biggest ones, had only offered the loud, fast and costly Modified classes. With most manufacturers and many racers eager to reduce the costs of fielding expensive Mod racers, Stock racing became a priority for many.

Opening Shots
Stock racing had meant family trail sleds with mostly fan-cooled engines, like Ski-Doo Olympiques, Arctic Cat Panthers, Polaris Chargers and AMF Ski-Daddlers. A dozen brands including Chaparral, Moto-Ski, Scorpion, Skiroule, Sno*Jet and Sno-Pony were represented among the USSA points leaders. Many more manufacturers ranging from recognizable names like Alouette, Ariens, Bolens and Mercury to obscurities like Poloron and Williamsburg filed models for USSA Stock competition.

Controversies over what was Stock were as old as snowmobiling itself, with many disagreements triggered

First corner Stock racing action in 1976

by Ski-Doo developments. But Rupp fired the first shot in this war. In 1971, the performance-oriented manufacturer dominated D Stock with their Magnum 400. Some USSA officials felt that the company had "snuck an engine over on them" as one put it privately. Rupp only had to build 100 units to qualify it, so hand finishing the exhaust ports on the handful of engines was easy.

Arctic Enterprises responded by attempting to list its EXT Modified racers for Stock classes, but was rejected. So Cat came up with an all-new racer that would change everything.

The sleek 1972 EXT with its purple laser striped hood was new from the ground up. Engineered to compete in both Stock and Mod classes, it was offered with eight free-air engines from a 250cc twin to a 650cc triple. A windshield and a 5-gallon gas tank made it a reasonable semblance of a trail sled even if the headlight was optional. And with over 4,200 of them built, these "hot Stockers" were widely available. But a technical dispute erupted, and USSA banned all 1972 EXTs from Stock competition. After a court fight, a compromise put the 250 and 400 back in Stock while the 290 and 340 were restricted to Mod competition. The 250 EXTs blew away everything else in the 250 and 295 classes, and the 400 topped its classes. Meanwhile, the new Rupp Nitro, also developed for Stock racing, dueled with the Polaris TX for 340 supremacy.

This season marked a transition in Stock competition, and in the future of the snowmobile. Family sleds were now useless as racers. Sleds engineered for Stock racing were now necessary, and they would quickly begin to influence trail models.

The 1972 EXT platform would become the most commercially successful race sled ever, continuing as the basis of the '73 & '74 El Tigré, the Arctic-built '75 Suzuki Fury, and all Jags through 1981, and with influence extending into other Cats.

How Many?

USSA wanted to insure competition between brands and availability of sleds to consumers, so it re-worked the build quantity rules for the 1973 season, settling on a sliding scale requiring anywhere from 1,000 to 3,000 units of a given model depending on overall production by its manufacturer. Although no one realized it, industry unit sales had already peaked, and overproduction meant unsold inventories were rising. Several brands, including AMF, Bolens and Sno-Pony, had already left the business, and many remaining companies lacked the resources to field competitive hot Stockers. With their trail sleds no longer competitive, most quit racing.

But staying in Stock racing was important for one very big reason: free publicity. Snowmobile racing was getting more attention than ever, both in enthusiast publications and in general media. With Stock racing now part of every event, the brands that did well received a tremendous amount of free publicity that helped sell sleds, particularly the models that were winning. But only the strongest companies would reap the benefits of this massive amount of free publicity.

Hostilities Escalate

Determined to avoid issues that dogged the 1972 EXT, Cat returned for '73 with the El Tigré, the same sled with a headlight and Kawasaki green instead of Arctic purple trim. Built in big numbers with four engine sizes, the El Tigré was promoted as a performance trail sled. Competitors gulped and retreated to their drawing boards and quickly created new machines to match the hot new Cat on the track and in the showroom.

Ski-Doo discarded its traditional engine-on-a-steel-tunnel format to create the T'NT F/A, a contemporary design to match the El Tigré. This new template with a front-mounted engine in an aluminum chassis would be used for all new Bombardiers going forward. Bombardier's Moto-Ski division concurrently introduced the similar S series, but it found scant success with just one USSA-legal engine. Meanwhile Polaris updated its TX to remain competitive on the track and in the showroom.

All these Stock racers used increasingly popular free air power for better performance. With AMF's Ski-Daddler gone, Rupp was the sole remaining fan-cooled contender. By mid-winter its Nitros weren't competitive. And worse, poor sales forced founder Mickey Rupp to sell his company in the spring while talented engineers and racers departed for other brands.

1975 Arctic Cat El Tigré 340

Tough Times

The Arab oil embargo of late 1973 hit all racing hard. Petroleum shortages limited travel and warmer than normal weather caused cancellation of numerous events while snowmobile sales tanked.

Nevertheless, the new Sno Pro Mod circuit headlined the 1974 racing season. Unhappy with the Stock production quantity rule, and now unable to field new Mods for non-Sno Pro racing, Sno*Jet sued USSA and lost. Big Blue did proceed with its new ThunderJet F/A Stock racer and a heavily-promoted $1 million dollar contingency program, but it didn't run in USSA because the company didn't build the required 1,000 machines.

Meanwhile, Mercury stole the Stock show with its all new Sno-Twister, a sled that was very different from any previous Merc and rumored to have originally been a Rupp. About 1,100 of the free air D Stock Twisters were built, and they owned their class in '74. The fan-cooled Trail Twister followed the next year, but with depressed sled sales continuing, it wasn't enough to carry Merc's snowmobile business much longer. Meanwhile, Ariens, Chaparral and others left the industry while Skiroule and Scorpion were both sold by their conglomerate owners.

By 1975 things were improving some, and the Stock rules were changed to reflect the realities of the still soft snowmobile market. The 295s were dropped, the 400 class became 440, and build minimums were dropped to a tiny percentage of a manufacturer's total production, with a minimum of 500 units for any class.

Bombardier introduced a new machine, the Ski-Doo T'NT 245 RV and companion Moto-Ski Sonic 340 RV. These successful racers were notable for their extreme width and for Bombardier's abandonment of 2-up capability in favor of the shorter single seat configuration. Both quickly evolved into successful trail sleds that sold well for the rest of the decade. But 1975 was also the end of Sno*Jet racing as Big Blue's sales continued to slip. By now, manufacturers were abandoning the snowmobile business in droves, and Sno*Jet would soon be sold to Kawasaki.

The 1976 season saw the first liquid-cooled hot Stockers from Cat, Mercury and Yamaha, with Polaris liquids appearing in cross-country competition. Merc's new Sno-Twister pushed the Stock rules to the extreme, resulting in a sled that simply was not trail-worthy. The featherweight machine had steering arms outside the belly pan, handlebars that were only straight in a left turn, and other features that made it a pure racer. It dominated the track like no sled has before or since. But at the height of its glory, Mercury quit the snowmobile business. Meanwhile, Yamaha made a huge splash by winning the Eagle River World Championship with a 1976 SRX Stocker that would also evolve into a good selling trail performance sled.

1976 Mercury Sno-Twister

1975 Moto-Ski RV 340

It's All Different

USSA changed the rules again for 1977, conceding that Stock racers were now pure race sleds. Meanwhile, the Stock Racing War had completely changed the snowmobiles that people were buying. At the beginning, fan-cooled 2-up family sleds were the big sellers for virtually every brand. By the end, single-seat performance sleds, many with free air engines, had risen to sales dominance while family sleds were in permanent decline. And most of the old brands were now history. Only the biggest manufacturers had survived, and some that had made it this far, notably Rupp, had little time left.

So who won the Great Stock Racing War? Arctic Cat, Polaris, Ski-Doo and Yamaha all used it to develop superior product and gain vast publicity and share of the consumer's mind from their competition successes.

And we riders certainly won because we got much more powerful machines with much better handling, improved ride quality, upgraded ergonomics, and above all else, significantly better reliability. Plus we had a lot of fun getting there and we're still reminiscing about it today.